AFTER THE EXPLOSION,
THE REAL DANGER WAS UNLEASHED....

The explosion prior to the *John Harvey* blast had startled the people crowded along the water's edge, but only a small number had been injured by the resultant flying debris. The explosion of the *John Harvey*, however, not only wiped out Captain John Knowles, his crew, and the military personnel on the ship, but it also killed most of the Italians huddled along the shore. There was no time to run, no time to hide, no time for anything. One moment the inhabitants of the old section were rejoicing in their good fortune for escaping from inside the wall, the next they were dead.

But those who lived through the flames, survived the explosions, and avoided the flying debris faced a greater hazard, although they did not know it. The cloud of smoke carrying the mustard gas released from the hundred tons of chemical bombs permeated the atmosphere over the old section and those that were still breathing filled their lungs with this lethal mixture....

THE BANTAM WAR BOOK SERIES

This series of books is about a world on fire.

The carefully chosen volumes in the Bantam War Book Series cover the full dramatic sweep of World War II. Many are eyewitness accounts by the men who fought in a global conflict as the world's future hung in the balance. Fighter pilots, tank commanders and infantry captains, among many others, recount exploits of individual courage. They present vivid portraits of brave men, true stories of gallantry, moving sagas of survival and stark tragedies of untimely death.

In 1933 Nazi Germany marched to become an empire that was to last a thousand years. In only twelve years that empire was destroyed, and ever since, the country has been bisected by her conquerors. Italy relinquished her colonial lands, as did Japan. These were the losers. The winners also lost the empires they had so painfully seized over the centuries. And one, Russia, lost over twenty million dead.

Those wartime 1940s were a simple, even a hopeful time. Hats came in only two colors, white and black, and after an initial battering the Allied nations started on a long laborious march toward victory. It was a time when sane men believed the world would evolve into a decent place, but, as with all futures, there was no one then who could really forecast the world that we know now.

There are many ways to think about war. It has always been hard to understand the motivations and braveries of Axis soldiers fighting to enslave and dominate their neighbors. Yet it is impossible to know the hammer without the anvil, and to comprehend ourselves we must know the people we once fought against.

Through these books we can discover what it was like to take part in the war that was a final experience for nearly fifty million human beings. In so doing we may discover the strength to make a world as good as the one contained in those dreams and aspirations once believed by heroic men. We must understand our past as an honor to those dead who can no longer choose. They exchanged their lives in a hope for this future that we now inhabit. Though the fight took place many years ago, each of us remains as a living part of it.

DISASTER AT BARI

GLENN B. INFIELD

BANTAM BOOKS
TORONTO · NEW YORK · LONDON · SYDNEY · AUCKLAND

DISASTER AT BARI

*A Bantam Book / published by arrangement with
Macmillan Publishing Company*

PRINTING HISTORY
*Macmillan edition published 1971
Bantam edition / September 1988*

*Illustrations by Greg Beecham.
Maps by Alan McKnight.*

PRINTED IN THE UNITED STATES OF AMERICA

O   0 9 8 7 6 5 4 3 2 1

To Ethel Marie

CONTENTS

ACKNOWLEDGMENTS

To gather material for this book it was necessary to travel to Italy where I not only visited with survivors of the disaster at Bari, a beautiful, thriving city on the Adriatic Sea, but also saw the crypt of Santa Claus; to Germany to talk with former Luftwaffe pilots who had bombed Bari the night of December 2, 1943, pilots whom I had opposed myself during World War II when I was a pilot for the USAAF; to England to speak with British medical and military personnel who were at Bari that tragic night.

There was a great deal of reluctance among the British military establishment to discuss the Bari incident or to cooperate with the writing of this book, but individuals who had firsthand information about the affair were exceptionally helpful and their accounts were invaluable.

Persons such as Rose B. Coombs, librarian, Imperial War Museum; Judith S. Hornabrook, senior archivist, National Archives, New Zealand; Paul Deichmann, Hamburg; General Kurt Student, Bad Salguflen; D. M. Mettig, Bremen; Oronzo Valenti, Bari; D. Lawson, Naval Historical Section, London; Hubert Blasi, Sontheimer Landwehr, Germany; Robert Kowalewski, Germany; Antony E. Brett-James, London; Lieutenant Colonel K. H. Millahn, Germany; Michele Ficarelli, Bari; Nicola Sbista, Bari; Willi Bohn, Frankfurt; and Charles Blyth, London, spent many hours giving me an insight into this event and its aftermath.

In the United States I received full cooperation from the military in spite of the fact that secrecy is always the byword when chemical warfare is mentioned. The Office of the Surgeon General, Department of the Air Force, United States Coast Guard, Office of the Chief of Naval Operations, U.S. Army Office of the Chief of Military History, the National Archives in Washington, Edgewood Arsenal, and the Adjutant General's Office are only a few of the organizations which gave me outstanding help in writing this book. To each I am grateful.

However, the bulk of the material, of necessity, came from those men and women who were in Bari the night the S.S. *John Harvey* exploded. Hundreds of these individuals, from all parts of the world, responded to my request for information regarding the Bari disaster. Without these personal accounts, there could have been no written account of the tragedy. There are too many to name each one on these pages, but they have all received my personal thanks.

Without the cooperation of two men, the book would not have been complete. Dr. Stewart F. Alexander of Park Ridge, New Jersey, the medical officer who discovered that the mustard was causing the mysterious deaths at Bari, permitted me access to his files on the disaster and made arrangements for me to obtain valuable information from the Edgewood Arsenal in Maryland. Captain Otto Heitmann, master of the ill-fated S.S. *John Bascom,* spent a great deal of time with me explaining details about the harbor at the time of the bombing, what happened during the hours immediately after the raid, and also permitted me access to his private reports referring to the Bari disaster. To both I express my appreciation.

To Robert Markel, my editor, "Thanks."

PREFACE

One of the best kept secrets of World War II is the fact that on the night of December 2, 1943, over one thousand Allied military personnel and unprotected Italian civilians died at Bari, Italy, when one hundred tons of poison gas was unleashed. It was mustard gas, the deadly chemical used so successfully by the Germans in World War I and still regarded at the time as the ultimate in hideous weaponry in a world as yet unacquainted with the horrors of the atomic mushroom cloud.

The bombing at Bari was the worst shipping disaster suffered by the Allies since Pearl Harbor. Seventeen ships were totally destroyed by the Luftwaffe bombers that night and eight others were damaged. Yet the greatest tragedy of the bombing occurred when the merchantman S.S. *John Harvey* exploded and her approximately one hundred tons of one hundred-pound mustard bombs were blown apart. Liquid mustard began spreading across the harbor, some of it sinking, some burning, some mixing with oil floating on the surface, and some of it evaporating and mingling with the clouds of smoke and flame. The crew of the *John Harvey* who knew about the secret cargo died when the ship exploded. The men struggling in the harbor waters, the civilians enveloped in the deadly clouds of smoke, and the rescuers working on the docks were all unaware of the presence of the mustard. Many of them died still not knowing about it. Others were blinded or burned. Hospital personnel treated the survivors for shock and exposure, not realizing that they had been subjected to a chemical agent. It wasn't until many of the patients died without obvious cause that an investigation was launched and the true reason for the deaths learned.

This is the story of the secret poison gas tragedy at Bari.

DISASTER AT BARI

1

"HERE COMES ANOTHER CONVOY!"

Captain Otto Heitmann, a slender veteran skipper for the Moore-McCormack Lines, left his Liberty ship, the S.S. *John Bascom,* at exactly 1:30 P.M. on the afternoon of December 2, 1943, to report to the War Shipping Administration office in Bari, Italy. He was contented, pleased that he had brought his ship across the Atlantic, through the Mediterranean, and up the Adriatic Sea to the port of Bari without a serious attack by the U-boats or Luftwaffe. The *John Bascom* was now moored with both anchors and the stern made fast at berth thirty-one on the East Jetty. The only concern Heitmann had that sunny afternoon was the number of ships in Bari harbor waiting to be unloaded. He had counted thirty merchant ships waiting their turn and it was rumored that another convoy was due that evening. It did not appear that he and his crew would be back in the United States for Christmas. Looking across the harbor toward the old section of the city, however, the skipper grinned. He could see the roof of the Basilica of San Nicola in the distance. The tomb of Santa Claus was in the crypt of San Nicola. At least if they could not get home in time for Christmas they would have something to remind them of the holiday.

Ensign K. K. Vesole, USNR, commander of the Armed Guard Unit aboard the *John Bascom,* was not grinning. He wanted to get back to Davenport, Iowa, to be with his wife Idamae and young "Butch," his son, for Christmas. The *John Bascom* had plenty of time to make it back to the United States if they could unload their cargo. Just as his skipper had done, Vesole counted the ships docked in Bari harbor and he did not like the situation. Every dock was occupied; at every

1

pier and for the entire length of the seawall ships were anchored and waiting. Lying at anchor for as many as five days in a port so crowded that the ships frequently touched each other whenever the wind shifted, their holds filled with eight thousand tons of war cargo, was not Vesole's idea of security. He shuddered at the thought of what German bombers could do to the ships in Bari harbor. The only consolation was the assurance of the British military officers in charge of the harbor that no Luftwaffe plane could possibly breach the air and ground defenses assigned to protect the port. Checking to make certain that Donald L. Norton, seaman, second class, and William A. Rochford, seaman, first class, were standing by their guns, the ensign returned to his quarters.

Three berths to the south of the *John Bascom*, the S.S. *Joseph Wheeler*, another American Liberty ship, tugged against the lines holding her to the East Jetty. Fred McCarthy of the navy gun crew on the ship was not particularly worried about Christmas at the moment. He was more concerned about getting ashore, since he had liberty that afternoon and he was anxious to visit the city of Bari. When the ship had docked the night before, after crossing from New Jersey, McCarthy had been broke, but fortunately he had been able to borrow ten dollars from a buddy and he was ready for an afternoon of relaxation after the long trip across the Atlantic. Just as the small boat that was to take McCarthy and his friends to shore was lowered the gunner spotted a white streak high in the blue sky over the Adriatic Sea.

"What's that?" he asked "Bouncer" Ryan, another member of the gun crew.

Ryan shrugged, but Captain Patrick Morrissey, skipper of the *Joseph Wheeler*, knew immediately that it was the contrail of a high-flying aircraft. Could it be a German reconnaissance plane taking pictures of the crowded harbor? He waited patiently for the British antiaircraft guns to open fire or some of the RAF fighter planes stationed nearby to intercept the lone plane; when they did not he decided that it must be an Allied aircraft. For some reason, however, the sight of the contrail and the fact that the lone plane disappeared to the north made him uneasy.

McCarthy, though, promptly forgot about the strange plane as he climbed into the boat heading for Bari. He had other things on his mind at the moment.

About the same time that Fred McCarthy of the *Joseph Wheeler* stepped ashore at Bari and started down Corso Cavour, another navy gunner, Robert R. Kirchhoff, aboard the S.S. *Hadley Brown* felt like cheering at the top of his lungs. The *Brown*, a merchant ship under lease to the British, had also arrived in Bari harbor late on the day of December 1. She had loaded in England and was carrying ammunition, trucks, army clothing, and mail for the British Eighth Army, under the command of Field Marshall Bernard L. Montgomery. The original aim of the Eighth Army was to secure a bridgehead on the toe of Italy to enable the Allied naval forces to operate through the Straits of Messina. It was not initially planned that the Eighth Army would go further than the Catanzaro Neck, a distance of about sixty miles from Reggio. Later, however, Field Marshal Montgomery received an urgent request for help, to push on up the spine of the Italian peninsula and pressure the German forces attacking General Mark Clark's U.S. Fifth Army at Salerno. He did as asked, but his Eighth Army moved so fast that he soon outran his administrative staff and overextended his supply route. The *Brown* was carrying the much needed supplies for the Eighth Army and, for that reason, she did not have to stay moored at the East Jetty very long. On December 2, after only one day on the breakwater wall, the *Brown* was called dockside for unloading. That was the reason Gunner Kirchhoff was elated. Not only did it appear that he would make it back to London, at least, if not his hometown of Sumner, Iowa, for Christmas, but he was glad to get away from the ships jammed together at the East Jetty. The British security agent who had boarded the *Hadley Brown* the previous day had emphasized how safe the harbor was, that the protection was the very best, with radar and guns aplenty. He had even insisted that the gunners cover and secure all the guns. The Britisher had not convinced Kirchhoff or his mates. Consequently the order to leave the East Jetty for unloading was welcome.

As the *Brown* moved toward the dock, Captain E. A. McCammond, skipper of the U.S.S. *Pumper YO-56*, watched carefully to make certain that a sudden change of wind would not cause a collision in the crowded harbor. The *Pumper* was a U.S. Navy tanker with a half-million-gallon capacity which carried aviation gasoline from Bari to Manfredonia, the seaport of the Foggia airfield complex further to the north.

McCammond, a member of the "old school," had been skipper of the *Pumper* since November 28, 1942, and most of his crew were veterans of the sea... and the war. For awhile the ship had operated out of Trinidad, B.W.I., providing aviation gasoline to British, Dutch, and French Guinean air bases. During the summer of 1943 the *Pumper* joined a convoy to Algiers, North Africa, and later was part of the invasion of Sicily. While transporting gasoline from Bizerte to Sicily, McCammond and his men were attacked three times by German bombers and, although one bomb hit within seventy yards of the ship, the *Pumper* had escaped serious damage. After Sicily was under Allied control, the tanker had been ordered to duty at Bari.

When McCammond arrived at Bari the British port director signaled him to moor along the East Jetty. The veteran skipper took one look at the long line of ships along the breakwater wall and asked Lieutenant, Junior Grade, J. H. Ritter, his executive officer, to send a message requesting permission to anchor further north since they would be getting underway the next day. Permission was granted.

"The mole mooring is a rat hole," McCammond muttered.

His premonition not only saved his own life but the lives of many others that night.

Captain W. R. Hays was another worried skipper the afternoon of December 2, 1943. His tanker, the U.S.S. *Aroostook*, was loaded with a cargo of nineteen thousand barrels of hundred-octane gasoline and was lying at anchor in the harbor about 300 to 350 yards distant from the concentrated shipping moored at the East Jetty. After lunch Hays boarded a small boat and went ashore for an appointment at the Psychological Warfare Board Headquarters in Bari. He was determined that as soon as he finished his business there he was going to the British port director's office and register another complaint about the long delay at anchor while loaded with the hundred-octane gasoline. He had complained several times before but there had been no change in procedure, so he made up his mind he was going to keep pestering the port director until some action was taken on the situation.

Hays was disappointed to learn later that afternoon that the port director was away from his office, so the skipper of the *Aroostook* decided to confer with Captain McCamey, U.S. Army, the liaison officer between the Petroleum Section of the Allied Force Headquarters and the Adriatic Base Depot

Group. Perhaps McCamey could help him get his ship out of the harbor, since the aviation gasoline was badly needed at the Allied Airfield to the north. By the time he located McCamey, however, it was too late to do anything to help the *Aroostook*.

The man who had the greatest interest of all in the aviation gasoline aboard both the *Pumper* and the *Aroostook* was sitting in his quarters in the building which formerly had been the headquarters of the Italian Air Force. General J. H. "Jimmy" Doolittle had arrived in Bari only the day before from North Africa and was still trying to get accustomed to his new quarters in the huge building along the waterfront. From the windows facing east he could see a long line of ships anchored in the harbor; but, because of his pressing problems with the newly formed Fifteenth Air Force, Doolittle paid little attention to the merchant ships, except to hope that some of them carried supplies for his airfields at Foggia north of Bari. He also knew that some of the personnel of the units being transferred from the Twelfth Air Force in North Africa to his Fifteenth Air Force were aboard some of the vessels.

Since early in 1942 a major consideration of Allied planners had been the capture of airfields from which their planes could reach important targets in northern Italy, Germany, Austria, and the Balkans. As soon as the southern part of Italy had been conquered, the captured airfields were immediately repaired and new ones were constructed for use by units of the Northwest African Strategic Air Force which was still operating from bases in Tunisia. Many of these bases were in the Foggia area northwest of Bari, approximately forty kilometers inland from the Adriatic Sea. At the same time pipelines for carrying aviation gasoline were laid from the port of Manfredonia, on the Adriatic Sea, to Foggia and, when completed, these lines were capable of moving one hundred sixty thousand gallons of hundred-octane gasoline each week. Large tankers unloaded their fuel at Bari onto smaller tankers such as the *Pumper* and *Aroostook* which carried it to Manfredonia where it was pumped through the pipelines to Foggia.

The development of air bases in Italy not only created problems of airfield construction and of moving gasoline, but also of handling other supplies for Doolittle's new air force. Eastern Italy was under the jurisdiction of the British because their Eighth Army was operating there and the English depots were altogether unsatisfactory for supplying the American air units. This problem was solved by establishing the Adriatic Depot at Bari and by December 2 it was just beginning its operation.

Doolittle, after leading the famous raid on Tokyo, had been assigned various command positions in the USAAF. In March, 1943, he became commanding general of the Northwest African Strategic Air Forces, a position he held until November 1 that same year when the Fifteenth Air Force was formed to operate from the Italian air bases. As soon as he received this new assignment, Doolittle sent his headquarters commandant at Tunis to Foggia to lay out a new headquarters. Bruce Johnson, the commandant, discovered upon his arrival at the city in southern Italy that there was no suitable building still standing so, in his jeep, he went from town to town looking for a headquarters site for Doolittle. At Bari, seventy miles southeast of Foggia, he discovered scores of buildings and hotels still unscarred by bombs, since this city of about two hundred thousand had practically been untouched by Allied bombers prior to the surrender of Italy. Johnson selected the huge building which had formerly housed the headquarters of the Italian Air Force for the new command post of the Fifteenth Air Force and, over the protests of an Italian general who still had his office there, began making plans for the move.

Early in November Doolittle called Johnson into his office and notified him that he was moving his whole headquarters and accompanying units to Bari on December 1 and that he wanted the move accomplished in one day! This meant that over two hundred officers, fifty-two civilian technicians, and several hundred enlisted men had to be moved, and there had to be a place ready for them when they arrived in Bari. The commanding general, his chief of staff, personnel, operations, intelligence, material and maintenance, war plans, adjutant general, air inspector, ordnance, public relations, provost marshal, weather, chaplain, engineering, communications, quartermaster, and many other units had to be in Bari ready to do business by dark on December 1. Johnson made plans for part of the personnel to fly to Italy from North Africa on that date, part to arrive in Bari harbor aboard ship on December 1, and for the remainder to be sent to Bari as soon as possible by any means of transportation possible to help set up headquarters for Doolittle and his staff and establish supply depots for the large amounts of material that would be arriving at the port of Bari.

Robert M. Flynn was one of the early arrivals. Attached to an ordnance company assigned to help the Fifteenth Air Force get underway, Flynn arrived in Bari in the middle of November. When he first arrived he was billeted in a large modern building along the waterfront directly across the Lungomare from a former Fascist headquarters building that had a statue of Mussolini on its facade. The stone face of the former dictator seemed to stare directly at him every time he looked out the window, so Flynn was not sorry when, after a week, his unit was moved to a small three-story building at the northeast corner of the port, a building previously used as a school by the Italians. During the latter part of November Flynn saw the contrails of a high-flying plane many times over the city. Once or twice the antiaircraft guns fired at the aircraft but the shells burst far below it. The radar screen on the Margherita Theater at the water's edge at the end of Victor Emmanuel Street followed the plane until it was out of sight, but no British interceptors appeared in the sky. On the afternoon of December 1 and again the next day Flynn saw the lone plane, but by this time he paid little attention to it. The antiaircraft guns were silent on the afternoon of December 2, indicating that the British gunners were not worried either.

Late in the afternoon of that fateful day Flynn stretched out on an army cot in his room on the third floor of the former school building for a rest. Within a few minutes he dropped off to sleep, a sleep that was destined to be disrupted a short time later.

John H. Kiser was busy as usual on December 2 handling the supplies that were piling up at the warehouses of General Depot Number Five, half a mile north of Flynn's billet. He, too, had been at Bari several weeks. The depot was originally an automobile manufacturing plant and the large storage areas made an ideal place to store the material arriving at Bari to support the operations of the Fifteenth Air Force. At times the volume of the supplies arriving was so great that the trucks were lined up a long distance along Corso Vittoria, the street bordering the harbor area. Kiser was recovering from an attack of yellow jaundice and still was not feeling strong. Earlier in the day he had considered going to the sports stadium that was near the depot to watch the motorcycle races. The stadium was called "Bambino Stadium," a nickname it received because Mussolini had given it to the city of Bari as a reward for having more male babies in a certain period of time than any other city of its size. Feeling weary as the afternoon passed, however, Kiser changed his mind about going to the stadium and headed instead for the squadron day room where a religious service was being held.

He took a chair in the day room and joined the others singing several old-time-religion songs. After the singing ended a debate was started on the sins of gambling, an unusual topic for the majority of the card-playing, wine-drinking GIs, and the argument became hectic after a few minutes. When a sergeant, well known for his women-chasing habits, was asked if he thought life was a gamble, he did not answer. A minute later another GI asked the sergeant if he thought the chance that a man would live long enough to get out of bed the following morning was a gamble. Kiser grinned. Before the sergeant could answer, however, it became obvious to every man in the day room that they were on the short side of the gamble of whether they would live to see another daybreak or not.

At the headquarters building which brusque Bruce Johnson had selected for Fifteenth Air Force commander and his staff, William Blau of the Adjutant General's Section was busy moving the newly arrived equipment into place on the afternoon of December 2. He had arrived in Bari only three days earlier and was still behind in his work. He knew that Doolittle was anxious to get the new air force operating efficiently as soon as possible so he did not mind the extra-long hours that were required. By late afternoon, however, he had most of the equipment in the proper location so, when two of his co-workers, Ray Donahue and John Wood, suggested that they take a walk into Bari and look the city over, Blau was quick to agree. Just as he was leaving the headquarters, though, he was called back by an officer. Telling his two buddies to wait for him at their quarters, he went back into the building.

A few minutes later, after completing his conference with the officer, Blau rushed down the street to the former Technical and Agricultural School where he was quartered. Donahue and Wood were not in their room so he grabbed his mess kit and hurried to the mess hall. Unfortunately—or so he thought at the time—Blau had to wait for the second serving. While he was still in the chow line he spotted his two friends leaving the mess hall for their quarters. After he was finally served Blau rushed through his meal, dashed back upstairs to his room with his mess kit, and looked for Donahue and Wood. They had disappeared from sight. Disappointed and a little angry, Blau stretched out on his bunk.

"They could've waited a few minutes," he muttered.

Because they did not wait that afternoon of December 2, Blau lived.

Flight number 501, Air Transport Command, had arrived at Bari airport at exactly 5:00 P.M. on December 1. One of the passengers who stepped from the C-47 that day was Leroy T. Eure, a specialist in unloading operations. That night he was assigned a room at the Hotel Spa and early the following morning he reported to the docks to begin work with the 1095 Dock Operating Company of the British Army. It was Eure's job to oversee the unloading of ammunition and bombs transshipped by the U.S. Army from North Africa to Bari for the Fifteenth Air Force. December 2 was a busy day for him. From morning until late afternoon he supervised the unloading of the military supplies from the ships at dockside. After the ships were empty they were moved to anchorage inside the breakwater until the next morning. At about 5:30 P.M. another convoy of ships from North Africa and the United States arrived and started to enter the harbor. Eure knew that these ships would have to be moored to the East Jetty, since there was no room at the dock; he knew, too, that they would not be unloaded for several days. Looking at his watch, he saw that it was 7:05 P.M. He decided to return to the Hotel Spa. As he walked along Molo Foraneo he saw the lights on the cranes and all along the harbor turned on one by one. It seemed strange to be able to turn on the lights instead of having to maintain a strict blackout as was often required in North Africa, but the British port director had said it was safe, that no Luftwaffe plane could penetrate the defensive screen around Bari. Eure hoped the Englishman knew what he was talking about.

The convoy that Eure had seen just before he started his walk back to the hotel included the Liberty ship *Samuel J. Tilden* commanded by Captain Joseph L. Blair. The ship had loaded personnel of the 376th Bomb Group, the 98th Bomb Group, and several medical units at Bizerte, North Africa,

C–47

and sailed to Taranto, Italy, late in November. Also on board were trucks filled with full gasoline tanks in numbers four and five holds, two tractor-trailer units containing six thousand gallons of high-octane gasoline stowed in number two hold, one hundred tons of ammunition in numbers four and five holds and on deck. Among the members of the 376th Bomb Group on the ship was D. M. Fly, a technical sergeant who had tried to get a seat on a C-47 flying from North Africa to the Foggia area but had been outranked and had to make the trip by sea. Fly could see the lights of Bari from the rail of the *Samuel J. Tilden* as the Liberty ship stopped just inside the entrance to the harbor. In fact, the beam of a high-powered searchlight from shore nearly blinded him as it shone on the ship. He did not like the situation. He did not feel comfortable sitting in the middle of a spotlight, surrounded by other ships with their lights shining brightly, and with the enemy still well within bombing range. The British were too confident to suit him. Much too confident. He wished he could get his feet on solid ground again. At that moment he heard an airplane and looked up. It was a C-47 with USAAF markings and Fly relaxed. For a moment he had thought it might be the Luftwaffe.

C-47s had been arriving all day at Bari airport, carrying

cargo and personnel from North Africa to Italy. Edward M. Borsarge, a pilot attached to the Fifty-second Troop Carrier Wing, brought his aircraft over the jammed harbor in midafternoon; he got a very good view of the ships since he had to make his approach to the airport runway directly over the masts of several of them. As soon as he landed and reported to operations, Borsarge and several of his crew, including Robert L. Burelson and Junior Carr, went into Bari to find a room for the night and to check on the entertainment possibilities. It did not take them long to find both. After making certain they had a place to sleep, they visited the bars along Corso Cavour—so many of them, in fact, that finding a rest room soon became an absolute necessity. Unable to locate one fast enough, the trio went into one of the air raid shelters in the middle of the street and relieved themselves. The shelter was a concrete tunnel about fifty feet long with steep steps leading into it at each end. Borsarge noticed that there was approximately eighteen inches of water lying on the bottom of the shelter and shook his head in disgust.

"A guy could get trapped and drown inside one of these shelters," he told Carr.

Later, as he sat in the Oriente Theater watching an American movie, Borsarge did not dream that within an hour he would be fighting for his life inside that very air raid shelter.

December 2 was a very busy day for another pilot of the Fifty-second Troop Carrier Wing. James A. Oleman had flown his C-47 from Trapani, Sicily, to Palermo, Bizerte, Foch, and finally to Bari. Tired, but not so exhausted that he wanted to stay all night at the airfield outside of the city, Oleman caught a ride on a truck going into Bari. After registering for the night at the Grande Albergo delle Nazioni and getting a room on the fifth floor, he decided to go to the theater next door to see the movie *Springtime in the Rockies* starring John Payne and Betty Grable. He knew the words would be in Italian, but had no doubt that Betty Grable would look just as good as an Italian as she did as an American. Jens L. Lerback, his roommate, agreed. As they walked from the hotel to the theater they could see the ships in the harbor tied up so close together that they were touching each other; Oleman remarked that the harbor was as crowded as the airfield they had landed at earlier. Entering the theater, the pair promptly forgot about the ships. They would remember them within a short time, however, long before Betty Grable made her last appearance on the screen.

About the same time that Oleman and Lerback left the Grande Albergo delle Nazioni to see *Springtime in the Rockies*, Walter Logan stepped from the same hotel and headed toward the harbor. Logan was a naval correspondent attached to a squadron of four British destroyers, the *Quilliam*, *Quail*, *Queensborough*, and *Loyal*. Normally he lived aboard the *Quilliam*, but he also maintained a room at the hotel. He had stayed in the city the night of December 1, but decided to return to the British ship early on the evening of December 2. It was a clear, starlit evening and as he approached the harbor Logan could see the ships anchored in every available space within the breakwater. Their navigation lights were visible. So were the bright lights on the cranes unloading the ships at the dock and the other lights scattered around the harbor for various purposes. In fact, the harbor was so brightly lit that he could even see the ships moored at the far end of the East Jetty—including the S.S. *John Harvey*.

Of all the ships in Bari harbor the night of December 2, 1943, the *John Harvey* was by far the most important to the inhabitants of the city, the military personnel in the area, and the Allied plans for the future conduct of the war. It was the bombing of the *John Harvey* that perpetrated the worst poison gas tragedy of World War II.

2

"PUT THE CARGO IN THE HOLD AND PRAY"

The *John Harvey*, similar to the multitude of other Liberty ships built and launched during World War II, was a long way from being a luxury liner. Constructed by the North Carolina Shipbuilding Company, she was completed on January 19, 1943, and destined to exist less than a year. From the date of completion until sunk, the *John Harvey* was operated under a General Agency Agreement by Agwilines of New York. The ship was named for John Harvey who was a member of the Continental Congress in 1777 and a signer of the Articles of Confederation; some of her crew swore that she was just as stubborn and independent as her namesake. With a deadweight of 10,617 tons, a gross tonnage of 7,176, and a speed of slightly more than twelve knots, the *John Harvey* served her purpose, but had a rough life while doing so.

The skipper of the *John Harvey* on her final voyage was short, stocky Elwin F. Knowles. Born in South Thomaston, Maine, the forty-three-year-old Knowles had nearly lost his life early in the war on a convoy run to Murmansk. The convoy was attacked by German U-boats and Norwegian-based German dive bombers as it moved through the North Atlantic and twenty of the thirty ships in the convoy were sunk. Knowles, aboard the *Ozark* as first officer, managed to get his ship hidden in a fogbank before the submarines and aircraft could sink her. With no radio communication possible, since Knowles knew that the German U-boat commanders and Luftwaffe pilots would monitor the airwaves and quickly home in on any message he transmitted, he made for

Iceland. Long before the *Ozark* reached the port of Reykjavik, the vessel and the crew were given up for lost. In reward for his heroic action, Knowles was given command of the *John Harvey*. It was a fateful assignment.

Shortly after Captain Knowles was given command of the *John Harvey* the combined Allied forces invaded Sicily and the long-awaited drive toward the Axis-held Continent began. The step-by-step path planned by the Allies was obvious to Adolf Hitler and his staff: Sicily, Italy, southern France, perhaps the Balkans. The crucial problem facing the Nazi dictator was how to stop the powerful Allied forces with the men and weapons still remaining to him. His Luftwaffe was hard pressed day and night by the USAAF and the RAF; the fall of Mussolini on July 25, 1943, had deprived Hitler of between thirty and forty Italian divisions that he had depended upon to oppose any invasion of Italy; and the remaining sixteen German divisions in Italy were spread so thinly that, unless they were at the exact invasion spot at the right time, there was slight hope of repulsing an Allied landing.

Near the end of July ominous reports began to reach Washington and London, reports that indicated Adolf Hitler, in a desperation move, was planning to resort to the use of poison gas to repel any attempted invasion of southern Europe. Allied agents verified that the Germans had a quarter of a million tons of toxic munitions east of the Rhine, including a new gas called Tabun. Colorless and almost odorless, Tabun reportedly attacked the human nervous system through the lungs or eyes causing death within one to five minutes. In Report 353.6, dated September 11, 1943, issued by Major Stewart F. Alexander, consultant, chemical warfare medicine, assigned to Headquarters, North African Theater of Operations, the subject of chemical warfare activity in the Sicilian operation was reviewed. Item number five of the report stated: "Significant amounts of vesicant agent were captured. Analytic procedures are now in process. It seems probable that the majority of the agent is a mixture of fifty percent phenyl dichlorarsine and fifty percent mustard. It is believed that this mixture is of Italian manufacture. There was no evidence of tactical use of this vesicant."

In August, 1943, President Franklin Delano Roosevelt, alarmed by the reports of the imminent use of chemical agents by the Axis, issued a statement outlining Allied policy on the use of poison gas.

* * *

From time to time since the present war began there have been reports that one or more of the Axis powers were seriously contemplating the use of poisonous or noxious gases or other inhumane devices of warfare. I have been loath to believe that any nation, even our present enemies, could or would be willing to loose upon mankind such terrible and inhumane weapons.

However, evidence that the Axis powers are making significant preparations indicative of such an intention is being reported with increasing frequency from a variety of sources. Use of such weapons have been outlawed by the general opinion of civilized mankind. This country has not used them, and I hope that we never will be compelled to use them. I state categorically that we shall under no circumstances resort to the use of such weapons unless they are first used by our enemies.

As President of the United States and Commander-in-Chief of the American armed forces, I want to make clear beyond all doubt to any of our enemies contemplating a resort to such desperate and barbarous methods that acts of this nature committed against any one of the United Nations will be regarded as having been committed against the United States itself and will be treated accordingly. We promise to any perpetrators of such crime full and swift retaliation in kind and I feel obliged now to warn the Axis armies and the Axis peoples in Europe and in Asia that the terrible consequence of any use of these inhumane methods on their part will be brought down swiftly and surely upon their own heads. Any use of poison gas by any Axis power, therefore, will immediately be followed by the fullest retaliation upon munition centers, seaports, and other military objectives throughout the whole extent of the territory of such Axis country.

More than words were needed, however, to prepare against the possibility of such an attack by the Axis. After careful consideration, permission was granted by the White House to ship an adequate supply of chemical bombs containing mustard to the depot at Bari, Italy, to be used by the Allies in retaliation in case the Nazis resorted to gas warfare during the planned invasion of Italy. The *John Harvey* was chosen to carry the shipment and Captain Knowles received orders to report to the docks at the Curtis Bay Depot in Baltimore, Maryland, immediately. He was not exactly overjoyed with the orders. He had been enjoying himself in New York City, spending some of the money he had saved during the long weeks at sea, doing the things he had dreamed about doing while on the long, bitter cold Murmansk run. He really had not expected to sail again until after Christmas, but, as he told the attractive woman who accompanied him to the train station, "They wouldn't have ordered me out again so soon if it wasn't important."

Laura LaFoe nodded. A descendant of a seafaring family herself, she was accustomed to rush sailings at unexpected hours. She handed him a coat. "At least you shouldn't get cold on this trip."

Knowles grinned as he looked at the new sheep-lined coat she had bought for him. It was khaki-colored, heavy and warm. As he walked away after bidding Laura good-bye, his limp was obvious to anyone watching him. Knowles was sensitive about the clubfoot with which he had been born and usually managed to move so that few knew of it. When he was tired, however, it became more noticeable.

At approximately the same hour that Captain Knowles received his orders to report to Baltimore, First Lieutenant Howard D. Beckstrom of the 701st Chemical Maintenance Company was alerted for movement overseas. Beckstrom was one of a select group of officers trained to handle large-scale shipments of toxics, including mustard. The maintenance, storage, and shipment of such toxics involved a number of special problems arising from the nature of the materials. Mustard itself required particular attention. In the form produced during most of World War II, the so-called Levinstein H mustard contained about 30 percent of unstable impurities which caused trouble when it was left in storage for any length of time. It evolved gases at a rate that sometimes built up dangerous amounts of pressure within the bomb casings where it was often kept. Handlers had to learn techniques for testing pressures in the containers, venting them when necessary, and cleaning them when drained.

Beckstrom had completed a course in the handling of

toxic agents at a training center established at Camp Sibert, Alabama. When he was assigned to accompany the two thousand M47A1 hundred-pound mustard bombs to Italy aboard the *John Harvey*, the lieutenant selected several enlisted men to help him. Under his command on the *John Harvey* were Sergeant Broadus J. Jamerson; Private, First Class, Bennie G. Taylor; Private, First Class, Charles N. Thompson; Private, First Class, Fred Wilson; Private Wilson Bodie; and Private Willie Tensley. All were experts in the handling and transporting of toxic agents.

The mustard bombs, developed by the Chemical Warfare Service in the 1930s, were a constant source of worry to Beckstrom and his men from the moment they were loaded on a train at the Eastern Chemical Warfare Depot in Maryland until the *John Harvey* arrived in the harbor at Bari. The bombs did not appear nearly as deadly as they actually were. Only slightly more than four feet long and eight inches in diameter, the bombs held from sixty to seventy pounds of mustard, enough to contaminate an area from fifteen to forty yards in diameter. From the depot to the Baltimore Cargo Port of embarkation, the lieutenant rode the train caboose. At each stop he made a quick check of the bombs to determine whether there was any evidence of contamination due to leaks in the casings caused by corrosion or vibration. He also had to check the pressure inside the casings to make certain they were not building up to a dangerous peak that might cause an explosion and destroy the entire train, kill everyone aboard, and contaminate the countryside. By the time Beckstrom and his detachment arrived at Baltimore with the lethal cargo they needed a rest.

There was no time for rest, however. The *John Harvey* was already in port taking on her more conventional portion of the cargo—munitions, food, and equipment. Captain Knowles was anxious to get everything on board, since he did not want to miss sailing with the convoy scheduled to leave within a few days. He had already decided that if everything went all right he might get the *John Harvey* back to the United States for Christmas, and he wanted to spend the holidays in New York if possible. Consequently he kept pressing Beckstrom to get the cargo he was shepherding on board. Officially Knowles was not notified about the exact nature of the cargo, but the veteran sea captain was well aware that his ship was carrying mustard bombs. When

Lieutenant Thomas H. Richardson of the U.S. Army Transportation Corps arrived with the manifest listing of the cargo it was quite obvious to the entire *John Harvey* crew that they were carrying a special load. Richardson was the cargo security officer and his questions left no doubt in anyone's mind that the holds of the *John Harvey* were filled with dangerous materials. Just what, none of the seamen were sure, but they sensed the concern of their captain. Just prior to sailing, Chief Engineer John J. White turned to Second Officer Myron E. Young and shook his head, "I don't like it."

Young shrugged, "Just put the cargo in the hold and pray. We don't have any other choice."

The crossing from the United States to Oran, Algeria, was uneventful despite the fact that German U-boats infested the Atlantic Ocean. The first hint of the final tragedy that was destined to strike the *John Harvey* occurred on November 18 at Oran when Seaman Cecil C. Croxton was killed while attempting to secure number two starboard boom. He fell from the foremast crosstrees and died instantly. Knowles left his crewman there, buried in plot J of the American Cemetery, but he could not overcome the uneasy feeling he had after the accident. To him it was a bad omen. Very bad.

On November 20, Knowles eased the *John Harvey* out of the harbor at Oran, a part of a convoy headed for Augusta, Sicily. He was apprehensive about the trip through the Mediterranean, since he had learned about the new tactics the Germans had used against an Allied ship-train headed for Italy earlier in the month. At Oran the port director had told Knowles that Convoy KME25A, transporting tons of war supplies and thousands of troop reinforcements for the American forces of General Mark Clark, had been unmolested along the Algerian coast as it followed the sea road which led to the narrow waist of the Mediterranean. When the convoy reached the Tunisian War Channel, however, it had to string out in a column, since the channel was too narrow for the preferred columns of three ships each. Traveling at a speed of twelve knots, it had reached the eastern end of the channel when the enemy struck. Diving out of the darkening sky—it was 1800 hours—the Luftwaffe hit hard and with a new killer weapon.

A gunner aboard the destroyer *Davison* was the first to notice a strange object heading toward his ship. At first glimpse he took it for a midget airplane. At close range, however, it resembled a winged rocket, a streak of red light with a flaring green tail. Actually the gunner was witnessing a surprising new weapon that had been hatched in the dark secrecy of Nazi Germany, the radio-controlled glider bomb known as the "Fritz X." It was a dwarf descendant of the murderous "buzz bomb" and, while it did not have the range of the "buzz bomb", nor carry as big an explosive charge, it was an appalling danger to ships at sea. Knowles recognized that fact as soon as the new weapon was described to him in Algeria. The "Fritz X" could be aimed by a man in the high-level bomber that launched it. It had a control mechanism that responded to the radio signal transmitted to it from the "mother" plane and, under the right conditions, could be sent into a meteorlike dive straight for a slow-moving ship such as the *John Harvey*. The Luftwaffe had inflicted serious damage on Convoy KME25A, sinking two transports and one destroyer. Knowles shuddered when he thought what such an attack could do to his convoy.

However, the *John Harvey* reached the port of Augusta on November 25 without incident. There had been several wolf pack scares and four German aircraft had been spotted high in the sky south of Sicily, but there had been no actual attacks on the convoy. When he reached Augusta, Knowles relaxed a little. He felt that the worst of the trip was over. From Sicily across the Ionian Sea, through the Strait of Otranto that separated Italy from Albania, and up the Adriatic Sea to Bari seemed easy after the trip across the Atlantic and through the Mediterranean. The remainder of the sea routes were under control of strong Allied ground, sea, and air forces. Of course, there was still a chance that a lone U-boat might make a suicidal attack on the convoy or that a formation of Luftwaffe planes might sneak through allied defenses and attack the ships, but it was unlikely. Very unlikely.

Beckstrom did not have time to relax at Augusta as Captain Knowles did, however. He and his detail of 701st Chemical Maintenance Company experts were busy checking on the hundred-pound mustard bombs. Each bomb casing was examined closely for any leaks or split seams. Although some seawater had sprayed into the holds, there was no indication of corrosion. Nor did Beckstrom and his men find any dangerous pressures building up inside the casings. Everything had worked out much better on the trip than the lieutenant had expected, and he was happy. All they had to do now was make the short trip to Bari and unload the mustard bombs. That was the easy part of the trip . . . or so Beckstrom mistakenly thought.

Lieutenant Richardson, the cargo security officer, was the man who was worried. In Augusta he had talked with a navy officer who had just returned from the port of Bari; his report had been discouraging. The harbor, according to him, was crowded with ships and the docks were jammed with supplies waiting to be taken away. He stood on the deck of the *John Harvey* and studied his manifest, his eyes lingering on one item: two thousand M47A1 hundred-pound mustard bombs. Richardson knew that the silver bars of a first lieutenant that he wore would not make much impression on the British port officials, but somehow, someway he had to make certain that the mustard bombs were unloaded immediately upon reaching Bari.

On November 26 the convoy moved slowly out of Augusta harbor and set course for Italy.

Two days later the fifteen-ship convoy entered the breakwater of Bari harbor, passing through the submarine nets strung between the Molo Nuovo and Molo San Cataldo. Captain Knowles shook his head in frustration when he saw the condition of the harbor. Every place he looked—along the two moles he had just passed between, along the shorter finger of the Molo Pizzoli, the blunt Molo San Vito, and the Molo Foraneo—ships were moored. It was obvious to him that the *John Harvey* was not going to be permitted into the inner breakwater of the new port, that he was going to have to anchor his ship along the already crowded East Jetty. As if reading his mind, the semaphore station relayed his orders at that very moment.

"Moor at pier twenty-nine."

The following five days were the type of days that no merchant seaman likes, the type he dreads, in fact. Since the *John Harvey* had to wait her turn to move to dockside for unloading, there was little work for the men to do. Shore leave into the city of Bari was granted to part of the crew each day, but even this break in the monotony grew tiresome to men who wanted to head back for the United States so they could be home in time for Christmas. Captain Knowles made many trips to the War Shipping Administration office at the Stazione Marittima, but his efforts did nothing to move up his unloading date. He wanted to tell the British port director about the mustard bombs on the *John Harvey*, but, since he was not supposed to know of them officially, he was stymied. Secrecy about the transporting of poison gas to the war zone was paramount. Only a few people other than the military personnel on the *John Harvey* knew about the mustard bombs nestled below the decks. No one else must know. So Knowles kept quiet, despite the danger to his ship and crew.

One man that knew all about the bombs, Lieutenant Richardson, was a bundle of nerves by dusk the evening of December 2. He had done everything possible, had contacted every military officer he could locate stationed at the port of Bari, but the mustard bombs were still aboard the *John Harvey*. For five days he had sweated out the situation. He did not feel he could take much more of it. He gazed at the lights burning on the port wall and felt uneasy. There were lights glinting in the city, too, even though it was now dark enough for a few stars to become visible. Bari was really asking for it, he thought.

"Look!"

Richardson turned as Captain Knowles's voice reached him. The skipper of the *John Harvey* was staring skyward and

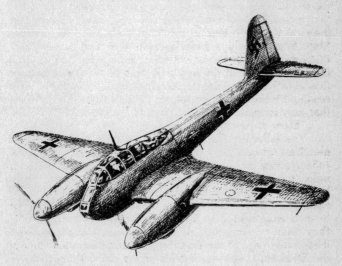

Me–210

the cargo security officer followed his gaze. There, high in the sky where the last rays of the sun still glinted from its winds, was a lone plane crossing directly over the harbor area. It moved slowly, lazily, and Richardson wondered if the men on the aircraft whoever they were could see the ships so far below them.

High above Bari harbor the Luftwaffe pilot in the lone Me-210 knew the answer. Oberleutnant Werner Hahn not only could see the ships in the jammed harbor, he could even count them, and when he reached a total of thirty he knew the time had come. Banking his plane northward, the Luftwaffe reconnaissance pilot streaked back toward his base in northern Italy to report to his General der Flieger. The stage was set for tragedy at Bari.

3

"THE TIME TO STRIKE IS NOW"

Field Marshal Albert Kesselring, commander in chief of the German Troops in Italy, had been looking for a target such as the harbor at Bari for several weeks. He desperately needed an air strike that would delay the advance of the British Eighth Army on the east coast of Italy and hamper the organization of Doolittle's new Fifteenth Air Force. Kesselring knew that he was asking the next-to-impossible because the Luftwaffe was lacking both planes and experienced pilots in Italy since the country surrendered to the Allies, but he had no intention of giving up on the idea. With this plan in mind he arranged a conference at Frascati late in November. Among those attending the meeting were Field Marshal Freiherr von Richthofen, commander of Luftflotte Two, Major General Dietrich Pelz, an outstanding German expert on bombing techniques, and Werner Baumbach, general of the bombers.

At Frascati, Kesselring's headquarters, the food was fine, the wine of the best quality available in all of Italy, the meeting room warm and comfortable despite the coldness of the Italian winter. The news from the front, however, was bad. The British Eighth Army had advanced nearly ninety miles during the previous fifteen days and reached the Sangro River. The Fifth Army, after forcing passage of the Volturno River, had fought its way to the entrance of the Liri Valley, which led to Rome. For the moment the Americans were checked in front of the natural strongholds of Monte Camino, Monte Lungo, and Monte Sammucro which dominated the Capua-Cassino road, but as soon as reinforcements arrived, the battle would be renewed. Some way had to be found to slow down both the British and American forces.

One of the men upon whom Kesselring depended to come up with a plan was Werner Baumbach. Baumbach was tall, slender, blond and looked every inch the skilled flyer that he was. Yet his main value to the Luftwaffe was not so much his flying skill as his overall planning ability and talent to see the entire picture and not just one small corner of it. He had been convinced since the beginning of the Italian invasion by the Allies that the main purpose of the thrust was to tie up German ground and air forces on the peninsula so that these forces could not be used to oppose the main invasion of the Continent that would come along the shore of France later. He was right, of course, but in the winter of 1943 very few German officers agreed with him. His record was outstanding. He had fought the RAF, the USAAF over the Continent and the Mediterranean, both as a pilot and as a commander of a bomber *Gruppe*. Based on this experience he had been assigned the task of completely reorganizing the German bomber fleet to meet the turn of the tides of the war. For this service and for his previous combat action, Hitler awarded Baumbach the Oak Leaves with Swords to the Knights Cross, the highest distinction given to a German bomber pilot in World War II. Now he was being called upon again to come up with an aerial miracle.

Another outstanding Luftwaffe officer present at the Frascati meeting was Dietrich Georg Magnus Pelz, a great favorite of Adolf Hitler. Pelz had pioneered the "Pelz Doctrine" that had been used so successfully by the Luftwaffe earlier in the war. This was the technique of hitting a single target with a massive formation of planes rather than spreading the force thin over a number of targets. In 1939 Pelz was an Oberleutnant. Four years later he was a Generalmajor because of his fine record. During the winter of 1940–41 he flew seventy-seven sorties over England. He also flew many missions over Poland, Greece, and Russia. Now, in late 1943, the Führer had ordered Pelz to Italy to command all the bomber units in the country.

Freiherr von Richthofen was a veteran of air wars, having been in command of the Condor Legion at the end of the Spanish Civil War, led the blitzkrieg of Poland in 1939, hammered the British at Dunkirk, aided in the planning of the Battle of Britain, and finally after a disagreement with the Luftwaffe commander in chief Hermann Goering ended up as commander of Luftflotte Two in Italy. He was a

Oak Leaves With Swords

mercurial, independent general who was ready to try any air strike at any time if the odds were at least fifty-fifty for success.

These four German officers and their staffs and aides sat around a large oak table and each presented his ideas. The conference was extremely lively. Pelz was not entirely convinced that Italy, especially the southern portion of the country, should be defended at all. He was discouraged because the airfields at Foggia had fallen into Allied hands. Those fields, he felt, were the most vital military installations in southern Italy and, since they had already been captured by the enemy, what was the use of trying to hold onto the boot?

Kesselring had no intention of giving up southern Italy without a struggle. He felt that, if the supplies and reinforcements for the Allied ground forces fighting their way up the penisula were delayed long enough for him to get his troops and weapons in place and establish the Bernhard Line, a defense position crossing the narrowest sector of the Italian Penisula between Gaeta and Ortona south of Rome, he could stop the Allied drive in its tracks.

"If we can do this we stand an excellent chance of recapturing the entire Foggia airfield complex," the tough-minded Kesselring told Pelz.

The question was, of course, where to hit the Allies to hurt them the most, to halt the flow of supplies and men north.

Pelz admitted Kesselring's plan had merit. German agents had revealed to Berlin that the planes and supplies for the newly established Fifteenth Air Force were arriving very slowly. This was good, he said, because the ultimate aim of the Allies was to use the heavy bombers of the Fifteenth Air Force in conjunction with the U.S. Eighth Air Force and RAF long-range bombers in England. With the Fifteenth hitting vital German factories, oil refineries, airfields, and other installations that were out of range of the British-based bombers at present, it would require drawing back several Luftwaffe units from western Europe to cope with this new threat. This would serve the Allies in two ways. It would spread the German Air Force much thinner and make it more vulnerable. Secondly, the move would weaken the western air defense and this was exactly what the Allies wanted to do in preparation for the anticipated cross-channel invasion of the Continent.

Consequently Pelz agreed that anything Kesselring could do in southern Italy to delay or destroy the newly formed Fifteenth Air Force was vital. But the question still remained as to how this could be accomplished. The Luftwaffe was outnumbered in Italy, forced to use makeshift fields in the northern part of the country. Was it still possible, under these conditions, to launch an air strike which would result in slowing down the Allies on the ground and in the air? For the answer the German officers at the meeting turned to Richthofen, commander of Luftflotte Two.

Richthofen shrugged, "The only planes I have left for such an attack are my Ju-88s based in the north. Perhaps I could put 150 in the air at one time on a good day."

It was not an optimistic report, but Kesselring had not expected it to be. Ignoring the small number of bombers available, he asked for target suggestions from Pelz, Baumbach, and Richthofen. All three had different ideas. Baumbach immediately suggested the Allied planes and men at the former German airfield complex at Foggia. Pelz was in favor of a mass air raid against the advancing Allied Fifth Army in hopes of making the GIs dig in further south and stop their advance northward. The veteran Richthofen wanted to bomb the Allied ships and harbors, destroying their much-needed supplies before the material reached the ground and air forces.

Kesselring was too smart to commit himself at the outset. Instead he asked each man for further details on his suggestion and, following this, all four of the officers discussed each idea separately. At first glance the airfields at Foggia seemed likely targets, the most direct way to stop the American heavy bombers from striking deep into the underbelly of Germany and splitting the Luftwaffe forces. Baumbach had been a Wing commander in Italy late in 1942 and had seen how the Luftwaffe had been drained to its present weakened condition by searching the seas for the periscopes of American or British submarines and by strafing and bombing the elusive Allied transports on the sea. The sea campaign had been a failure. The German Air Force had been squandered while the Allied ground, air, and sea forces became stronger. Baumbach had no desire to waste the remaining Ju-88s on such targets. Consequently, he favored hitting the airfields at Foggia. If a large percentage of Doolittle's bombers could be caught unprotected on the ground by a surprise air strike and destroyed, the new Fifteenth Air Force would be blotted out before it got started.

Richthofen, however, pointed out the fallacy of the theory. There were too many airfields in the Foggia complex, so many that his handful of bombers would be spread much too thin to accomplish any real and lasting damage. If his entire Luftflotte Two concentrated on one single airfield the Flying Fortresses and Liberators on the other bases would go unharmed. Pelz, a disciple of saturation bombing, agreed with Richthofen.

On the other hand, Baumbach was strongly against trying to stop General Mark Clark's Fifth Army advance by using the remaining Ju-88s. He pointed out that the soldiers were not massed at one area, but were scattered over a wide section of the peninsula. There was no one focal point to bomb, no single mass of troops that could be wiped out and stop the Allied advance toward Rome. Certainly, he agreed, the Luftwaffe could make life miserable for the Fifth Army, but stop it? Absolutely not!

Kesselring next turned to Richthofen. He was convinced that the dynamic little general knew more about the day-to-day operations of the Luftwaffe in Italy than any other man. Richthofen did not hesitate to give his opinion. Supplies, he insisted, were the key to the current situation in Italy.

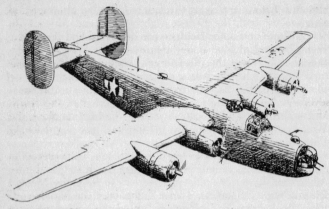

B–24

Already the Fifth and Eighth armies were slowing down because they had overextended their supply lines. An agent of the Abwehr, the German counterespionage section, had verified the shortage of supplies in his last report from Salerno. If the supply line could be cut—even temporarily—the results would be much more advantageous than the mere bombing of an airfield or a ground unit.

Kesselring nodded. He understood Richthofen's reasoning. "Do you have a specific target in mind?"

Richthofen did. "Bari."

The air general had been sending a reconnaissance Me-210 over the harbor at Bari every day for a week. Each day the pictures the plane brought back revealed more and more ships moored in the port. Baumbach looked at the aerial photographs that Richthofen displayed on the conference table and added that he had learned a few days earlier that Bari was the port for imcoming supplies and men destined for the Fifteenth Air Force.

The field marshal was immediately interested in the possibilities of bombing Bari. For the next hour the four German officers discussed the port and its importance to the Allies. Aides quickly obtained reports compiled by German agents pertaining to activities at the city on the Adriatic Sea. It became obvious that Bari was the main port for the Allies on the eastern coast of Italy, that not only were supplies for the

Fifteenth Air Force passing through the city, but also men and materials for both the British Eighth Army and Allied Fifth Army. These and other factors were discussed and finally the feeling was unanimous among the men at the Frascati conference that Bari was the ideal target. They agreed that an air strike on Bari harbor was a gamble, but one that must be taken. The British had hundreds of fighter planes in the area, several antiaircraft units composed of veterans of the North African fighting, and an excellent radar installation along the coast that could give ample warning of any approaching planes.

Despite the odds, however, Richthofen was ordered to gather all available bombers based in northern Italy and have them stand by for the mission. He was to have the Me-210 continue its daily reconnaissance flights over the harbor and, when the pictures and reports indicated the opportune time had arrived, the raid was to be launched.

On December 2 Oberleutnant Hahn crossed over the harbor of Bari at twenty-three thousand feet in his 370 mph reconnaissance plane heading south and then circling out to sea and flying over the inner breakwater on a westerly course on a second pass. The veteran Luftwaffe pilot could see the ships moored side by side on the East Jetty, anchored so close to each other, that they nearly touched. At the dock several other merchant ships were being unloaded. There did not appear to be an open space in the entire harbor, and Hahn knew that the time to strike had come. Banking his Me-210 steeply, he headed north to give his report.

As the sound of Oberleutnant Hahn's plane faded, a slim, dark-haired British officer stepped from the small building housing the Office of Harbor Defense and watched the contrail high in the sky drift with the wind. Captain A. B. Jenks swore softly as he stared at the telltale condensation trail. Jenks had the thankless job of trying to organize a proper defense system for Bari harbor and he was the one man who knew that he had neither the necessary manpower nor weapons to do so. He had tried to get this point across to his British military superiors, but they had dismissed him curtly, explaining that even if they did lack sufficient men and materials it really was not important. The Germans were not foolish enough to try and attack Bari. British Air Marshal Sir Arthur Coningham, commanding officer of the British air forces supporting the Eighth Army, even held a press conference the afternoon of December 2 to assure one and all that the German Air force in Italy had been thoroughly defeated and absolutely did not have the resources to intervene in any future Allied operation in the area.

"I would regard it as a personal affront and insult if the Luftwaffe would attempt any significant action in this area," he stated.

Jenks was not convinced, but, when he related his misgivings to a fellow officer after the press conference, the man laughed at him.

"The trouble with you, Jenks, is that the Germans have you scared. Ever since you lost your ship you've been a pessimist."

Shortly after the port had been opened for Allied shipping Jenks was assigned to a Q-class British destroyer with the task of sinking enemy boats that appeared along the heel of Italy. The mission sounded important but it really was not, since few enemy ships were in the area. The most dangerous part of the assignment was getting in and out of the harbor through the mine fields that the Italians had planted prior to surrendering. One morning Jenks's destroyer and three others came into the harbor in line. The first three destroyers passed through the channel safely but Jenks's ship hit an enemy mine.

The destroyer managed to stay afloat by some miracle, but everything aft of the stern gun position was badly damaged and thirty-two crewman were killed. Jenks maneuvered the destroyer into the dock, but the ship was a total loss. It was after he had lost his ship that Jenks was assigned to the harbor defense position. He realized that this experience might have made him overly jumpy, yet he felt he had evidence to support his contention that the Germans were still capable of fighting back. The German long-range bombers from northern Italy had stepped up their activity during the last days of November. They had staged air strikes against Naples which, with its surrounding facilities of Bagnoli and Torre Annunziata, was handling nine thousand tons of shipping per day. The Luftwaffe had attacked this area four times, using as many as 110 planes on one mission. While there had not been much damage to the shipping facilities, it was a clear indication, at least to Jenks, that the German Air force still was a danger.

In addition, the enemy bombers had renewed their attacks on Allied convoys. DO-217s and He-111s had sunk four ships off the coast of Oran during a raid in mid-November. On the twenty-fourth of the month the Luftwaffe had hit again, bombing La Maddalena, while two days later more than thirty German planes attacked another convoy off Bougie and sent a troop ship to the bottom. This last raid was made by the huge He-177 twin-engine monoplane, the first time this aircraft had appeared in Italy. To Jenks this was another warning that the Germans were trying to build up their forces on the penisula.

He was well aware that Bari had no real defense, that the city and the harbor were both vulnerable. The American heavy bombers of the Fifteenth Air Force were strictly offensive weapons and were of no use in defending the port city. The RAF had no fighter squadrons based on the Bari airfield, and those scattered throughout the heel of Italy and within range of Bari had escorting or attack assignments, not defensive missions. There was a single light antiaircraft squadron, Number 2862 AA Squadron, in the city. Since this unit made so much racket with their guns during practice sessions, few people in the city, even military personnel not familiar with the defensive setup, realized the small number of guns

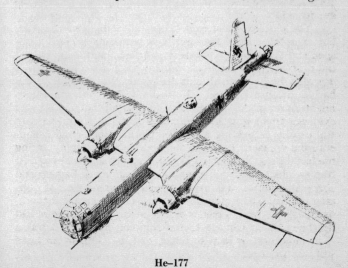

He–177

available in case of an air strike by the Germans. Number 2856 AA Squadron was assigned to Bari, but it had not yet arrived in full strength. Jenks also knew that the gunners assigned to the single antiaircraft unit in Bari depended upon the radar installation located on the Margherita Theater at the end of Victor Emmanuel Street to give them ample warning of approaching enemy aircraft. Unfortunately this installation, operated by the Number 548 Mobile Signals Unit, was not serviceable and had not been for several days. Technicians of the Number 305 Mobile Signals Servicing Unit had been working feverishly to get it back in operation, but by December 2 they still had not been successful. The radar screen was blank, the "eyes" of Bari harbor blind.

That old handmaiden of disaster, multiple command, also worried Jenks. There were too many "responsible" authorities in Bari. The British controlled the port. At least on paper the British were in command, but in reality who was giving the orders just depended upon what the situation was at a given time. So many Americans were in the city by December of 1943 that Bari appeared, at times to be dominated by them. And there was no question in Jenks's mind that the independent Yanks did just as they pleased anyway. He had been with the British naval officer who boarded the American Liberty ship *John Bascom* and he had to turn his face to hide his laughter at the remarks the U.S. Navy gunners made when they were told to cover their guns and not to fire at any time unless ordered to do so by a British officer. One young, redheaded Yank gunner looked at the British lieutenant and grinned, "I don't need no Limey to tell me when to start shooting. The first time anybody shoots in my direction, I'm shooting back."

Besides the multitude of devil-may-care Americans who resented taking orders from anyone except their own officers, Jenks wondered about the Italian officers and troops in Bari. Although these troops were aligned with the Allies now, it made him uneasy when he remembered that less than six months previously they had been fighting on the other side. Not that he did not like Italian officers such as General Nicola Belomo, commandant of the Presidio; small, debonair General Nicola Pascazio, chief of the SIM (Security Service); and bull-chested, rugged Captain Alfredo Spilotros who was deputy commander of all Italian defense troops along the southern coastline of the Adriatic Sea. They were friendly, cooperative, and always seemed willing to follow any orders given them. Yet, it was not an ideal situation for Bari or the Allied troops in the city or on the harbor who had to depend upon them to ward off any German attacks.

At 7:10 P.M., an hour after Oberleutnant Hahn made his final reconnaissance flight over Bari harbor, Jenks left the Stazione Marittima on the waterfront and walked toward the British officers' mess along the Lungomare. He felt that he had done everything within his power to warn his superiors about the vulnerability of the city's defenses. None had taken him seriously. In fact, as he headed for dinner, he was almost convinced that he was worrying over nothing, that the other officers were correct in their assumption that the Germans would not dare attack Bari. Almost, but not quite.

4

"LET'S GO TO THE CONCERT"

As Captain Jenks walked along the sea toward the British mess he passed many Italians hurrying toward the Chiesa San Domenico opera house on Victor Emmanuel Street. Among the concert-goers that December evening were Ruderi Francesco and his wife Pier. The Francescos rarely missed a concert, war or no war, and December 2 was no exception. Ruderi, a short, heavy Italian, was born in Milan, but had moved to Bari five years before the war began to work in the Bank of Italy, the beautiful marble-pillared building in the center of the city; he had never regretted it. Music was his avocation and, until the start of hostilities, he and his wife had traveled to France and Germany as well as all over Italy to hear their favorite concert artists. The surrender of Italy to the Allies in the fall of 1943 had not altered their habits in the slightest. The concerts, a part of Italian culture from the beginning, were held regardless of what nation controlled the country. Tonight Francesco had tickets to hear a little-known basso from Venice, but both he and his wife were looking forward to the concert with pleasure.

So were several other citizens of Bari that night. Paola Bartole, the restaurant owner who found the influx of GIs and British soldiers excellent for his business, was happily walking from his apartment on Abate Gimma toward the Piazza Liberta, whistling so loudly that others on the street turned and stared at him. Bartole had reason to be happy. That very afternoon he had made a deal with an American supply officer, a "you scratch my back, I'll scratch yours" type of deal that would keep his restaurant well stocked with meats, potatoes, eggs, and even some butter. In return he would make certain that the officer had an apartment to house his Italian mistress. War was hell—sometimes.

A block to his left Carlo Abbati and his crippled wife were moving slowly along Via Piccinni. Rose Abbati, nearing sixty years of age, knew firsthand the horrors of war, having been within twenty yards of an exploding hand grenade a year earlier. The fragments had nearly cut her left leg off, but the doctors had saved it. Now, as she limped toward the opera house on Victor Emmanuel Street, each step was a chore. Still, she enjoyed the evening out and in a gesture of gratitude to her hard-working husband she took his hand in hers. Carlo Abbati, a solemn-looking man with a large, hooked nose, smiled.

"It's not much further and we have plenty of time."

He had just finished speaking to his wife when he saw four young Italian men coming down Via Piccinni abreast. Realizing that the quartet did not intend to give him and his wife any room on the sidewalk, Carlo maneuvered his wife into a narrow store entrance. The stocky Italian nearest the old man bumped Carlo hard on the shoulder, spinning him around and nearly knocking him to the sidewalk.

"Watch where you are going, old man," the youth called as his companions laughed uproariously.

Abbati knew that they were ex-soldiers now working on the docks unloading Allied ships, roughnecks who never had been good fighters and were now overjoyed that they were a long way from the front. Angry, the old man rubbed his nose in the age-old sign of contempt. The four stopped, mutttered among themselves, and started back. At that moment, however, two American MPs stepped from the doorway of the Ficarelli Photo Shop and intercepted the four young men. A few words were exchanged and the quartet, looking sheepish, turned and hurried down the street. Abbati nodded solemnly to the Americans, took his wife's hand, and started slowly down the street again. He did not want to be late for the concert.

Bari, always a pleasant, peaceful city, was little changed by the war. While the Axis troops occupied the city there had been a few Allied air strikes, but most of these raids had been against the Bari airport on the outskirts where the Italian Air Force and Luftwaffe planes were based. A few scattered bombs had hit the city itself, but damage had been slight.

The Allies, planning the invasion of Italy, had wanted the city intact for their own use once the landings were accomplished; consequently it was bypassed during the heavy preinvasion bombardment southern Italy suffered. The city and the harbor were both divided into the *vecchia*, or old, and *nuova*, or new, sections. The old part of Bari, with its labyrinth of alleyways, was built on a peninsula washed by the sea on three sides. Narrow, winding streets, giving off to pleasant roads and squares, filled with such historical sites as the Arch of Marvels, Basilica of San Nicola, Piazza Ferrarese, and Largo San Pietro gave the old section a medieval aspect, even in 1943.

A long asphalt ribbon—two promenades—joined the old section to the new section of the city. New Bari was started in the year 1813 and, in contrast to the old city, had long, wide streets and modern buildings. The center of the new city lay between Victor Emmanuel where the opera house was located, Corso Cavour, a gay street lined by trees and fountains and home of the Petruzzelli Theater, one of the largest in all of Italy, and the railroad station at Piazza Roma. It was in the new Bari that the well-to-do businessmen and their families lived, where the elite hotels were located, the area where the concerts, art shows, and the university activities took place.

Traditional festivities such as the historical pageant commemorating Saint Nicholas always took place in the old section, however, where the fishermen and their families lived. Elio Dante was weary the night of December 2 because he had been out on the Adriatic Sea all day in his small blue fishing boat, but he had promised his sister Sophia that he would take her to church. Dante, wearing a faded blue shirt, dark pants that were one size too large for him, and shoes that were still wet from the seawater, picked up Sophia at her apartment on Via Venezia in the old city at 7:00 P.M. They walked through the Piazza Mercantile, cut north at the far end of the park, and hurried toward the Basilica of San Nicola. The old city was crowded as usual. The narrow streets were the playgrounds for the kids and there were soccer games in progress on every block. Dante yelled at several of the kids who threatened to run into his sister, but he was not angry. He had played at the same sport when he was younger and had been yelled at the same way. The old city did not have open areas for playgrounds, did not have backyards to hang up the washing. The two- and three-story houses were jammed together on each side of the narrow streets and the washed clothes hung from windows, on porches, and on roofs to dry. Many times Dante had wondered if anyone in the old city would survive if enemy planes bombed it. There were no shelters, no place to hide. But he no longer had to worry about such a disaster he decided. With the city swarming with American and British troops, the harbor filled with Allied ships of all nationalities, the mention of a German air strike only brought derisive hoots from his friends. They were probably correct.

Mass was scheduled for 7:30 P.M. Dante and his sister Sophia reached the church early, but Renzo Zanelli and Umberto Vona, coming from the other side of the old city, did not think they would make it in time. They had worked late on the docks unloading the merchant ships that had come into Bari harbor in a steady stream the past week or so. Both men had wanted to quit work at 6:00 P.M., but the British officer in charge of the unloading had insisted that they stay an hour longer. Now, as they hurried across Piazza Pietro toward the Basilica of San Nicola, they were too short of breath to continue talking about the plane they had seen circling above the harbor less than one hour earlier. At the time, however, both men had been concerned. Months earlier they had been stationed with an Italian infantry unit south of Naples when an American P-38 had circled overhead in the same manner. Later that same day the infantry unit had been bombed and strafed by American fighter planes and Zanelli had been badly wounded. Neither man had ever forgotten the attack—nor the reconnaissance plane that had marked them as a target.

As the pair reached Piazza San Nicola, Vona asked the question that he had asked half a dozen times since he had seen the plane over the harbor, "Do you think it was a German aircraft?"

Zanelli shrugged, "It was too high. Stop worrying. The port director saw it, too. He will do what is necessary."

Antonio Urbani, Giovanni Tomei, and Silvio Zugno could not have cared less whether a plane had flown over Bari harbor that day or not. They had fewer worries at age seventeen than the older citizens of the city and, as they left the old city and rode along the harbor front on their motorcycles, their main concern was whether or not they could get into "Bambino Stadium" to see a baseball game that was to be

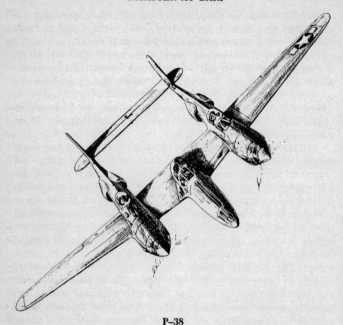

P–38

played by two American teams composed of soldiers from
General Depot Number Five. The trio worked at the depot
for the Americans, so they decided they might see one of the
GIs they worked with and he could get them into the game.
Urbani loved baseball, ever since he had discovered an old
book explaining the game in the university library. His companions were soccer fans, but had agreed to accompany him
to "Bambino Stadium" in order to get out of the congested,
noisy old section of the city. To many of the younger genera-
tion, the wall completely surrounding the old city seemed to
be a hated barrier and they crossed it everytime they had a
chance. At seventeen years of age, they were too young to be
in the army, too old to play in the street. They needed
excitement and the ball game offered it to them on December 2. The furthest thing from their minds was the threat of a
Luftwaffe air strike on Bari. They never even considered such
a possibility.

Neither did the tall, blond girl lounging on the corner of

Via Napoli and Via Pizzola. Maria's only real experience with war was the men it brought to Bari. Germans, Americans, British—she did not really care what nationality they were as long as they were friendly and, more important, had money. Since Italy had surrendered and the Americans had arrived in Bari, she had led a more interesting and profitable life. Lonely Americans, enlisted soldiers and officers, liked the company of beautiful women and, since she was beautiful and cooperative, for a price, deals had been easy to make. At 6:45 P.M. on the evening of December 2 Maria was waiting to close another deal, one that she had made two nights earlier in a bar on Corso Cavour with an American sergeant from General Depot Number Five. As she waited, she glanced at the air raid shelter in the middle of the street and smiled. Since there were no air raids to be concerned about, no one went into the shelters, so where could a lonely sergeant and a willing Italian girl find a more suitable place to comfort each other? After all, Maria decided, there was no use allowing the air raid shelters to be completely wasted.

Giacinto Iusco also had an appointment with an American, but his business deal was of an entirely different nature. An artist, Iusco had been working with an Allied training unit painting posters, illustrating instructive material, and making sketches for training booklets. When an American colonel visited the unit and spotted Iusco at work, he offered to pay the artist to paint a portrait of him to send back to the United States. Iusco agreed and the appointment was set for 7:15 P.M. on the evening of December 2 at Iusco's apartment a block from the waterfront. By 7:00 P.M. he had his brushes and paints ready, had the chair for the colonel placed where he wanted it, so that the light would hit the officer correctly, and had opened a bottle of wine. Iusco loved to paint and he hoped that nothing would interfere with this portrait sitting. He hated interruptions.

Another Italian who hated interruptions was Bruno Vigorelli, a dockworker who had fallen from the deck of a ship into a hold the morning of December 2 and was taken to Three New Zealand General Hospital for treatment. It was discovered that his left leg was broken and Vigorelli was unhappy when Matron M. E. Jackson informed him that he would be a patient for at least two weeks. After thinking it over, however, he decided that he was a lucky man to have been admitted to the Three New Zealand General Hospital.

Doctors and nurses were still scarce in the Bari area, since all the hospital equipment and personnel to operate the Allied hospitals had to be transferred from North Africa to Italy and transportation facilities were overburdened. Combat personnel took precedence on the ships and aircraft, with medical personnel getting whatever space was left over. Vigorelli realized that he could have been treated briefly at a first aid station on the dock and left to shift for himself instead of being assigned a bed at the huge Three New Zealand General Hospital south of the city.

The Three New Zealand General Hospital personnel had arrived from Tripoli on November 1, 1943, on board a merchant ship and had been taken immediately to the Bari Polyclinic three miles south of the city. The Bari Polyclinic was one of Mussolini's grand schemes that had never been completed. He had planned to use the complex of buildings for the furtherance of the public health of all the citizens in southern Italy. The main group of buildings was in the form of a horseshoe with wings jutting from it in all directions. Within the curve of the horseshoe was a large, two-story building that had obviously been intended as an administration headquarters for the whole clinic. Near the open end of the shoe was a connecting verandah and in its center a tall tower which Mussolini intended to be a solarium. There were also several large, detached buildings, all within the same grounds, composing twenty complete blocks in all.

When Colonel G. W. Gower, CBE, commanding officer, and the personnel of the Three New Zealand General Hospital arrived from North Africa they were allotted a couple of the blocks jutting out from the central horseshoe of the Bari Polyclinic. The smaller block was for surgical and the other for medical patients. Gower, Staff Sergeant A. J. Taylor, and Lieutenant Colonel L. A. Bennett, the officer in charge of the surgical division, promptly nicknamed the two buildings "Tripoli" and "Beirut." On November 5 the first patient was admitted to the Three New Zealand General Hospital, the following day thirty-two more came, and, by November 11, Gower had three wards ready, equipped with a total of 205 beds.

By the end of the month Three New Zealand General Hospital had admitted 656 patients and discharged 237, mostly medical cases from a New Zealand Division operating in the north. It was obvious to Gower that his unit needed more beds, more doctors, more equipment, and each day he checked the docks at Bari harbor in an effort to learn whether the arriving ships carried any of his requirements. On December 2 the critical shortage was once again brought to the colonel's attention. A convoy of casualties was due to arrive at the railroad station off Piazza Roma at 7:00 P.M., wounded from the front, but already the three wards of Three New Zealand General Hospital were crowded. Gower finally decided that, if necessary, he would put stretchers in the unfinished part of the Bari Polyclinic, even if there were no lights, no water, and no sanitary arrangements in the section. He had to put the men someplace.

Sergeant Major A. J. Robson and Sergeant Major T. M. McCauley, waiting for the wounded from the hospital train to arrive, were in the patients' recreation room arguing about the merits of soccer and rugby. Robson, a tough, long-legged soccer player, was insisting that his favorite sport was more rugged than rugby football, that a good soccer player needed more skill than a football player. They were so loud that the other members of the hospital staff and the patients in the room trying to watch the movie on the small screen complained. Finally Robson looked at his companion and grinned, "We'll settle this argument once and for all in the morning."

Neither man realized that long before the dawn of the next day they would be too busy to recall what they were even discussing.

A few blocks south of the Bari Polyclinic where the Three New Zealand General Hospital sergeant majors were arguing, Kathryn Salo, a U.S. Army nurse attached to the newly arrived American Twenty-six General Hospital detachment, was still trying to get accustomed to Italy. The Twenty-six General Hospital personnel had already seen a lot of the world. The medical detachment had landed in Liverpool, England, in October, 1942, took a train to Birmingham where it stayed until moving to Oran, North Africa, in February of the next year. Later at Constantine, the Twenty-six operated a tent base hospital of more than two thousand beds. On November 25, 1943, the unit arrived at Taranto, Italy, leaving the next day for Bari. In Bari, Kathyrn Salo and her companions took over the Ospedale Militare, a former Italian sanitorium on Via Bonomo, and began getting it ready for use as an American medical hospital. After months in North Africa, living in tents, the nurses immediately, upon arriving at Bari, decided to go shopping for furniture to use in their quarters

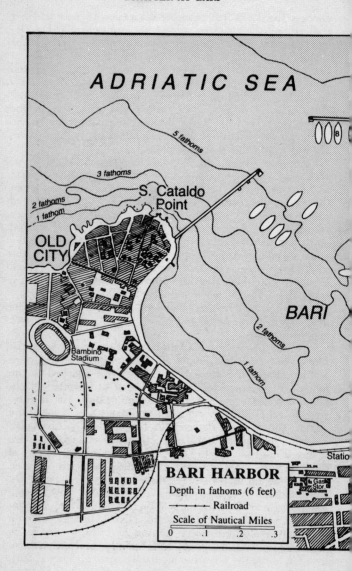

ADRIATIC SEA

5 fathoms

3 fathoms

2 fathoms

1 fathom

S. Cataldo
Point

OLD
CITY

BARI

2 fathoms

1 fathom

Bambino
Stadium

Statio

Gas
Stor.

BARI HARBOR

Depth in fathoms (6 feet)

———•——— Railroad

Scale of Nautical Miles

0   .1   .2   .3

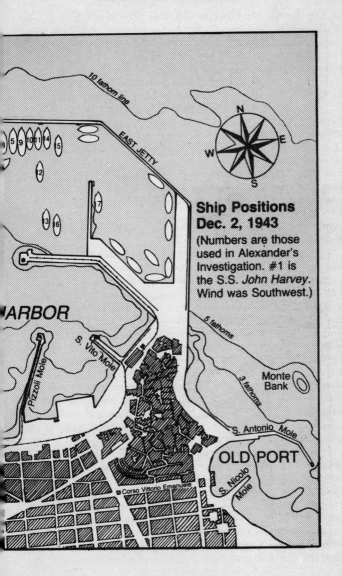

**Ship Positions
Dec. 2, 1943**
(Numbers are those used in Alexander's Investigation. #1 is the S.S. *John Harvey*. Wind was Southwest.)

at the Twenty-six General Hospital. For more than a year Kathyrn and the other nurses had not even had a chair to sit on and now that such things were available they were determined to buy them. They ordered desks, chairs, chests of drawers, and lamps and impatiently waited for delivery. Salesmen had been waving their arms and spouting promises in Italian, but the furniture never arrived. Finally, however, on the afternoon of December 2, many of the items were brought to the hospital and Kathyrn spent several hours arranging the furniture in her quarters, enjoying the task, as it had been a long time since she had had the opportunity to do such work.

After dinner she was preparing to rest, but it was such a nice evening that when an infantry officer who had been reassigned to the Twenty-six General Hospital staff asked her to go for a walk she agreed. At 7:10 P.M. they sauntered down Via Bonomo unaware that the quiet of the evening at Bari was very near an end.

John Shifflet, a baker at the hospital, saw the nurse and her companion disappear down Via Bonomo and wished that he had the time to go for a walk himself, but he did not. He had work to do in the kitchen, especially now that one officer and nineteen more enlisted men were arriving to help staff the Twenty-six. Word had arrived that the Liberty ship *Samuel J. Tilden*, carrying the medical personnel, had entered Bari harbor and that the men would soon disembark. He was certain that they would be hungry. Men such as Buster Long, Pete Gasparich, Steve Corey, and Leo Kaczmarczyk seemed always to be hungry and Shifflet was determined to welcome them to Italy with a good meal. Forgetting about the walk he would like to take, he went back to the stove and opened the oven door. It was time to go to work, he decided, since it was going to be a long night. A very long night.

Other people were waiting for the *Samuel J. Tilden* to dock, too. Clifford Price of the Fifth Medical Supply Depot was just across the railroad yards from the harbor preparing a space in the depot building for the medical supplies arriving on the *Samuel J. Tilden*. The Twenty-six General Hospital could not begin operations until the X-ray equipment, beds, drugs, bandages, and other items were delivered to Bari. The Fifth Medical Supply Depot was also assigned the task of keeping the Fifteenth Air Force medical detachments supplied, a task which was impossible as long as the depot buildings were empty.

"I hope they unload the *Tilden* as soon as the anchor is wet," Price muttered as he cleaned the debris out of the corner of the building. "We had more medicine back in St. Mary's than we have here."

Price was referring to the small town in the hills of West Virginia where he was born.

At an Italian warehouse on the outskirts of Bari the men of the Fourth Medical Supply Depot were also preparing for the delivery of medical supplies from three transports that were scheduled for unloading at the harbor on December 2. Walter R. Anderson, executive officer of the unit, had arrived in Italy on November 6 and had been trying to get the depot organized in Bari in order to service the medical groups responsible to the Foggia airfield complex. The main section of the Fourth Medical Supply Depot was stationed at Naples and a second section was located at Casablanca. It had been a difficult assignment for Anderson to get his depot operating at Bari. Ship transportation was scarce and, since the British controlled the port, ships carrying supplies for the British Eighth Army and other English units were scheduled for unloading long before those ships carrying cargo destined for American units. Now, however, it appeared that he was finally going to get the long-awaited medical supplies. His ships were in the harbor. In fact, they were at the unloading dock.

In order to discuss the final details of the depot organization, Anderson had invited two officers of his staff who had arrived from Naples that afternoon to his room on the top floor of the Hotel Miramar, located a short distance from the harbor. Donald McGregor and John V. DeLuca made their final plans for handling the medical supplies after listening to the briefing by Anderson about the situation in Bari. They were so interested in their discussion that it was not until DeLuca looked out the hotel window that any of the men realized it was getting dark. He looked at his watch. It was exactly 7:25 P.M.

Fifty miles northeast of Bari Oberleutnant Gustav Teuber looked at his watch, too. It also read 7:25 P.M. At one-thousand-feet altitude above the Adriatic Sea, Teuber still

Ju–88

could not see the lights of Bari through the cockpit window of
his Ju-88, but he knew that he and the other Luftwaffe
bombers in the formation were nearing their target—the
harbor at Bari. At that moment the flight leader started a
gradual descent toward the water below, Teuber eased the
nose of his plane down slightly and followed. The plan was to
get under the radar screen operating at Bari, to completely
surprise the British defenses at the port. He hoped the plan
worked. Reconnaissance pilot Hahn had promised the harbor
defenses were not alert, that the sneak attack would be
successful. Within minutes Teuber knew he would find out
whether Hahn was right or not.

5

"LOOK! A PIECE OF TINFOIL!"

German reconnaissance pilot Werner Hahn flew straight north after making his final pass over Bari harbor in the Me-210 on December 2. He knew that Richthofen was eagerly awaiting his report, that all available Luftwaffe bombers were gassed and loaded with bombs at the scattered airfields in northern Italy, ready to take off at a moment's notice for Bari if the word was given. Hahn stayed away from land, flying over the Adriatic Sea, hoping to avoid any Allied fighters that might be hunting his aircraft after being alerted by the Bari defenses. He also maintained his altitude, planning on starting a steep descent north of the Manfredonia spur. Looking at his panel clock, however, Hahn saw that it was getting late, that his reconnaissance flight had taken longer than anticipated. If the bombers were going to reach Bari just at dusk, as desired, he would have to speed up his return to base. With this in mind, the oberleutnant rolled the trim tab forward on the Me-210 and started a slow descent that also permitted him to pick up some extra airspeed. He was still south of Manfredonia instead of being north as planned.

At five thousand feet he crossed the coastline directly west of Foggia, a mistake that very nearly cost him his life. A flash of an object in the sun suddenly caught his attention. He stared toward the spot where he had first seen the flash, but the sky seemed clear. He kept observing the area for several seconds and finally decided he must have imagined the flash. Then, just as Hahn was about to forget the incident, he saw two small black dots far to the west of his Me-210.

"Fighters!"

It soon became obvious to the Luftwaffe flier that the

two dots in the sky were rapidly growing bigger, a definite indication that they were moving in on him. Using maximum power, Hahn headed back out to sea, but he was too late. The next time he looked at the dots he could clearly see that they had two engines and twin tail booms. The dots were now P-38s and the Lightnings were racing after him, gaining on his Me-210 every second. He decided to "hit the deck."

Flying only a few feet above the water at maximum manifold pressure and rpm, Hahn kept his aircraft in a constant twisting, turning course in an effort to avoid the guns of the Allied fighters. Several times he saw spouts of water at the side of his plane where the shells from the P-38 guns had hit after narrowly missing the Me-210, but, fortunately for the reconnaissance pilot, no damage was inflicted on his aircraft and east of Vasto the two Allied fighters gave up the chase and turned south. Hahn maintained maximum power and returned to his base at treetop height.

Hauptmann K. H. Millahn was waiting when the Me-210 touched down in northern Italy. Millahn, a veteran Ju-88 pilot of Bomber Wing Seventy-six, was temporarily grounded for a few months for a rest from flight operations and was assigned to staff work. He was well aware of the planned air strike on the shipping in Bari harbor. Not only were the available bombers of Bomber Wing Seventy-six prepared to make the mission, but so were the aircraft of the other wings still remaining in northern Italy: Twenty-six, Thirty, Fifty-four, Seventy-seven, and One Hundred. Pilots such as Hans Feich, a former Stuka flier who had flown hundreds of missions against Russian targets; Hugo Glatt, who had bombed London night after night earlier in the war; Klaus Grabow, a survivor of a night's swimming in the English Channel after his bomber had been shot down by a Spitfire over Land's End; Alfred Kathner, Ewald Izler, and Herbert Krenz, a trio who had spent hours in the air over Crete and Malta on air strikes against Allied installations; and Lothar Lintow, a pilot who had flown many missions in He-111s against British and American shipping in the Mediterranean Sea and had accompanied the renowned Robert Kowalewski on several "Swedish turnip" forays.

The "Swedish turnip" system was a special method of attacking enemy ships developed by Kowalewski and Martin Harlinhausen, X Fleigercorps chief of staff, in 1940. It was based on the ancient naval axiom that ships present the best target when approached from the beam. And the lower the aircraft's approach, the higher the target stands out of the water, and the clearer becomes its silhouette against the horizon. The last applied particularly at dusk, but also on moonlight or starlight nights. Kowalewski was one of the few pilots who had nerve enough to use the system at the beginning, but later other pilots such as Lintow, now stationed in northern Italy, had learned the technique.

It was not easy. Usually Kowalewski would approach the ship to be attacked at a speed of about 200 mph and an altitude of forty-five meters. It was difficult to maintain such height, especially at dusk or after dark, since most barometric altimeters were too unreliable. The altimeter often indicated that the plane was flying several feet under the water. Consequently, Kowalewski had to fly perfectly level once he established the correct height and not permit the nose of the bomber to dip even a few inches. He had figured that at that speed and altitude a bomb would fall five meters the first second, fifteen meters the second second, and twenty-five meters the third second after release, or a total of forty-five meters in all. In this time the bomber covered a distance of two hundred forty meters so, in order to hit the target, that was the exact distance from which the bombs must be released. During the three seconds the loss of momentum for the bombs was minimal; they at first flew with the bomber and below it, then dropped against the target in a gentle arc.

During the early part of the war Kowalewski had succeeded three times in sinking two ships on one sortie by using this technique. He was credited with sinking more than a hundred thousand tons of Allied shipping and his system was used by Luftwaffe crews in all the theaters of combat, although none of the other pilots reached Kowalewski's peak of perfection. Now, as the air strike on Bari was planned, his "Swedish turnip" system was once again in the limelight. Richthofen had suggested that the 105 Ju-88 crews that he had managed to gather for the proposed raid use Kowalewski's technique, hoping to get underneath the radar screen at Bari and to reach the harbor before the British defenses in the area were alerted.

Richthofen had another surprise for the British defenses. His Ju-88s were supplied with a large quantity of *Duppel*. This was the German name for a secret radar jamming technique developed by the British in 1942 and consisted of strips of tinfoil cut to certain lengths and widths. When dropped from the air each of these strips looked like an aircraft on the radar screen and made it impossible for the ground gunners to distinguish between the strips and the actual aircraft. The British had first used the tinfoil strips that they called "Window" on Hamburg in July, 1943, and its effect surpassed expectations. For some months after the initial use of "Window," British bomber losses dropped to nearly half. Goering was quick to realize the advantages of the new device and ordered his Luftwaffe bombers to use it when the occasion arose. Richthofen decided that at Bari the *Duppeler* technique would be of benefit and a large supply, cut to the required wave length to dupe the radar installations along the Adriatic Sea, had been provided to Lintow, Teuber, and the other pilots assigned to make the daring air strike.

The 105 Ju-88s, including several carrying flares to bathe Bari harbor in brilliant light, took off from the various temporary airfields used by the Luftwaffe in northern Italy shortly after Hahn landed his Me-210 reconnaissance plane and gave his report. The field order called for the aerial strike force to fly east until they were over the Adriatic Sea then fly south until they reached the Bari area. Richthofen was confident that the British and Americans did not expect a major air strike on the city or harbor, that the nuisance raids that had been carried out by one or two German planes earlier had conditioned them to ignore any serious threat to Bari. The field marshal also knew that the British ground defenses were geared to attacks from the north since the Luftwaffe had been driven from the air bases at Foggia to a line above Rome by December, 1943. Little thought had been given to the few fields used by the Germans in the Balkans. While Richthofen planned on using the Ju-88s based in northern Italy, he decided to make it appear that his planes had come from the Balkans by using a few Ju-88s from Yugoslavia. Thus, retaliatory raids against the more important German bases in northern Italy might be avoided at the expense of such Allied air strikes against the less important bases in the Balkans. Consequently he ordered his pilots to attack Bari from the Adriatic Sea, to come in from the east, skimming the water at low level just at dusk. The planes from Yugoslavia joined the formation out at sea.

At 7:25 P.M. Oberleutnant Teuber made the turn west

that put his plane on course for Bari. He looked at his instruments. Altimeter, forty-five meters. Airspeed, 200 mph. Compass reading, 270 degrees.

Teuber's estimated time of arrival over the target: 7:30 P.M.

The unloading at the docks in Bari was proceeding well on the night of December 2 and Votl Lienhard, officer in charge of Ordnance Section (Advanced) AAF, Mediterranean Theater of Operations, was pleased. It appeared to him that finally, after days of waiting, the bombs and ammunition destined for the air bases at Foggia were going to be removed from the merchant ships and loaded onto the trucks waiting to take the cargo north. Lester V. Light, Mediterranean Theater of Operations ordnance officer, had been pressuring Lienhard to get the supplies to Doolittle's new air force. This would relieve some of the pressure. He smiled contentedly as he watched the unloading proceed at dockside, completely oblivious to the fact that Richthofen's Ju-88s were almost within earshot to the east.

Lienhard did not hear the German bombers, probably because of the noise at dockside; but approximately sixty miles to the north of Bari Lewis W. McIntyre thought he heard a strange noise. McIntyre was civil affairs officer for the Allied military forces in charge of the Gargantian Peninsula. He had his quarters at a small summer beach a few miles south of Manfredonia. That evening he was invited to have dinner at the officer's mess of the British unit in charge of the antiaircraft battery located near his headquarters and had just sat down at the table when he heard the sound of airplanes. Glancing out the window toward the west, toward the airfields at Foggia, McIntyre saw nothing. The sky was empty. Since it was approaching dusk, however, he decided that he must have missed the American formation that had passed over the mess. One question bothered him? Why would the daylight bombers of the Fifteenth Air Force be flying so late in the evening? Unfortunately, neither McIntyre nor the British officers eating with him looked to the east or they might have seen Richthofen's Ju-88s streaking south over the Adriatic Sea toward Bari.

Forty miles south of Manfredonia, William P. Jones, Jr., was working in his office at Fifteenth Army Group Headquarters located at the small village of San Spirito on the coast of the Adriatic Sea. Fifteenth Army Group Headquarters was under the command of Field Marshal Sir Harold R. L. G. Alexander, but was an integrated British-American headquarters that commanded the British Eighth and U.S. Fifth armies in Italy. Jones lived upstairs in the villa used for the headquarters building, while his office was downstairs in a room with a huge glass door that gave him an excellent view of the surrounding area. He, too, heard the sound of aircraft on the evening of December 2, but, since more and more Allied fighter planes and bombers were based in Italy every day, he paid scant attention to them as they passed near the villa. At this moment, when the sound of the planes reached the ears of Jones, Oberleutnant Teuber and his fellow German pilots were only minutes from the ships in Bari harbor.

Donald J. Reap, an American attached to a British Eighth Army unit at San Spirito, was not aware of the German aircraft flying toward Bari fifteen miles to the south either. Previously Reap had been assigned to an American antiaircraft outfit near Orna in North Africa and he was an expert in plane identification and ground defenses against low-flying aircraft, but this experience was of no use to him this evening, since he was completely unaware of Richthofen's Ju-88s.

Secrecy was the keyword of the Luftwaffe raid against Bari, and at a very small village twelve miles east of Bari, Alexander J. Repke, commander of the First Platoon of A Troop, 117th Cavalary Reconnaissance Squadron, well knew the value of the word. His unit was a mobile, armed security platoon assigned to provide protection for the Advanced Command Post, Allied Forces, that was located in the small village of Bitonto. The Advanced Command Post was top secret and only high-ranking officers of the British and American military forces were aware that it existed. General Dwight D. Eisenhower held many of his strategic conferences at this headquarters that had the code name "Mayfair." Repke and his men furnished the protection for the field marshals and generals attending such conferences, as well as making certain that the headquarters was concealed from the public eye. "Mayfair" was not being used for a conference on the evening of December 2, but the men of the 117th Cavalry Reconnaissance Squadron, including Repke, were stationed in the vicinity of the post. As he made his rounds that evening at dusk, Repke could see the glow of lights at Bari harbor twelve miles away and knew that dockhands were working throughout the night. Seeing the lights in a combat zone had concerned him when he first arrived at Bitonto, but now, after several weeks of the procedure without incident, he took for granted the Luftwaffe had given up trying to stop the Allies from using the port of Bari. He was soon to find out he was wrong.

Roy E. Gibson, a radio operator of the 416th Signal Company, had arrived in Bari from Naples early in the morning of December 2 by truck convoy. That same evening, after getting his billet assignment in an Italian schoolhouse across the street from the seawall of the harbor, Gibson was assigned to duty at the Fifteenth Air Force Headquarters. The radio room was in the wing of the building extending away from the street on the ground floor. As he took his chair in front of his radio set, Gibson did not give an instant's thought to the possibility of a German air attack, even though the Bari area was entirely new to him. He had had a full day and was tired. To add to his troubles, he had difficulty copying messages from wing headquarters at Foggia because of static. He had so much trouble with the crackling in his headset that he did not even notice that the other operators were hurrying from the radio room at first. He kept struggling with his radio, desperately trying to clear up the reception, but it was no use. At this moment he decided to ask the operator next to him for help, but when he turned to him he discovered that the chair was empty. Gibson looked around the room and discovered he was alone. There were no other operators in the entire room. Slipping his headset off his ears, he suddenly heard a large gun stationed behind the headquarters building fire, heard other guns firing in the distance, heard the roar of a plane flying over the building at low level. He returned to his radio set and sent "Q," the signal for air raid.

A few minutes before Gibson sent the signal over the radio from Fifteenth Air Force Headquarters, an Italian schooner loaded with a cargo of olive oil had slipped its mooring in the old harbor of Bari where the fishing boats anchored and headed out to sea. In command of the schooner was Michael A. Musmanno, a U.S. Navy officer who had been on the staff of General Mark W. Clark, but was now military governor of the Sorrentine Peninsula of Italy, a territory that embraced about fifteen towns and a population of some two hundred

thousand. Of Italian descent himself, Musmanno had quickly
agreed with the inhabitants of the area that the available food
was unpalatable without olive oil. Since there was no olive oil
in the area of the Sorrentine Peninsula, Musmanno decided
to make a sea trip to Bari to obtain a supply. He was using a
schooner owned by merchant Francesco Merefredo that had
been raised from the bottom of the port of Castellammare
after being sunk by the Germans when they evacuated the
peninsula ahead of the Allied advance. Musmanno and his
crew of three—Giuseppe Barcelli, Giovanni Catella, and
Fabiano Menorisini, all Italian fishermen—had repaired the
hull, calked the seams, erected the masts and reinstalled the
125-horsepower diesel engine that had been removed by the
Germans. They then set sail for Bari, going down the western
coast of Italy, through the Straits of Messina, and heading
northward to Brindisi and their destination. The *Inaffondabile*,
as they had named the schooner, arrived at the harbor of Bari
at 8:00 A.M. on the morning of December 2 and, after
Musmanno made a few contacts with officers he had known
previously, he obtained the olive oil. Late in the afternoon
the cargo was loaded aboard the schooner. Shortly after 7:00
P.M. that night he made a final check of the three hundred
quintals of olive oil stored in the vats on deck, wrapped his
blue scarf around his neck, and gave the signal to his crew to
set sail for home.

The sky was dark enough that Musmanno could see a
few stars as the *Inaffondabile* moved slowly out of the old
harbor at Bari. Suddenly he felt hungry and remembered
that he had been so busy hunting the olive oil that he had
forgotten to eat. Reaching into his pocket, he pulled out a
candy bar he had bought at the American exchange and
started eating it. As he stood with one hand gripping the
helm, the other holding the candy bar, he felt a soft fluttering
object hit his face. Dropping his candy bar, he snatched at
the unknown object thinking it was a large flying bug. Holding it in his fist, he turned the beam of the flashlight on it.
He stared at it a second and broke out laughing. It was a
piece of tinfoil that came from his candy bar, although he was
puzzled as to how the wind could have lifted it from the deck
where it evidently had fallen and blown it fore instead of aft,
the direction the wind was blowing. Before he could solve
that puzzle another piece of tinfoil, this time a very long strip
of it, drifted onto the deck. Musmanno glanced about and

saw the silvery ribbons of tinfoil descending everywhere. Barcelli came hurrying toward him clutching a fistful of the tinsel in his hand. It was then that Musmanno understood. It was "Window."

"Fermate macchine! Stop the engine!" he exclaimed. "It's from German planes. Get down!"

He threw himself behind an olive oil cask.

The disaster at Bari was only seconds away.

6

"I SEE A FLARE!"

Aboard the Liberty ship *John Bascom* Captain Heitmann had finished paying his crew from the two thousand dollars he had drawn from the U.S. Army Finance Section, Sixtieth Service Group, in Bari that afternoon and granted shore leave to some of them. He was putting the remaining $1,268 in the ship's safe just as Chief Engineer Dean M. Herrick started down the gangplank followed by the seventeen other crew members leaving for an evening in Bari. Glancing toward the stern of the ship he saw some of Ensign Vesole's gun crew frowning and he knew the reason. None of them were permitted to go ashore because of an 8:00 P.M. curfew for gun crews serving as armed guard units on the merchant ships. In a way Heitmann felt sorry for them, knowing that it had been a difficult and dangerous crossing the *John Bascom* had just completed, but there was nothing he could do to help. Military orders could not be changed by a captain of a merchant ship.

Kay Vesole was also aware of the disappointment felt by his twenty-eight gunners and two signalmen, but he knew they would soon get over it. They were a fine crew, well-disciplined, dedicated. Once the *John Bascom* was unloaded he would see that they got shore leave, too. Vesole, thirty years of age, was a former member of the Iowa State Guard, but had been in the U.S. Navy since 1942. Born in Poland, he was brought to the United States when he was seven years old, graduated from the University of Iowa, and was an attorney prior to entering the U.S. Navy. He was considered one of the best gunnery officers in the service and had the complete confidence of his men. Heitmann, not a skipper to

56

lavish praise on a man very often, thought Vesole was the finest ensign he had ever known. The feeling was mutual.

Otto Heitmann had begun his career on the sea as an ordinary seaman in 1922 and was a veteran skipper for the Moore-McCormack Lines at the outbreak of World War II. In December of 1942, while en route from Trinidad to Rio de Janeiro, Brazil, as captain of the S.S. *West Maximus*, Heitmann had spotted what he first thought was an enemy submarine, but turned out to be an empty lifeboat. Checking further in the submarine-infested waters, he discovered two small boats carrying survivors from a British ship that had been sunk by a torpedo. During the evening of December 2 at Bari, as he stood on the deck of the *John Bascom*, he fingered the silver cigarette case that had been presented him for the rescue. He knew without looking the words that were engraved on the cover: "Presented to Captain Otto Heitmann, Master of the American M.V. West Maximus, by the British Community of Rio de Janeiro as a token of appreciation of the services of himself, his officers and crew in rescuing at sea 41 survivors of the British M.V. Teesbank lost by enemy action. December, 1942."

"Flare! I see a flare!" The bellow jolted his reminiscing.

Heitmann rushed to the bridge of the *John Bascom* when he heard the warning shouted by his second officer, William Rudolph. He immediately spotted two steady white lights suspended in the sky east of the harbor and knew at once that they were parachute flares dropped from aircraft. There was no reason for Allied planes to use such flares over the harbor of Bari. It had to be German aircraft. He glanced at his watch. It was exactly 7:35 P.M.

"Battle stations!"

As soon as his order was relayed to the crew members remaining on board the *John Bascom*, Heitmann searched the sky for some sign of the German planes, but from his position on the port wing of the bridge he could not see any. Shore battery antiaircraft guns started firing and almost simultaneously Vesole's gun crew on the *John Bascom* went into action. The dark blue sky over the harbor was soon densely covered with tracer bullets and the noise caused by the gunfire made it impossible for the captain to hear any enemy planes.

"Bomb hit on the starboard!"

The first explosion was off the harbor, in the city, and flames were visible above the rooftops of the business buildings on Corso Cavour. He guessed that the bombs had hit on either Via Abate Gimma or Via Sparano di Bari. Later he discovered that both streets had been hit. Heitmann did not have time to stand and watch the burning city, however, since the German bombers had already discovered their error and were "walking" the bombs out into the water straight toward the line of ships anchored at the East Jetty. Yard by yard the bombs came closer, working their way up the moored Liberty ships one by one from south to north. The *Joseph Wheeler* took a direct hit and burst into flames; moments later the *John L. Motley*, anchored next to the *John Bascom*, took a bomb on its number five hatch and the deck cargo on the ship caught fire. Heitmann saw the crew of the *John L. Motley* begin dousing the burning cargo with water from the fire hoses.

"Rudolph! Collins! Get the fire hoses ready for use."

As Rudolph and Allen G. Collins, the third officer of the *John Bascom*, supervised the unreeling of the fire hoses, the captain studied the situation in the harbor. He knew that unless he could move the *John Bascom*, it was going to be hit by the attacking planes. He considered letting go of both anchor cables, cutting the mooring lines, and steaming out of the harbor. He soon realized, however, that this action was impossible under the conditions that confronted him. The wind was on the starboard side and with only about thirty feet clearance between his ship and the *John L. Motley*, there was no chance he could get the *John Bascom* away without a collision. Since the *John L. Motley* was burning fiercely at this time, there was a possibility that her cargo of bombs and high-octane gas would explode. A collision with her would be fatal to the *John Bascom*. Besides, about fifteen hundred feet ahead of Heitmann was a ship at anchor, loaded with ammunition, and to the north of that ship was another. Even if the *John Bascom* cleared the flaming *John L. Motley*, he could not avoid colliding with these two ships. There was no escape.

At Pier Twenty-nine a small fire had started on board the *John Harvey*!

On the bridge of the *John Bascom*, Heitmann shook his head in frustration as the blazing merchant ships lighted up the entire harbor. Beside him, staring at the havoc, were

Third Officer Collins, Purser William B. Lesesne, Second Officer Rudolph, and First Assistant Nicholas Elin. For the next few minutes there were no more bombs dropped and it appeared that the air raid was over. Then, without warning, a string of explosions ripped the *John Bascom* as the attacking planes renewed the strike. The ship was bombed from aft to forward. One bomb hit the forward end of number four hatch; one bomb went through the top bridge and the radio operator's room into the vessel; one bomb landed in number three hatch; and one hit between numbers one and two hatches. There was a flash of fire from number three hatch when the bomb exploded and Heitmann was lifted completely off his feet and slammed hard against the wheelhouse door. The door broke off its hinges and both the captain and the door hit the deck.

When Heitmann regained his senses and discovered where he was, he got to his feet. The first person he saw was Purser Lesesne lying on the deck of the wheelhouse moaning. He helped him to his feet. A few feet away the captain spotted Elin sprawled on the deck, blood seeping from a cut across his temple. Both men were nearly nude, since the force of the explosion had ripped their clothes and even their shoes off. Heitmann's face and hands were bloody, but he ignored the blood as soon as he discovered that he could still walk, could still move his arms. Moving as fast as he could through the debris littering the deck of the *John Bascom*, the captain returned to the port wing of the bridge and surveyed the damage to his ship. Half of the bridge was torn off and the plates were hanging loosely; the forward deck was caved in; all hatches were open and minus hatch beams; life rafts were blown away; and the port side lifeboats were demolished. From the starboard wing of the bridge, Heitmann noticed that number one lifeboat was still usable but number three lifeboat was completely destroyed.

"Rudolph, get number one lifeboat ready."

As soon as the second officer and his men lowered the lifeboat even with the deck, the captain ordered Rudolph to put the wounded in it. Those who were wounded, but still able to walk, were ordered to line up on deck and wait for further instructions. After Heitmann was certain that this procedure was being followed and that there was no panic among the crew, he and Lesesne returned to the wheelhouse and examined the wounded Elin. After a close examination,

the captain found that the man was dead. Covering the body
with a half-burned blanket, he checked the other men in the
wheelhouse, Anthony J. Hughes, first mate, was obviously
badly hurt. His head was badly cut on top, his forehead skin
was lacerated, and his shoulder was broken. Heitmann and
Lesesne made their way down through the ship to the
medicine locker in the hospital below deck, passing many
crew members who were standing half-stunned, others who
were wounded. Heitmann directed those physically able to
help the wounded get to the lifeboat, discovering that as soon
as the shocked men were spoken to and given an order they
regained their confidence and self-control and carried on as
well as they were able.

Heitmann and Lesesne were startled to find that there
were clouds of dense steam in the hospital area and it was
difficult to breathe. Covering their faces with handkerchiefs,
the two men felt their way to the medicine locker and the
purser chopped it open with a fire ax. Using his flashlight,
Heitmann managed to find several rolls of adhesive tape and
cotton, but little else. Taking these with him he hurried back
to the bridge to find that the lifeboat was ready for use and
that the wounded were being loaded in it as he had directed.
Vesole, commander of the Armed Guard on the *John Bascom*,
reported that all his guns had been knocked out of action.
The captain stared at the ensign a moment and then ordered
him into the lifeboat.

"You're badly wounded yourself. Get in the boat."

Vesole said nothing, aware that his left shoulder and arm
were broken, but instead of going directly to the lifeboat he
went back to his gun crew and ordered them to line up on
deck with the survivors of the *John Bascom* crew.

After speaking with Vesole, Heitmann walked back toward his quarters. Outside his damaged quarters he found
Cadet-Midshipman Leroy C. Heinse lying on the deck. The
twenty-three-year-old cadet was covered with blood and all
his clothes had been blown off. His stomach was covered with
lacerations. Heitmann washed the wounds with water from a
nearby bucket and then tried to pull the worst wounds
together with adhesive tape. As he did, he recalled that a
short time before the bombing he had seen Heinse at the
starboard forward top bridge gun reloading the magazines
and, since the cadet had not been lying in this spot when
Heitmann went to the hospital area earlier, he had apparently

gotten there by walking. He wondered how he had gotten that far before he collapsed.

Down the line of ships anchored at the East Jetty, the *John Harvey* was a mass of flames. It was 8:00 P.M.

Hughes, the first mate, was on the settee that still remained intact in the chart room. Heitmann took another piece of adhesive tape from the roll he was carrying and tried to bandage the man's head. It was very difficult to get the tape to stick since the captain's hand was very bloody and it was then that Heitmann noticed the blood was still running down his face in a steady stream. Also his left hand hurt where a piece of shrapnel had pierced it. He finally managed to get Hughes's head bandaged, however, and the wounded man was helped to the lifeboat which was being loaded with the seamen injured the most seriously. Collins and Heinse were also assisted to the lifeboat. On his way topside, Heitmann stopped once more to check Elin and assure himself that the man was dead.

The scene at the lifeboat satisfied the captain when he arrived on deck. Everyone was standing at attention in a perfect line, awaiting orders, while the seriously injured were already in the boat. The capacity of the lifeboat was thirty-two men, and already Rudolph had loaded fifty-two men into it. Heitmann decided it was time to get underway.

"Lower the boat into the water."

After the lifeboat was in the water beside the *John Bascom*, Heitmann directed additional men on deck to climb down the side of the ship and get into it. After a few minutes Rudolph reported that the lifeboat was beginning to settle too deeply into the water, that the gunwale was close to the water's edge. The captain acknowledged the warning and ordered all operations stopped immediately. It was a difficult decision to make, because many of the men still standing on deck beside him were injured and were unable to attempt the long swim to the seawall or to land. The *John L. Motley*, next to the *John Bascom*, was a raging inferno and, to complicate the situation, the stern lines of the *John Bascom* had burned away and the ship was drifting toward the *John L. Motley*. He had to do something.

"Get into the water," he ordered "and hold onto the seine floats at the gunwale of the lifeboat."

After making certain that no one was left aboard except the body of Elin, Heitmann climbed into the lifeboat and gave the orders to cast off. He told Rudolph to hold the tiller and steer for the East Jetty while he helped a seaman in front of him handle a broken oar. Fortunately the men on the port side had a good oar to use. Even if there had been additional oars, they could not have been used because of the overloading of the lifeboat with the wounded. There were so many men in the boat that it was hardly possible to move. Wounded were lying between the thwarts and on makeshift stretchers placed across the thwarts, using every inch of available space. Since only one good oar and one broken oar were in use, progress was slow as the crew of the *John Bascom* attempted to move between their ship and the *John L. Motley* to the jetty to which both ships had been moored. The surface of the harbor was a sheet of flame as the oil from broken petroleum lines, debris from the ships, gasoline, dunnage, and other cargo dumped into the water by the bomb explosions burned. This sheet of flame was gradually gaining on the slowly moving lifeboat, threatening to catch it long before the lifeboat reached the East Jetty.

As they got closer to the jetty, Heitmann saw that it was impossible to get to the landing stairs because the stern lines and cables of a nearby vessel were slack in the water and blocked their path. By careful maneuvering, the captain managed to guide the lifeboat alongside the smooth stone wall of the jetty, but it was five-and-a-half feet straight up to the top. Even if some of the uninjured managed to climb up the glass-smooth wall, the wounded were in too much pain to consider passing them to those on top. Yet, there was no other way, so Heitmann ordered the attempt made as the flames on the surface of the water bore down on the lifeboat. It was an agonizing job, since some of the wounded screamed at the touch of a hand on their bodies, but finally, by using makeshift stretchers made out of boards found on the jetty, everyone was ashore.

It was now 8:20 P.M. and the *John Harvey* was beyond saving. It was only a matter of time now until the flames reached the mustard bombs stored in the holds.

As soon as Heitmann was certain that everyone was on the top of the jetty wall he ordered them to head for the lighthouse at the north end of the jetty. When they reached the lighthouse area the men discovered two open shelters in the seawall. The floor of the shelters were dirt and sand and there was considerable debris in the openings, but the less-injured men soon had the shelters cleaned out and the wounded were placed inside on the floor. There were approximately fifty other men already assembled near the lighthouse and others climbed over the seawall from time to time. The East Jetty was the only place the men from the ships in that area could find refuge, since burning ships and the flaming debris on the surface of the harbor cut off any escape toward the unloading dock and the city. It was not an ideal refuge, however, since the men trapped on the north end of the jetty were approximately a mile out to sea and there was no way to get around the flames blocking their path to land unless a boat was sent to pick them up. Heitmann was quick to realize that he and the others were trapped, but he said nothing.

Vesole gave the captain a package of hypodermic capsules that he had in his pocket which Heitmann quickly used on those in greatest pain. Since he was the only captain among the group of survivors huddled on the north end of the jetty, he took charge, detailing some to help the wounded and others he ordered to make certain that everyone was in one of the shelters. He expected several of the burning ammunition ships in the harbor to explode at any second and he knew the blast would have force enough to blow a man off the jetty into the Adriatic Sea if he was in the open. It was obvious also that not only the surface fires were coming closer and closer to the East Jetty, but that several of the blazing ammunition ships were drifting toward the men grouped near the lighthouse. The most serious hazard was the *John L. Motley,* since it was very close to Heitmann's men and, with its mooring lines burned completely away, the ship was free to drift with the wind and the wind was carrying it directly toward the lighthouse.

"She's going to hit," Vesole yelled to Heitmann as the burning ship neared the jetty wall.

The captain had only time to nod and throw himself flat before the burning ship smashed hard against the seawall and exploded. The force of the blast picked Heitmann up and tossed him onto a pile of sand several feet away. Vesole and two of his men were also injured by the explosion, even though they had been lying prone. The ensign's head hit hard against a rock lying on the jetty and he was knocked unconscious. The entire harbor seemed to empty as the tidal wave caused by the explosion of the *John L. Motley* washed over the breakwater. Everyone on the seawall was thrown about violently by the water as it hit them and several of the merchant seamen were tossed back into the sea. Before Heitmann's head cleared there was another violent explosion followed a few minutes later by two lesser blasts. He realized that other ships in the harbor were exploding.

The violent explosion that followed the blast of the *John L. Motley* was the worst detonation Heitmann had ever experienced. From the depths of the harbor leaped a vast fountain of flame with multicolored jets streaming from its rim. It rose more than a thousand feet into the air. The blackness above it was slashed with streams of crimson, pink, rose, orange, and green, and then, in the terrible concussion that followed, he was knocked down again.

The *John Harvey* had blown up, taking with it Lieutenant Richardson, Lieutenant Beckstrom, and his six chemical warfare men, as well as the remainder of the crew on duty. The only men who could warn the others present at Bari that a large amount of deadly mustard had been released over the harbor were now dead.

While Heitmann was unaware of the mustard that was already at work, secretly, silently, he was worried about the blazing fuel oil that covered the harbor. The flames were now from forty to fifty feet high with the heavy, black smoke covering the East Jetty making it difficult to breathe. He would have been more worried if he had known that the mustard released from the ruptured bomb casings had become mixed with the oil on the water's surface and with the billowing clouds of smoke. As the flaming mixture curled over the top of the seawall the survivors of the *John Bascom* huddled closer together, their small island of safety becoming more minute each second. Heitmann and Rudolph watched the approaching flames, then checked the portion of the jetty that still remained clear. It was not much. They needed help.

"I'm going out to the lighthouse at the tip of the jetty," the captain said. "I'll try to signal a rescue ship."

While Heitmann was gone, Vesole recovered consciousness. The heat was suffocating, especially to the ensign, who was already badly injured. He tried to take a deep breath and nearly choked. But he got enough air into his nostrils to make a strange observation.

"I smell garlic," he muttered to Rudolph.

No one paid any attention to his remark because of the

other problems facing them. They were to remember it later, however. What Vesole was smelling was the deadly mustard which emitted a garlic odor!

Meanwhile, Heitmann was at the far end of the East Jetty, the furthest point from the safety of the dock and city, trying to spot a ship in the area that he could signal for help. There were no ships in sight. Walking to the seaward side of the seawall, he looked down into the sea in hopes that there would be jagged rocks along the water's edge as was the case with most breakwater construction. If there was he intended to lower as many men as possible on lines made from blankets brought with the wounded and order them to stand on the rocks while the fire burned over the top of the seawall. He was disappointed, however. The seawall dropped straight to the sea. There was no place for the men to stand and allow the fire to curl out to sea over their heads.

The only escape remaining was to swim out to sea and hope to reach the Northeast Jetty. He knew that very few of the men were in shape to attempt the swim in the cold water. Even those who were strong enough to give it a try risked a change of wind that would drift the blazing oil right into them and burn them to death. Heitmann refused to give the order, refused to condemn most of the men to death. He decided to wait, hoping for some kind of a miracle. Rudolph reported that he had discovered a flashlight in the pocket of one of the wounded men and he was going to try and signal to shore for help. Several signal men appeared and offered to assist in trying to contact shore with the flashlight. After several minutes of signaling there was still no indication that their light had been observed, however.

The fire was closing in gradually until finally the entire group on the East Jetty was forced to the very tip of it. They could go no farther... except to leap into the sea and start swimming. Several of the men wanted to dive into the cold water, but Vesole and Heitmann talked them out of it for the time being. Both men could tell by the spray that splashed over the seawall and soaked them that the Adriatic Sea water was paralyzing cold. Added to the frigid temperature of the water was the covering of oil that would definitely hamper swimming, even though this oil had not yet caught fire adjacent to the tip of the East Jetty as it had in the harbor area on the west side of the jetty. There was little chance that

any of the men could survive the half-mile swim to the
Northeast jetty. They did not know it, but the mustard mixed
with the oil made it near-suicide to try.

"A ship!"

At about 11:00 P.M. Heitmann saw a small Norwegian
coasting steamer approaching the breakwater to steam out to
sea. Rudolph quickly contacted the ship with the flashlight
and the vessel stopped and sent a lifeboat to the jetty.
Heitmann's joy was short-lived, however, when he was informed that the ship could not take anyone unless they were
able to climb a Jacob's ladder, because the ship had lost many
of its crew and they had no means to carry the wounded
aboard from a lifeboat. Despite his disappointment, the captain ordered all the Scandinavian survivors from other ships
that had been sunk to take advantage of this chance to escape
the seawall. The lifeboat made two trips, taking approximately sixty men to the steamer before the Norwegian captain
informed Heitmann that he could not stay any longer, fearing
that his ship would drift into the minefields close by.

There was only silence as the Norwegian steamer pulled
away from the East Jetty leaving the trapped crew of the *John
Bascom* behind with the survivors from other ships. Approximately four hours had now elapsed since the first German
plane dropped its bombs on the ships in the harbor and the
merchant seamen were no closer to safety than they had been
when the German planes started bombing.

Oberleutnant Teuber and the other Luftwaffe pilots were
much closer to safety, however, than Heitmann and the
seamen. The surprise air strike had gone perfectly. The
Ju-88s had kept out to sea until they reached a point directly
east of Bari and then turned toward the city. Feich, flying on
Teuber's left wing, had tightened up his position as the
formation dropped to an altitude of forty-five meters, according to the Kowalewski technique. Behind them, the oberleutnant
saw Glatt and Grabow nosing their planes down toward the
Adriatic Sea. Further back the other Ju-88s were strung out
in double and triple lines as they headed for the Allied ships
anchored in the harbor.

Since he was in the forefront of the formation, Teuber
anticipated that his plane would come under fire first. Shifting
his position until he was sitting as straight as possible in his

seat, the oberleutnant gripped the controls tightly. He was aware that a near-miss of an antiaircraft shell could cause enough turbulence to make him momentarily lose control of the Ju-88 and, at an altitude of forty-five meters, there was a possibility the plane could nose into the water before he could regain control of it. He had to be ready for instant action.

"Lights!"

Richthofen had told them at the briefing that the Allies at Bari were not blacking out the harbor at night because of the large number of ships to be unloaded, but Teuber was skeptical of the statement until, as he approached the city from the Adriatic Sea, he saw the lights with his own eyes. He saw the dock cranes moving back and forth between the piers and the ships, a light on top of each crane. There was a beam of light at the lighthouse on the seaward side of one of the jetties, many lights along the dock bordering the city, and scattered lights along Molo Foraneo and Molo Pizzoli. Further north, on Molo San Cataldo, where the main petroleum line was located, there were more lights. Accustomed to wartime blackouts, Bari harbor looked like Berlin's Unter den Linden on a New Year's eve to Teuber as he roared in from the sea at 200 mph. "There go the flares!"

He heard the bombardier's warning just as he banked the Ju-88 north. At that same moment he saw the ships lined up along the East Jetty. It was unbelievable! He did not have time to count them, but he guessed there were at least eighteen or twenty merchant ships anchored in a neat row, their hulls nearly touching, along the length of the jetty. The parachute flares that had been dropped by a pair of higher-flying Luftwaffe aircraft illuminated the row of ships just as though it was daylight and Teuber could see the gunners racing for the gun positions on board several of the vessels, could see some men on the jetty running toward the docks. He knew that they would never make it.

"Prepare to drop bombs!"

He had never flown a better mission. Keeping the airspeed needle on the 200 mph mark, the altimeter as close to forty-five meters as possible, the oberleutnant lined up a course that would take his aircraft directly over the row of ships from south to north. Just as he reached the first ship an antiaircraft gun on his left opened fire and he felt the Ju-88 rock violently as the shells exploded overhead. Despite this defensive fire Teuber kept his eyes on his instruments until he heard the bombardier's yell.

"Bombs away!"

Teuber, hearing the message, tried to turn right toward the water, knowing that the concussion of the bombs exploding underneath him would endanger his aircraft, but discovered that Lothar Lintow had his path blocked. There was not enough room to fly his Ju-88 between Lothar and the other Ju-88s strung out behind him, so the oberleutnant had no choice but to continue straight ahead. He had just braced himself for the blast when the plane was lifted skyward and tossed on its left wing like a toy being mishandled by a young boy. Fighting with all his strength to regain control of the Ju-88 before it slid off on the left wing and hit the water that now seemed so close he could reach out and touch it, Teuber cut the throttles and kicked right rudder. For a moment the plane refused to respond, just kept sliding through the sky to its left, barely missing several other Ju-88s that were also either out of control or just partially under control. Finally, however, the controls responded, the right wing dropped level, and at twenty feet over the water in a clear spot between the ships anchored on the East Jetty and those moored along Molo San Cataldo to the north, he slammed the throttles open and headed for the sea. Ground fire from the antiaircraft installations along the shore and shells from the gunners on the ships trailed him.

Circling out to the Adriatic Sea, Teuber looked back at Bari harbor. It was a sight that he would never forget. Ships were burning and exploding throughout the entire harbor area. Flames were reaching upward as high as a hundred feet in some spots. But it was the blasts that occurred periodically that made the sight reminiscent of a giant fireworks display. Red, yellow, green—every color that he had ever seen—was visible as the ammunition ships exploded and, even at a distance of several miles out over the sea, the oberleutnant could feel the violence of the blasts as they rocked his Ju-88.

As the last of the Ju-88s dropped their bombs, they, too, flew out over the Adriatic Sea and the entire Luftwaffe strike force headed for their home bases in the north. The ground fire had been relatively light and not one Allied fighter plane had appeared in the sky over Bari harbor to attack them. Two Ju-88s had gone down into the sea. Teuber had seen them crash into the water, but it was impossible for him to determine whether it had been antiaircraft fire or fire from the ships that had hit the Ju-88s. Now, as he headed northward, he was happy to be alive, amazed that there had been so little opposition. Looking toward the harbor one more time, he saw a tanker anchored near Molo San Cataldo and wished he had one more bomb with which to attack it. Oberleutnant Teuber felt, and rightly so, that the Luftwaffe controlled the skies over Bari harbor that night.

7

"THERE'S A LIGHT ON THE JETTY"

The tanker that Teuber saw anchored near Molo San Cataldo as he flew north over the Adriatic Sea was the U.S.S. *Pumper YO-56* commanded by Captain E. A. McCammond. As soon as he was notified by the watch on the bridge that a flare had just been dropped over the harbor, McCammond ordered his crew to battle stations and hurried to the bridge himself. Sizing up the confusing situation, he decided that the best defensive maneuver he could make was to order all guns trained to the seaward side at maximum elevation and begin firing.

"Pour it up," he called as soon as the gunners were ready.

Neither McCammond, Ritter, his executive officer at battle control number two, nor O. V. Darr, the engineering officer, could see the enemy aircraft that were dropping the bombs, but periodically they could hear one of the Ju-88s roar overhead less than a hundred feet above the ship. During the initial minutes of the raid the captain was concerned about the U.S.S. *Pumper* being hit by one of the bombs, but as the raid progressed and the line of ships along the East Jetty began burning, his worry shifted to the danger they presented. The gunfire from the tanker and from two other tankers anchored near the U.S.S. *Pumper* was the heaviest concentration of defensive firepower thrown up from the harbor and the German planes picked easier targets, staying away from the area where the tanker was riding in the water. The burning merchant ships that were drifting free of the East Jetty as their mooring lines parted made McCammond nervous. He knew that many of these ships carried ammunition, bombs, aviation fuel, and other explosive items that were more of a threat to the U.S.S. *Pumper* than the bombs from the enemy planes. He saw the *John Bascom* catch fire shortly after the *John L. Motley* began burning. On down the jetty he saw the *John Harvey* was a mass of flames. He did not, however, know about the lethal load of mustard gas bombs aboard the *John Harvey*. Very close to the U.S.S. *Pumper* the *Yug*, a small Yugoslavian coastal vessel about eighty feet long, was aflame, too, but McCammond ignored her, concentrating on the ships carrying war cargo, especially the *John Harvey*.

The *John Harvey*, loose now from pier twenty-nine, was drifting across the harbor directly toward the U.S.S. *Pumper*. McCammond could see the men aboard the ship fighting to douse the flames, saw a limping figure directing the battle with the fire. This was Captain Knowles fighting desperately to save his ship and his crew. Several of the crew members of the tanker wondered why the seamen on the *John Harvey* did not leap overboard, why they stayed and tried to keep the flames from spreading, unaware that Beckstrom and his detachment of the 701st Chemical Maintenance Company were staying in a final effort to keep the chemical bombs intact.

Radioman Carl M. "Pop" Keefe was in his general quarters station on the bridge when the raid started, having just returned from liberty ashore. "Pop" Keefe was the oldest man aboard the U.S.S. *Pumper* at forty-nine years of age. He had grown up on the Mississippi River, enlisted in the U.S. Navy during World War I as a landsman for Electrician (Radio) and, after attending a school at Groton, Connecticut, became a qualified listener on a device known as a "C" tube used for detecting submarines under the surface. He returned to shore after World War I, but promptly enlisted when World War II started and was assigned to the U.S.S. *Pumper* in December, 1942. Now, as he watched the *John Harvey* bearing down on the tanker, he wished he was back in Wisconsin punching a telegrapher's key for the C&NW Railroad as he had done between wars. He knew that if the *John Harvey* exploded, as it appeared likely she would, the U.S.S. *Pumper* was in a precarious position.

So did Coxswain A. M. Nikkila and Ship's Cook H. K. Olsen who were standing on the bridge watching the merchant ship moving closer and closer to the tanker. Momentarily an explosion on the south end of the East Jetty distracted the pair, but only for a minute. Stocky, quiet Nikkila shook his head slowly and muttered, "Nothing going to stop her from hitting us now."

Nikkila was not entirely correct, although, at the moment, the odds favored his prediction. The burning merchant ship bore down on the tanker as the ten-knot wind pushed her along. Once the *John Harvey* half-turned to the east, but slowly, inexorably the ship swung back on course for the U.S.S. *Pumper* and began closing the gap between the two ships. While she was still several hundred feet away, however, the flames reached the mustard bombs and the courageous fight to save the ship by Captain Knowles, Lieutenant Beckstrom, and the others on board the *John Harvey* ended abruptly. The ship exploded.

One moment the *John Harvey* was a huge mass of flames moving across Bari harbor from east to north, the next she was gone. To the men on the U.S.S. *Pumper* the world seemed to stand still for several moments when the merchant ship blew up. There was a whispering sound as the air around the tanker was sucked toward the center of the blast and a fraction of a moment of silence. Suddenly the violence of the explosion ripped the area. The initial crack of sound threatened the eardrums of every man in the vicinity and seemed to vibrate every bone in a person's body until even those who were not knocked off their feet found it difficult to keep their balance. Ritter, the executive officer on the tanker, was lifted completely off his feet at battle control two and tossed onto the deck below. He was knocked unconscious by the force of his fall and injured his back seriously. Shrapnel from the mustard bomb casings smashed into crewman James Heeg's mouth and a piece lodged in the buttocks of Coxswain Dale Johnson. The tanker rolled about thirty-five degrees to port from the concussion, throwing most of the crewmen of the U.S.S. *Pumper* to the deck. The ship was literally showered with nose fuses and small fragments of the *John Harvey*. One piece of hull plating that was nine inches wide went through a port on the bridge breaking out the glass and lodging inside in the superstructure.

Unbelievably, the closeness of the *John Harvey* to the U.S.S. *Pumper* saved the tanker from more extensive damage and prevented many deaths among the men aboard her. The merchant ship blew up with such intensity that most of the flying debris passed completely over the U.S.S. *Pumper* and hit other ships further away. The small Yugoslavian coastal

. The ladder that had to be climbed to get onto the
m the water was between the hull of the *Louis*
n and the dock and there was a possibility of a man
crushed to death if he did not time the climb just
Downey watched the ship swing out and back several
trying to get a feel for the rhythm of the boat so he
clamber up the ladder while the ship was on its
rd swing. The lifeless bodies of several seamen floating
water by the dock was evidence of what would happen
made a mistake.

While he was still watching the bow of the boat moving,
ney saw a man start up the ladder and knew immediately
the seaman had timed it wrong. The merchant ship
ted swinging toward the ladder before the man was
fway up it. He did not have a chance. At that moment,
wever, a British sailor standing on the dock grabbed a long
ard and held it between the ship and the side of the dock.
Vedged in this position, the board withstood the pressure of
he ship's hull and kept an open space around the ladder. The
seaman climbed to safety, followed by many others. By this
time, Downey decided that the damage aboard the *Loui*
Hennepin was not as serious as he had first believed, so he
and several others stuck with the ship.

The *Samuel J. Tilden* was not as fortunate as the *Loui*
Hennepin. Captain Blair and his crew had done everything
they could to save the bombed merchant ship, but it was no
enough. The *Samuel J. Tilden* had been anchored approxi
mately two miles out in the harbor, since she had arrived
from Taranto, Italy, carrying U.S. and British military passen
gers and loaded with supplies shortly before the Germar
bombers struck. Fly, the technical sergeant assigned to the
376th Bomb Group personnel being transported to Bari by
the *Samuel J. Tilden*, had been watching C-47s make thei
landing approaches directly over the ship ever since they ha
arrived in the harbor so it was quite a shock when the Ju-88
began dropping bombs. He had thought the roar of thei
engines indicated more C-47s heading for the Bari airport a
the outskirts of the city. So did most of the personnel of th
Twenty-six General Hospital who were aboard the ship
Lieutenant John H. Adamson, Jr., heard the engines an
turned to Leo Kaczmarczyk.

"I can't understand why we couldn't get a seat on

vessel *Yug* simply disappeared, a victim of the explosion.
Another tanker further north was also badly damaged and
drifted toward the torpedo nets at the entrance to the harbor.
The U.S.S. *Pumper*, however, once she had recovered from
the initial blast and rolled back on an even keel, appeared in
good shape to Captain McCammond. He immediately ordered a complete check of the tanker made by the engineering officer and, within a few minutes, Darr reported everything was under control and that the damage was not serious.
The captain had been worried about his ship being full of
aviation gasoline fumes, but, although the tanker was dented,
she had not opened up, so none of the fumes escaped.

The harbor, from the vantage point of the men aboard
the U.S.S. *Pumper*, was dotted with burning ships, flaming oil
and debris on the surface of the water, and hundreds of men
in the water trying to reach safety before another ship
exploded, the surface flames caught them, or they became
exhausted and drowned. Since the tanker was on the opposite
side of the entrance to the harbor from the East Jetty,
McCammond had a perfect view of the holocaust and it made
him sick. Every few minutes there was another blast, not
nearly as violent as the explosion of the *John Harvey*, but still
dangerous, especially to those on board the ships along the
jetty. He could plainly see that the crews of those vessels
were trapped. The flaming oil, dunnage, and other material
lying on the harbor surface cut off any escape toward the
U.S.S. *Pumper* from the East Jetty. The only hope for the
men was to climb onto the seawall of the jetty and await
rescue. The sailors on the ships nearer the dock or anchored
in the center of the harbor had more opportunity to reach
shore alive since they were on the land side of the flaming
debris covering the water. If they were strong enough or
lucky enough, they could swim to Molo Pizzoli or Molo San
Cataldo.

About an hour after the *John Harvey* blew up, Coxswain
Nikkila asked for permission to launch the whaleboat in an
attempt to rescue some of the men struggling in the water.

"There seem to be more men swimming now than there
were an hour ago," he explained. "Some of them are in bad
shape."

McCammond quickly gave his permission to use the
whaleboat.

Nikkila, Heeg, and Quartermaster, Third Class, W. E.

"Bill" Olson manned the boat, launching it within a few minutes after permission was granted by the captain. They moved through the darkness very slowly, picking up survivors as they went. Many of the men were in bad shape, so bad that it was nearly impossible to get them into the boat. They were burned so seriously that as Nikkila and his companions tried to lift them into the motor launch flesh came off parts of their body. The screams of the wounded could be heard above the explosions. Others seemed to be having trouble breathing and complained, as had Vesole and Rudolph on the East Jetty, that they smelled garlic. They, too, were completely unaware that they were breathing fumes from the mustard which was now mixed with the oil. On their first trip the men from the U.S.S. *Pumper* learned why there was so much oil on the surface of the harbor. One of the German planes had bombed the large petroleum line running along the north side of the harbor and the oil was pouring out of the breaks. This oil, added to the dunnage, the debris from the exploding ships, and the mustard made the waters of Bari harbor nearly impassable, especially for injured, exhausted, and shocked seamen.

The three men in the motor launch made three trips back and forth between the dock and the open areas of the harbor picking up survivors. As they prepared to make another trip, Olson suddenly pointed toward the north tip of the East Jetty.

"Someone is signaling with a flashlight from the end of the jetty," he said. "They must be trapped out by the lighthouse."

Nikkila looked toward the lighthouse and saw the blinking light that Rudolph from the *John Bascom* was using to try and get help for the men caught between the sea and the flaming ships along the East Jetty. After watching the light for a few moments, he looked at Olson.

"Think we can reach them?"

"We can give it a try."

It was a hazardous, slow trip for the three men in the motor launch as they made their way through the fires in the harbor, past the exploding ships, along the broken petroleum line that threatened to burst into flames at any minute, dodging floating sections of damaged ships that appeared out of the darkness without warning. The entire harbor area was bathed in a red glow, giving the men in the water covered

with the black oil a hideous appear[   ] tip of the East Jetty, Nikkila saw blac[   ] same reddish glow waving frantically [   ] the motor launch was going to turn [   ] stranded on the seawall. To his right, t[   ] U.S.S. *Pumper* noticed that the burning [   ] anchored along the jetty were free of their [   ] and were drifting toward the lighthouse [   ] seamen were trapped. The safe area on th[   ] getting smaller every minute.

On the East Jetty Heitmann saw the [   ] approaching and watched it closely. Turning t[   ] said, "Do you think they are coming for us?"

The second officer, his flashlight batteries [   ] shrugged. "I'm not certain. I thought they saw m[   ] after it went out the boat seemed to turn furth[   ] northeast. They'll miss the jetty entirely if they [   ] back soon."

The captain of the *John Bascom* heard several of t[   ] on the seawall yelling toward the motor launch that w[   ] moving almost parallel to the seawall, but he knew [   ] voices were drowned out by the crackling flames and [   ] intermittent explosions. There was nothing they could [   ] now but wait . . . and hope.

While Heitmann, his crew, and the other seamen waite[   ] on the tip of the East Jetty for rescue, crews and troops on [   ] other ships in the harbor were fighting to survive also. On board the merchant ship S.S. *Louis Hennepin*, Signalman Robert Downey had been knocked down several times by ships exploding nearby. Finally he decided to stay on the deck temporarily in an effort to regain his strength and also stay out of the path of the flying debris that was hitting the *Louis Hennepin* from all directions. He had not seen even one of the attacking planes, but that did not concern him as he lay on the deck of the merchant ship trying to decide on his next move. The two British warships that had been tied up beside the *Louis Hennepin* were badly damaged and burning. Downey knew that his best chance of escape would be to try and get off the ship onto the dock. There was only one trouble. The mooring lines of the *Louis Hennepin* had burned away and the ship was swinging on the anchor chain. Sometimes she was eight to ten feet away from the dock, but at other times the ship drifted in and hit the dock

broadside[   ]
dock fro[   ]
Hennep[   ]
getting [   ]
right. [   ]
times, [   ]
could [   ]
outwa[   ]
in th[   ]
if he [   ]

Do[   ]
that [   ]
sta[   ]
ha[   ]
h[   ]
b[   ]

plane," he said. "It sure would have saved us a lot of traveling time."

Kaczmarczyk did not even have time to answer. Several bombs suddenly exploded in the harbor west of the *Samuel J. Tilden* and the blinding flares lighted the entire harbor. Although the ship rocked violently, there was no damage during the initial moments of the air strike. A short time later, however, the Ju-88s made another pass over the *Samuel J. Tilden* dropping incendiary bombs. One of these bombs hit the ship immediately forward of the bridge. The explosion destroyed all wooden bulkheads, bulged the metal bulkheads, buckled deck plates over the engine room and completely destroyed the engine room skylight. Fire broke out immediately and spread forward to the bow and then aft.

Captain Blair was furious because a British Naval Control searchlight from the mole was still burning and illuminating the *Samuel J. Tilden*. When he had brought his ship through the entrance of the harbor just prior to the raid, the beam of the searchlight had focused on her to aid the harbor pilot to board. Now, seven minutes after the first bombs had been dropped, the light was still outlining the *Samuel J. Tilden*, making her an excellent target for the Ju-88s. Blair had never entered another port controlled by the British where such a practice was used. In addition, as soon as the air raid began, the shore batteries, also controlled by the British, had opened fire with their 40 mm guns. Because of misdirected fire or unsuitability of the guns for antiaircraft defense, the *Samuel J. Tilden* and her crew were subjected to a continuous rain of shells from these batteries, destroying equipment, killing and wounding men, and rendering the ship incapable of defending herself. Since it was impossible for the gun crew to stay at their positions due to this shore fire, they were ordered to take cover. Because of this shore fire, the searchlight, and the Ju-88s that were now strafing the decks of the *Samuel J. Tilden*, since the German pilots could see so clearly by the beam of the searchlight, the captain considered moving his ship to a new position. Finally he decided that it was better to remain stationary than try to maneuver in the unfamiliar, crowded harbor among the exploding ships. The fire spread throughout the vessel, and at 8:45 P.M. he gave the order to abandon ship. Blair immediately went to his quarters, put the secret codes in a perforat-

40 mm Bofors Gun

ed metal box, returned to the bridge and dropped the box into the water. He then went to oversee the abandoning of the ship, knowing that this was the first time at sea for many of his 209 passengers.

The men of the Twenty-six General Hospital were below deck when the incendiary bomb hit the *Samuel J. Tilden*. Lawrence H. Buys was knocked down by the blast, but quickly regained his feet and rushed to aid some of the others who had been injured. A huge icebox had been overturned, pinning down several of the men who had been trying to make their way to the deck. Buys, Adamson, Byron A. Bell, Stephen Corey, and others put their shoulders to the icebox and managed to lift it high enough for the pinned men to pull themselves free. Once topside, the medical personnel of the

Twenty-six General Hospital joined the men of the 37th and 98th Bomb Groups lining up for the available lifeboats and rafts. Number three lifeboat had been destroyed by the attacking planes, but the remaining boats were in good condition. Fifty-six men boarded the lifeboats while eighty others got onto the rafts. One hundred and fifteen more of the passengers and crew took to the water on floats.

Once off the ship the survivors of the *Samuel J. Tilden* found the harbor a maelstrom of fire, blasts, screaming men, and drifting ships. Some of the lifeboats were towed toward shore by harbor motor launches, but the others found the going very difficult because the surface of the water was thick with oil. The rafts were at the mercy of the wind and every time a ship in the harbor exploded, the rafts were tossed in a different direction. The men in the lifeboats, rafts, and on the floats were doused continually by the dirty water that was stirred up by the explosions. It went into their eyes, up their nostrils, down their throats. After awhile they felt their skin burning and many of the men found it difficult to breathe. The mustard was taking its toll.

The *Joseph Wheeler* and *John L. Motley* had disappeared. There were no survivors except the men who had been ashore. Chester B. Filewicz, Utility, aboard the *John L. Motley,* was in Bari when he heard the ack-ack guns begin firing. As soon as possible he and a companion, Osmond Jackson, made their way to the harbor, but all they could see when they arrived where the *John L. Motley* had been moored was fire and smoke. The closest he could get to the site was approximately two city blocks, but that was close enough for Filewicz to be convinced that he no longer had a ship. Another member of the *John L. Motley* crew who was on shore leave that evening, Deck Engineer Carl Smith, arrived at the dock about the same time as Filewicz, saw that his ship had blown up, and began searching among the hundreds of wounded and exhausted men already on the dock for survivors from the ship. The only one that he located was Radio Operator Melvin H. Bloomberg who was severely injured. Stopping a British soldier driving past in a jeep, he loaded the injured radio operator on the vehicle and started for the nearest hospital.

Fred McCarthy from the *Joseph Wheeler* had just started to spend the ten dollars he had borrowed from a friend aboard ship. He had found a place to get a bottle of wine and was negotiating the deal with the Italian operating the place when the antiaircraft guns began firing nearby.

"What's going on?" he asked the Italian shopkeeper.

The man shrugged, "The British are practicing again."

When the firing continued, however, McCarthy decided to investigate. As soon as he stepped into the street he knew that it was no practice session. It was the real thing. Planes were roaring overhead, bombs were exploding on Via Abate Gimma, and shrapnel was slamming into the street all around him. Running from doorway to doorway, McCarthy made his way back to the dock where he was supposed to board the motor launch for the trip back to the *Joseph Wheeler.* The motor launch was not waiting. No one even stopped to answer his question. The dock was in utter confusion with men running in all directions, injured men lying everyplace, shocked survivors walking around in circles talking to themselves. While he was still trying to decide on his next move, there was a violent explosion out in the harbor and McCarthy was knocked over backward. As he lay stunned on the dock, he suddenly wondered what had happened to his friend "Bouncer" Ryan who had remained behind on the ship. McCarthy did not know it, but Ryan was already dead.

Chief Mate Roy J. Newkirk of the *Joseph Wheeler* had gone ashore early on the morning of December 2 after being relieved by the second mate. He, too, hurried toward the dock as soon after the German air strike as possible, but it was impossible to get out onto the East Jetty because of the burning ships. The flames blocked his path completely. Instead of returning to the city, Newkirk helped pull survivors out of the water and also cut one tanker loose from its mooring lines so it could escape the inferno along the jetty. Choking from the smoke and fumes in the area, the chief mate then returned to the boat pool area.

The *Hadley F. Brown* had reached dockside for unloading prior to the air strike by the Luftwaffe, but Robert Kirchhoff was still nervous thinking about the crowded harbor conditions. He had been in many ports since the beginning of the war, but he had never seen one as jammed as Bari harbor was on the night of December 2. Nor had he ever seen one lighted at night as this harbor was; he did not like it, did not like it at all. He was in his quarters aboard the ship discussing the situation when the general alarm suddenly sounded. His first thought was that it was another drill, but within a few seconds he heard a bomb explode along the East Jetty and knew that it was no drill. Racing to his gun position, he completely ignored the port rule that the guns aboard ship were to remain covered. Grabbing his machine gun, he began firing at the flares hanging above the *Hadley F. Brown* and twice he got off a few shots at German aircraft that flew over the ship at mast level. By the time the Ju-88s left the area Kirchhoff had used all the available ammunition and was hunting for more.

He had been so occupied with his gun that he had barely paid any attention when a bomb hit the port bow of the *Hadley F. Brown*. Now that he had more time to look around, he discovered that he and the remainder of the crew were in a precarious situation. The hull was badly damaged and the gangplank that had been in use was completely smashed. Two ships nearby along the dock had also been hit. One was an ammunition ship, the other a tanker. Both were burning furiously and the tanker, its hull ruptured, was spraying fuel over the *Hadley F. Brown*. Kirchhoff was still worrying about the fuel saturating the deck of his ship when there was a terrific explosion. The *Hadley F. Brown* keeled over on its starboard side, slammed into the dock, then rolled the opposite direction. Bodies flew through the air mixed with a wide assortment of debris and ship sections. Kirchhoff felt something hit his life jacket directly below his chin and reaching down, picked out a two-inch, jagged piece of shrapnel. It was his souvenir from the *John Harvey*. The shrapnel, fortunately, did not hurt him, but the unseen mustard from the same ship was moving toward him mixed with the smoke and fumes in the sky, the oil on the surface of the harbor.

Captain Hays of the U.S.S. *Aroostook* had tried to get permission to move his tanker to the unloading area, but the British port director was too busy to be concerned about one more ship, even one loaded with nineteen thousand barrels of hundred-octane gasoline. Hays was just leaving the Psychological Warfare Board Headquarters in Bari to go to the Petroleum Section of the Allied Force Headquarters to continue his efforts to get his tanker unloaded when the first flares were dropped over the harbor by the Ju-88s. He immediately ordered his driver to take him to the port area, arriving there within eight minutes. Every effort by Hays to get a motor launch to take him back to the U.S.S. *Aroostook*

failed, since the rescue of the men floundering in the flaming
harbor took priority. He decided to try and proceed to the
outer end of the fueling quay which would take him to within
a few hundred yards of his ship, but a direct bomb hit about
one-third of the way out the quay blocked him. The bomb
ruptured one of the main gasoline pipes and a raging fire
prevented Hays from going any further. After waiting a few
minutes, the determined captain lowered himself to the side
of the seawall opposite the fire and crawled past the flames.
Once he was beyond the fire, he climbed back onto the
fueling quay and hurried to the outer end of it where once
again he found himself trapped and unable to reach his ship.

The sky was bright as day and Hays could see the men
aboard the U.S.S. *Aroostook* fighting to save the ship. While
he was not close enough to see the details of the damage
suffered by the ship, he knew that the German planes had hit
her. Actually the U.S.S. *Aroostook* had suffered considerable
damage, but was in no immediate danger of sinking. Both
Wellin lifeboats had been pierced by shrapnel; a hole had
been made in the deck amidships; all doors, officer's country,
passageway, and stateroom had been blown off; the six-inch
fueling hose was pierced by shrapnel; all windows in the
lower wheelhouse were blown out; and the starboard diesel
engine was damaged. Hays considered swimming to his ship
from the quay, but he gave up the idea because the fires on
the water were spreading rapidly. All he could do was stand
and watch his crew fight to save the U.S.S. *Aroostook*.

Two ships anchored within four hundred yards of the
U.S.S. *Aroostook* sustained direct hits and immediately sank
in six fathoms of water, the upper decks and superstructure
still burning fiercely. Despite the nearness of the flaming
ships, however, the men of the U.S.S. *Aroostook* refused to
quit battling. Boatswain K. R. Groote remained at his station
in the completely exposed firing control tower, ducking the
burning debris and shrapnel flying through the air, and
directed the firing of the ship's guns. The effectiveness of the
barrage from the ship was evidenced by the fact that the
Ju-88 bombed nearby ships instead of risking another pass on
the U.S.S. *Aroostook*.

Hays was still on the fueling quay when the *John Harvey*
exploded and was nearly blown into the sea by the force of
the blast. He suffered partial deafness from the blast and it
was several minutes before his head cleared. It was then that

he saw that the executive officer of the U.S.S. *Aroostook*, John Umstead, Jr., had managed to get his ship underway. He was maneuvering the ship through channels of burning oil and gasoline on the waters and sunken ships in the harbor to a safer anchorage further north. The captain, realizing that he could not reach his ship at that time, turned and started back the fueling quay toward the dock. Near the fire on the quay he discovered that several of the men from the U.S.S. *Aroostook* who had been on shore liberty and were unable to get back aboard were assisting in removing wounded to ambulances from boats that had picked them up from the harbor waters. The wounded were in various states of shock and exhaustion, but they all had one thing in common—they were covered from head to foot with the oil slime that was lying on the surface of the harbor.

None were aware that the deadly mustard was mixed with this oil slime.

8

"I SMELL GARLIC!"

"Stop the engines! Stop the engines!"

Michael A. Musmanno's voice was high-pitched and shrill as he yelled at his crewmen aboard the schooner *Inaffondabile*. He was still holding the tinfoil in his hand, too shocked by the realization that it was dropped from German aircraft above the harbor to release it. Musmanno had seen a great deal of fighting during the war, but this was different. This was a complete surprise, a German air strike where no German plane dared fly, where the Allies supposedly had an overwhelming fighter defense!

Fabiano Menorisini, the Italian attending the engines, immediately cut the power and the swishing sound of the propeller gradually stopped. "What is wrong?"

"Get down. Take cover. The Luftwaffe is attacking," Musmanno bellowed. He did not have time to explain further. Menorisini and the two other Italian fishermen aboard the schooner did not argue. They flattened out on the deck.

For a long minute Musmanno prayed that he had been wrong, that even the daring Luftwaffe pilots would not have nerve enough to attack as far south as Bari. It was a forlorn hope. Suddenly there was a blinding flash that lighted the area around the schooner as bright as the Golden Triangle of his hometown of Pittsburgh, Pennsylvania. Shrapnel ripped through the schooner, leaving jagged holes for the water to pour in, and a ship less than one hundred yards to the right slid under the surface of the harbor. Twisting his head, Musmanno looked toward the sky. Three huge parachute flares were drifting earthward, lighting every inch of the sky and outlining every ship in the harbor. He saw something else, too. He saw a Ju-88 silhouetted against the sky, its nose

84

pointed directly toward the *Inaffondabile*. Miniature geysers of water shot up all around the schooner as the German pilot opened fire with his wing guns.

"He's after us," Musmanno yelled. "Fire . . . fire."

Menorisini and Giovanni Catella grabbed the machine guns lying on the deck and began firing at the oncoming plane. It was a one-sided fight, however. A bullet from the German plane ripped into Menorisini's leg and he fell to the deck. Catella took one look at his wounded companion, glanced at the diving plane, and made his decision. He jumped overboard. Musmanno, also firing a machine gun, refused to give up so easily. He felt they still had a chance. He did, that is, until the bow of the schooner suddenly burst into flames.

"Abandon ship!"

Musmanno did not have to leap into the oil-covered water. Without warning the deck of the *Inaffondabile* disappeared from under his feet and he found himself flailing both arms in an effort to keep his head above the water. Floating debris kept hitting him until he was dazed, but he managed to keep afloat.

"Catella? Menorisini? Can you . . . ?"

A timber, thrown against him by the force of another ship exploding in the harbor, hit his head a glancing blow as he turned to look for his companions. Without a word he slipped beneath the slime on the surface of the harbor. Fortunately, the bitter cold of the water brought him back to consciousness and his eyes opened to a sight he would never forget. He was deep in the water. Above him on the surface a fire was raging, giving the blue waters of the Adriatic Sea an orange glow as he looked upward. By this time his lungs felt as though they were on fire, as if they, too, were going to explode if he did not get to the surface where he could take a deep breath. He fought his way upward, finally breaking through the oil slime into the flames. Frantically he swam toward an open spot in the spreading fire, splashing a path with his arms. Only the fact that he had surfaced where the olive oil from the broken casks that had been aboard the schooner had spread across the water with the other slime saved him. It kept him from being burned until he reached a clear spot.

A floating timber provided Musmanno a resting spot for a few moments, but it suddenly submerged as another figure

appeared out of the darkness and gripped it. The captain saw
that it was Menorisini. Both men splashed their way to a cask
floating nearby and, fortunately, the cask supported both of
them above the water. Musmanno continued to search the
harbor for Fabiano and Barcelli and finally discovered them
hanging onto another bobbing cask. The four survivors from
the schooner salvaged a third cask and maneuvered a timber
across the three casks that had contained their precious olive
oil only a few minutes earlier and improvised a raft with rope.
With sticks, found in the debris floating on the surface of the
harbor, and cupped hands the men of the *Inaffondabile*
started to paddle toward the shore that was at least a mile
away.

The attacking German planes had disappeared and
Musmanno felt more confident after the strafing ended. He
knew that it was a long distance to solid ground, but he saw
no reason that they could not make it safely if they avoided
the fires and burning ships. He was still congratulating
himself on being alive when there was an eye-popping explosion that shook the entire harbor. Clouds of smoke tinted
every color of the rainbow shot thousands of feet into the air.
Meteoric sheets of metal rocketed in all directions carrying
incendiary torches to other ships, setting off a series of
explosions that could be likened to Chinese firecrackers with
each firecracker a ship of from seven to ten thousand tons. In
addition to the ship explosions, the piers vibrated with the
detonations of artillery shells and sacks of gunpowder stored
on the dock. Occasionally small black objects could be seen in
the upward rush of flame and smoke and Musmanno shuddered
at the piteous fate of those sailors and dock workers who were
being hurled to their death—not realizing that the terrific
blast he had just witnessed was spewing a deadly chemical
toward him and the other three men on the improvised raft.

Hypnotized by the scene in the harbor, they forgot to
paddle and floated aimlessly. It was not until a siren sounded,
warning of another possible air strike, that Musmanno ordered his crew to grab some pieces of wood drifting nearby
and start paddling toward shore once again. He no longer was
as confident as he had been prior to the explosion of the *John
Harvey,* since their path seemed partially blocked in every
direction. Finally Musmanno guided the raft north toward
the ruptured fuel line that extended along the quay, hoping to
find a path that was clear. They entered an area that was not

burning, that was dark. The oar suddenly slipped from the captain's hand and as he groped for it in the blackness he was surprised to see it clearly as the whole ocean abruptly lighted up. He listened for the sound of planes, certain that the Luftwaffe had returned and dropped more flares, but he did not hear the roar of a single propeller. Turning to look back toward the quay, Musmanno could not believe his eyes. The sea had opened up like a drawbridge and as the two huge waves on each side started to fill up the void again the raft carrying him and the others from the schooner was directly in the middle. The raft bounced skyward like a hard-hit tennis ball, throwing the four men into the harbor.

An oil tanker along the fueling quay had exploded! Since light traveled much faster than sound, Musmanno had seen the illumination before he heard the blast. The concussion knocked him off the raft and into the oil slime covering the harbor and he choked and coughed as the black mixture went into his mouth, up his nose, and nearly blinded him. It was several seconds before he could see again, seconds during which he drifted nearer to the flames that were now spreading from the quay toward the middle of the harbor. Once he got the slime from his eyes, Musmanno grabbed a timber and made his way toward the improvised raft he and his companions had made earlier. Miraculously it still was in one piece, the casks lashed to the timber by the rope Menorisini had found in the water. Nearly exhausted, he climbed back onto the raft and was soon joined by the other three men from the schooner, all of whom were blackened by the slime of the harbor.

"I smell garlic," Musmanno said as they started paddling toward shore again.

Menorisini, a rag wrapped around his wounded leg, agreed. "I smell it, too. Must be from the supply ship."

Musmanno shook his head. "Since when would American ships carry garlic to Italy?"

Unknowingly, Musmanno had detected the odor of the mustard in the water and in the smoke drifting over the harbor, but in the confusion he promptly ignored the smell. He and everyone else who thought they smelled garlic. Musmanno's main concern at that moment was reaching the comparative safety of shore. Poison gas bombs never entered his thoughts.

* * *

The Italian schooner *Inaffondabile* was not the only ship in the harbor that night that did not belong to the United States. Besides the *Inaffondabile* the British merchant ships S.S. *Fort Athabaska*, S.S. *Testbank*, S.S. *Devon Coast*, S.S. *Lars Kruse*, S.S, *Crista*, S.S. *Fort Lajoie*, and S.S. *Brittany Coast* were anchored at Bari. So were the Norwegian vessels S.S. *Lom*, S.S. *Bollsta*, S.S. *Norlom*, and S.S. *Vest;* Dutch merchant ship S.S. *Odysseus;* Polish ships S.S. *Puck*, S.S. *Lwow;* and the Italian cargo vessels S.S. *Barletta*, S.S. *Frosinone*, and S.S. *Cassala*. Some were lucky that tragic night; some were unlucky.

One of the less fortunate ships was the British freighter *Fort Athabaska* which was anchored close by the American merchant ship *Joseph Wheeler*. The *Fort Athabaska* was loaded for departure to North Africa, carrying seventy-six tons of general cargo, 238 bags of ordinary mail for Algiers, and two captured thousand-pound German rocket bombs. When the *Joseph Wheeler* exploded, the *Fort Athabaska* caught fire and, despite the heroic efforts of the British crew, the German rocket bombs stowed in number two hold between decks were detonated by the extreme heat and flames, reducing the British ship to a shattered hulk. Of the total complement aboard of fifty-six, there were only ten survivors.

The British tanker *Devon Coast* was not any luckier. She was anchored southernmost in the harbor, moored stern on to the breakwater and blacked out, although her port lights, including the arcs, were on. Shortly after the air strike began a bomb hit the *Devon Coast* in number two hold causing a bright green flash that was followed by an explosion. Although the scene was brilliantly illuminated by flares and fires, the crew was unable to see for several minutes. They were temporarily blinded by the mustard that had been released by the explosion of the *John Harvey*, although at the time the crew did not know it. The Norwegian ship *Lom* that was moored alongside the *Devon Coast* had also been struck by a bomb and was on fire. Her bow moorings had parted and she was drifting perilously near, the wind blowing the flames right across the fore part of the *Devon Coast*. Within minutes the British tanker was burning and the crew abandoned the ship, despite the fact that they could barely see. Using life rafts as long as they were available and then leaping into the water, the seventeen sailors, two army gunners, and four navy gunners got off the *Devon Coast* minutes before she exploded.

The fate of the British freighter *Testbank* was directly connected with the explosion of the *John Harvey*. The *Testbank* was moored stern on to the jetty at number eighteen berth on the night of December 2 waiting for a convoy. Once the attack by the Luftwaffe began, so many of the ships along the jetty were hit and started burning that the *Testbank* was hidden from view by those on shore. The smoke and flames formed an effective screen to conceal the British freighter, but the seventy-five men aboard her quickly assessed the situation and began abandoning ship. They were too late, however. When the *John Harvey* exploded nearby, the *Testbank* was ripped apart and seventy of her complement were lost. The five survivors were ashore at the time.

A British Ministry of War transport, the *Fort Lajoie*, was also anchored in the harbor awaiting a convoy when the German aircraft made the surprise attack. She was luckier than many of the other ships. During the initial pass of the Luftwaffe Ju-88s over the harbor, bombs exploded on the port side of the *Fort Lajoie* but inflicted no damage. However, one of the illumination flares dropped by the planes fell into the starboard defensive gun position, setting it on fire. A fire party was immediately organized, but, before the men could put out the flames, the flare burned through the iron deck and set fire to the gunners' quarters beneath. When the *John Harvey* exploded, the *Fort Lajoie* was peppered with red hot splinters and several more small fires were started. Pieces of red hot metal blew into number four hold and started a fire among rubbish piled there. The forepart of the lower bridge was also alight which, together with fire in the Oerlikon nest, made three separate fires burning at the same time. All hatches fore and aft were blown off and tarpaulins were ripped to shreds. There were several large dents in the decks and one piece of plating ten feet by six feet by four feet wrapped itself around one of the winches. A large anvil weighing about one hundred pounds landed on the deck, blown there by the blast from another ship, followed a few seconds later by an ammunition box that cut through number four derrick and fell into number four hold. Six two-pound shells were found buried in the lagging of the boiler fronts, but there was no damage to the boilers.

Despite the terrible beating the *Fort Lajoie* took, the crew did not abandon ship. Instead they continued to fight the three fires and, at the same time, attempted to shift the ship out of the oily fires on the surface of the harbor. They discovered that this was impossible, since they could not knock the steel pins out of the cable shackles, so they sat out the raid at anchorage, treating their wounded and waiting for an opportunity to take them ashore to the military hospital.

Deck Cadet James L. Cahill of the *John Harvey* and Seaman Walter Brooks had been the first to leave the ship on the afternoon of December 2 to go into Bari on shore leave. They had enjoyed the sights of the city, had eaten and drunk their fill, and had started back toward the dock when the German aircraft suddenly appeared from over the Adriatic Sea and began the attack on the ships in the harbor. Cahill and his companion were about twelve blocks from the waterfront and near the railroad station when the first bomb was dropped; they immediately rushed into the nearest air raid shelter. When it appeared that the German planes had left the area, the pair emerged and once again started toward the dock, but within a few minutes an alarm warned them that more trouble was in the offing. At that time Cahill and Brooks were near an old fort that housed the headquarters of the British port authorities so they took refuge there until the all clear sounded. Later they were taken to dockside by a British major of Marines and asked to identify their ship.

"That's the *Joseph Wheeler*," Cahill said, pointing to a burning, blackened hull. "And that is the *John L. Motley*," he added as he indicated a bow sticking up from the water.

The deck cadet's face went blank and he looked around wildly.

"Where's your ship? Where's the *John Harvey*?" the British major asked.

For a moment Cahill did not answer, but finally he turned away from the harbor and said, "She's gone. The *John Harvey* is gone."

"A pity," the Britisher replied. "What did she carry?"

"Ammunition, I think." Cahill's face clouded. "And, and—"

"Yes?"

"I, I don't know. Nobody knew. It was a big secret."

The "secret" was already taking its toll out in the harbor and on the survivors stretched out on the dock, covered with the oily slime, waiting for transportation to the hospitals in the area. The secret of the mustard was kept to the bitter end by Beckstrom and died with him when the *John Harvey* exploded.

Far to the north Oberleutnant Teuber was throttling back the engines of his Ju-88 as he turned on the approach for the runway at his home base. He was tired but jubilant. The raid had been much easier than he had anticipated, the aircraft losses lighter, the results excellent. He knew that Richthofen would be delighted, that the wires between Italy and Berlin would be busy that night as an assessment of the damage inflicted on the ships in the harbor at Bari was relayed to the Führer. As soon as he cut the engines, Teuber stuck his head out into the clear night air of northern Italy and took a deep breath, filling his lungs to capacity.

"Now for a cold beer," he murmured as he climbed from the bomber.

Everything was fine with Oberleutnant Teuber. It was a wonderful night.

9

"THE SHELTER'S FILLING WITH WATER"

General "Jimmy" Doolittle was worrying, even before the German aircraft arrived the night of December 2. One of the main reasons his new Fifteenth Air Force had been organized was to split the enemy's defenses, especially the German fighter force, and help reduce the alarming casualty rate being suffered by the Eighth Air Force flying out of England and attempting to strike deep into the Reich. During the fall months the Eighth Air Force had taken a severe mauling, so much so that the loss rate reached prohibitive proportions. Washington was faced with the sobering fact that during the latter part of 1943 German fighter forces in the west were increasing, not decreasing as had been expected. There was concern also about the improvement in performance among German pilots, mostly due to improved fighter tactics and increased firepower on the FW-190. Doolittle had received a report that concluded that the entire American daylight bombing program against strategic objectives located deep in Germany would be seriously threatened unless steps were soon taken by the Fifteenth Air Force to draw off some of the enemy's fighter planes. Washington was looking ahead to the invasion planned for the spring of 1944 across the English Channel, an operation that could not possibly succeed if the Allies did not control the skies over Europe by that time.

Time was thus a critical element for Doolittle and his new air force. He was aware that the British had voiced strong opposition to the formation of the Fifteenth Air Force, chiefly because they believed it diverted bomber groups from the scheduled buildup in the United Kingdom in preparation

Fw–190

for the cross-channel invasion. Most British leaders believed the Italian project a doubtful venture. They pointed out the fact that only a small percentage of the Combined Bomber Offensive targets were closer to Italy and the Fifteenth Air Force than to the Eighth Air Force operations out of the United Kingdom. Even these could be bombed from England, if necessary. The heart of the German war machine was in the west and northwest, not the south. Nor did the British leaders think that the reputedly better weather conditions in Italy were a critical factor in daylight attacks by the American bombers, since it was the weather over the targets in Germany that really mattered, not the weather in the base area. Advances in weather forecasting techniques and navigation had made the weather in England a secondary problem. Any advantages that the Fifteenth Air Force might have because of longer hours of daylight during the winter months in Italy would be more than counterbalanced by the necessity of crossing the Alps where clouds and bad icing conditions were common at the great heights. These mountains also constituted a serious obstacle to the safe return of damaged aircraft. Many an Eighth Air Force bomber had been able to limp home to its English base, losing altitude gradually. The crippled Fifteenth Air Force bomber returning to Italy from a mission against south German targets would be forced to stay high or crash.

Doolittle knew that the odds he faced, both in his

operations against the Germans and in his relationship with the British, were stacked against him during the initial stages of the organization of the Fifteenth Air Force, but he was determined to prove the worth of his men and planes by the end of 1943. A spectacular mission to the Messerschmitt works at Wiener Neustadt on November 2, one day after the formal activation of the Fifteenth Air Force, gave the cocky, tough-minded general a good start, but, after this one day of glory, trouble began. Bad weather, lack of radar equipment, and a critical shortage of long-range escort fighters prevented the Fifteenth Air Force from bombing high-priority targets in southern Germany for the remainder of November. By December 2 Doolittle was so anxious to get his planes and crews into the air against vital targets in Germany that he literally walked the floor of his office in the former Italian Air Force Headquarters building near the harbor. Everytime he looked out the window and saw the ships waiting to be unloaded, ships that carried men and supplies for his new air force, he felt a sense of frustration that was nearly overwhelming. The needed bombs, crews, mechanics, ammunition, and fuel were so close to the bases at Foggia, yet so far. The growing pains were threatening "Jimmy" Doolittle's usual good humor.

The general was leafing through a debriefing report of a mission flown by the Eighth Air Force to the Solingen area the previous day when he heard the sound of aircraft approaching Bari. He did not get up from his desk to look at the oncoming planes. He did not feel it was necessary. All day long the C-47s of the Fifty-second Troop Carrier Wing had been ferrying his men to the city from North Africa and it made him a little happier to know that several more planeloads were arriving. He started to study the mission report again when suddenly his office seemed much brighter than it had been previously. At first, he thought the lights had, for some reason, become brighter, but when he glanced toward the window facing the harbor he saw the flares floating down toward the ships anchored in the harbor. He knew instinctively what they were, where they came from, what they meant.

Doolittle was still trying to get to his feet when the first explosion sounded. The windows on the side of the building facing the harbor were shattered instantly, the glass flying across the room. The door to his office collapsed into the room, narrowly missing the general. Standing by the shattered window closest to his desk, Doolittle looked out across the harbor. One look told him all he needed to know about the precious supplies he had waited for so long, the supplies— and men—that were on the ships in Bari harbor. They were lost. Already the ships were burning and, even as he watched, one exploded. There was nothing the general could do but stand and watch the destruction helplessly.

The first person Bruce Johnson, Fifteenth Air Force Headquarters commandant, thought about when the first enemy bombs exploded was his friend and commanding officer "Jimmy" Doolittle. Johnson had just started to walk out of the officer's mess hall when the initial blast occurred. Running outside, he reached the street as a low-flying Ju-88 dropped a string of bombs nearby. The concussion picked Johnson up and threw him approximately fifteen feet. He was stunned momentarily, but, as soon as he regained his senses, he got back on his feet and hurried to the Fifteenth Air Force Headquarters building to check on Doolittle. He found the general still in his office amid the broken glass and smashed doors staring at the scene in the harbor.

"We're taking a pasting, Bruce."

There was nothing else to be said.

In the wing of the Fifteenth Air Force Headquarters building extending away from the street, Radio Operator Roy Gibson sent the air raid warning over his transmitter and then ran to the front of the building. Through the large, glassed-in-lobby area he could see hundreds of tracer bullets, criss-crossing the sky toward the harbor area. While watching the tracers he noticed the brilliant flares light up the ships and he knew what was coming next. Turning to another radio operator he asked, "Where's the shelter?"

His companion had just arrived in Bari, too, and did not know any more about the layout of the headquarters building than Gibson. Realizing that they could not stay in the glassed-in-lobby, the two radio operators decided to go to the radio maintenance room in the basement of the building. Just as they turned to go the first bomb exploded and the glass front of the lobby was shattered by the concussion. When Gibson arrived in the basement, he noticed an opening at the far end of the maintenance room. Upon investigation, he discovered that a sloping driveway led up to a stone wall that surrounded the headquarters building and that two huge, thick, wooden doors formed a gateway through the wall. The doors were locked.

Stooping low, Gibson looked under the heavy doors. He saw that the sky was still filled with tracers and periodically he heard a bomb explode in the harbor area. He was still stooped down when there was an extremely loud explosion and the wooden doors were blown off their hinges, hitting him a glancing blow. Glass from the windows in the building behind him hit Gibson on the back and neck, inflicting minor cuts. He rushed back into the basement and took cover in the maintenance room. Finally, at midnight, he was told it was safe to go to his quarters in the Italian schoolhouse four blocks down the street. After four hours of listening to the violent explosions and feeling the headquarters building shake after each one, Gibson was grateful to get away.

The street was covered with glass fragments and stone and brick debris that had been blasted loose by the ship explosions, the bombs, and the machine-gun fire from the Ju-88s. He had no trouble finding his way to his quarters, however, since the fires burning in the harbor lighted the street with an orange glow. When he arrived at his room, the radio operator discovered that his bed was covered with broken glass and part of the ceiling was knocked down. After cleaning off his blankets, Gibson tried to get some sleep, but, despite the fact that he was exhausted, he could only doze a few minutes at a time. It was the most miserable night he ever spent. He even had trouble breathing as the smoke and fumes rolled inland from the harbor area...and from the *John Harvey*.

Cheedle V. Caviness of the Fifteenth Air Force Service Command was already stretched out on his bed in the school building on the night of December 2 when he noticed some peculiar light patterns on the ceiling of the room. The thought never entered his mind that the light came from flares dropped by enemy planes since he had been assured, as had the other Americans stationed or passing through Bari, that the German Air Force "was shot all to hell" and was nothing to worry about. When the lights continued to dance all around the ceiling of his room, however, Caviness decided to look out the window in an effort to determine what was causing the light. Just as he reached the window facing the harbor, he saw a geyser of water shoot a hundred feet into the air. This geyser was soon followed by several others. He had been in the USAAF long enough to recognize the cause of the geysers.

"Bombs! Bombs!"

Before he could decide on his next move a bomb landed in the rear of the building—one of the string of bombs that knocked the wooden doors off their hinges at the spot where Gibson was taking shelter—and the concussion knocked Caviness flat. Getting back on his feet, he headed for the air raid shelter in the basement of the building. He had just reached the entrance of the shelter when another explosion at the harbor let go and he was thrown headlong into the shelter. Fortunately, neither blast injured him.

When the all clear signal sounded, Caviness went back to his room and discovered that it was badly damaged. All the glass was missing, part of the front wall was blasted away, as was a section of the ceiling. He now had a very good view of the harbor and the scene fascinated him. The surface of the harbor was a mass of flames and he could see several ships that were burning along the East Jetty. Suddenly he saw flames shoot several hundred feet into the sky and before he could even lie flat on the floor the force of the blast of an ammunition ship exploding hit the school building. A large window frame was dislodged and hit him hard on the knee. Limping badly, Caviness headed for the basement and the air raid shelter again. This time he stayed in the shelter, not venturing out until daylight the next morning.

Harry Fischer of the Fifteenth Air Force Headquarters A-3 Section had arrived in Bari on December 2 from North Africa and was completely unfamiliar with the area. He, too, was quartered in the Italian school building. After eating in the evening, Fischer, Joseph Redden, and William Duncan went into the city, but, since it was getting dark and they were tired, the three men returned to their room early. Fischer was stretched out on his bed, just as Caviness was, when the first string of bombs exploded and the window glass of the building was shattered. He did not know where the air raid shelter was located, since no one had yet briefed him on its location, but he ran as fast as he could down three flights of stairs just to get out of the building. When he reached the street, Fischer discovered he had no shoes on so, as happens so often during such moments of danger, the unimportant seems important. Ignoring the bombs dropping in the area, he ran all the way back up the three flights of stairs, sat down on his glass-covered bed, and put on his shoes.

When he reached the street the second time his friends

had disappeared, so Fischer hurried to the beach about a
block away and fell flat on his face. He never prayed so much
in his life as he did during the minutes that followed,
especially when three bombs landed in the harbor near the
spot on the beach where he was stretched out. Dirt, sand,
and oil were blown on him by the blast, but he was not
injured.

William Blau, a friend of Fischer's, was also in the school
building resting on his bed, disappointed because his two
buddies, Ray Donahue and John Wood, had gone into Bari
without waiting for him. Without warning, Blau heard a
sound that reminded him of the roar of a big truck passing
the building and he hoped that all the convoys would pass
early in the evening so they would not keep him awake all
night. A moment later the antiaircraft guns along the harbor
opened fire and someone in the school building yelled to
Blau, "Get out! It's an air raid!"

Blau did not wait for a second warning. He raced down
the stairs, through the door, and into the street. Looking
toward the water, he saw what looked like a fountain spurting
skyward and redoubled his efforts to get out of the area.
Following a man in front of him, Blau raced up the street as
fast as he could run, turning right when his guide turned
right.

"Not that way," someone yelled from the darkness. "The
marshaling yards are down there."

Blau and his companion whirled around and raced the
opposite direction. Finally they ran into a small group of
soldiers behind a low wall and joined them. Gradually, the
turmoil seemed to quiet down some and as soon as the all
clear sounded, Blau went back to his quarters. He, too,
wanted to put his shoes on since he had run out of the school
building in his bedroom slippers. The room was a mess, so as
soon as he put his shoes on he went back to the street and
watched the ships burning in the harbor. He was still in the
street when the *John Harvey* blew up and the blast knocked
him down, just as it did everyone else in the open. Lying on
the ground, he watched the mushroom cloud of smoke drift
toward the city from the stricken ship completely unaware
that the deadly mustard fumes were mixed with the smoke.

Robert M. Flynn was asleep in the school building when
Oberleutnant Teuber and the Ju-88s arrived over Bari. The
noise of the nearby antiaircraft guns awakened him and he, as

Blau, Fischer, and all the others in the building, raced to the street below. He was still crouched in a doorway watching the burning and exploding ships in the harbor when an explosion so loud he "thought the world had blown up" echoed throughout the area and slammed him hard against the side of the building. By the time his head had cleared, a truck had stopped in front of the school building and the driver yelled to Flynn.

"Hop in. I'll take you into town."

Flynn and several of the other men climbed into the back of the truck, but they had gone only a short distance when the driver stopped. An English "fog" truck, a vehicle equipped to spread a concealing layer of chemical "fog" over the area, was at work and it was impossible to go any further along the road. The men got out of the truck and walked back to the school building as the smoke and mustard from the *John Harvey* combined with the "fog" and spread over the eastern part of the city.

Carl Orgel, a maintenance engineer with the Fifteenth Air Force, had left the Italian school building earlier in the evening and gone into Bari to see a movie. He finally settled for *Sun Valley Serenade* at the Oriente Theater, a plush Italian movie house in the center of the city. When he first heard the noise of the bombs exploding above the voices on the screen he thought it was a truck backfiring. Settling back in his seat, he waited for the noisy vehicle to move on down the street so he could enjoy the movie. He had just made himself comfortable when there was a second explosion and the huge chandelier hanging in the theater broke loose from the ceiling and crashed on the people below. Fortunately, Orgel was not hit by the light fixture, although some of the glass fragments struck him. The second floor balcony had protected him from a direct hit.

His first thought was to get out of the theater, but he soon discovered that everyone in the movie house had the same idea. People—soldiers and civilians—were crowding toward the exits, knocking each other down, trampling those that were unfortunate enough to fall. He could hear agonizing screams from those being stepped upon and from those being crushed against the seats or walls. Despite the fact that the thunderous explosions seemed to be getting louder and nearer to the theater, Orgel decided the safest thing to do was stay in his seat. He was more willing to take his chances with the bombs than he was with the hysterical people jamming the exits of the theater.

Finally, the crowd inside the Oriente Theater calmed down and when the all clear sounded they walked in orderly fashion out of the building. Orgel followed them and went back to his quarters in the school building, discovering the same mess that his buddies had discovered. The fact that he had been in the center of the city when the *John Harvey* exploded made him completely ignorant of the danger of the spreading mustard. Of course, no one else knew about the chemical that had been unleashed by the German bombers either.

James Oleman, the C-47 pilot who had brought a planeload of Fifteenth Air Force men to Bari late on the afternoon of December 2, was admiring the feminine qualities of Betty Grable in the movie *Springtime in the Rockies* when he heard noise in the distance. He and Jens L. Lerback, his companion, ignored the racket as they concentrated on the blonde bombshell on the screen, never dreaming that German bombs were exploding outside. A short time later Oleman heard a much louder noise and he turned to look at Lerback. Before he could say anything, however, a bomb exploded outside the theater in an alley and blew in the exit door along with some dirt and gravel. An antiaircraft gun on the roof of the theater began firing at the same time and the panic was on. He and Lerback hit the floor and rolled under the seats to keep from being trampled and waited until the crowd was out of the theater. They then started down the long corridor that joined the theater and the Grande Albergo delle Nazioni, the hotel where they were staying for the night. About halfway down the corridor another bomb hit close by and Oleman was terrified to see the "brick" wall collapse and fall directly toward him and his companion. He did not even have time to yell before the wall crashed down on his head.

The "bricks" hit him—and bounced off his head harmlessly. The wall was made from light-weight material painted to resemble a brick wall and it was quite a relief to the pilot. In the hotel lobby Oleman discovered that the glass front was badly damaged. The revolving door was pushed inside the lobby and there was broken glass all over the floor. Upstairs in their room there was practically no damage. The room had a double bed and a large mirror hung over the head of the bed. Neither were disturbed. Since the window facing the harbor had a large wooden shutter closed over it, the glass was not even broken. Grateful for a place to sleep, Oleman and Lerback got into the bed. Before they could get to sleep, however, the *John Harvey* was ripped apart when the flames reached the mustard bombs. The heavy wooden shutters flew through the window, hurtled across the room and smashed into the mirror above the bed. The glass from the mirror showered down on Oleman and Lerback, cutting them slightly in several places. Through the open space where the window had been, Oleman saw an unbelievably large cloud at least three thousand feet high over the harbor drifting slowly inland. The cloud was full of fire and all kinds of burning objects. It was also full of mustard, the invisible menace from the *John Harvey*.

Another pilot who had brought a planeload of cargo for the Fifteenth Air Force into Bari that same day was Edward Borsarge. He and two companions were in the Oriente Theater when the bombs were dropped and they managed to get outside within the first few minutes of the air strike. When he reached the sidewalk outside the movie house, Borsarge found himself caught in a milling crowd of Italians and Allied soldiers, each person seeming to want to go a different direction. Some were running toward the docks, others were running away from the docks. Others were just running back and forth. Borsarge fought his way into the middle of the street and headed for the nearest air raid shelter. When he got to the entrance of the shelter it was jammed with people. A young boy was on the ground and hysterical Italians were trampling over him. Borsarge helped get the boy back onto his feet, but when he tried to go into the shelter an old man stopped him.

"Don't go in there. It's filling up with water."

The flier turned and raced back to the lobby of the theater. On the way he passed another pilot he recognized. This pilot was standing in the street yelling and shaking his fist at the low-flying German bombers, bolstered by the large amount of Italian wine he had consumed earlier. Borsarge dragged him into the lobby before he got killed. They had just stepped inside the theater when the *John Harvey* exploded. Both Borsarge and his drunken companion were knocked down by the blast, but neither was injured seriously. Deciding the lobby was the safest place in the area, Borsarge sweated out the remainder of the air raid there.

Ralph A. Scheer arrived at Bari on December 2 aboard a C-47. He was on his way from La Senia Air Base in North Africa to join the 376th Bomb Group at San Pancrazio, southern Italy; after registering at the Grande Albergo delle Nazioni, he decided to retire early. The sirens interrupted his sleep within a few minutes, however. He jumped out of bed and turned on the lights, but at that moment the hotel's power was knocked out. The same explosion blasted the toilet in his room off its base and water poured across the floor. Feeling his way out of the dark room, Scheer found the corridor leading to the lobby and followed it. Once he reached the hotel lobby he was swept up by the mass of humanity racing through the hotel on their way to the air raid shelter in the street and was carried along with them. The shelter resembled a subway tunnel and, with the rest of the crowd, he entered the tunnel. The moment he got inside he knew that he had made a mistake, but there was nothing he could do about it. The entrance he had just come through was the only opening into the tunnel and there was no way he could get through the crowd following him to get back out of the shelter. The room was jammed with Italians. Babies were crying, old men were coughing, women were wailing, and the smell of garlic nearly made him sick. Within minutes water began seeping into the shelter from the street and he feared it would drown them all.

Fortunately, after what seemed an eternity, the all clear sounded and Scheer was able to get back to the street. He hurried to his room in the hotel and even the bed with one leg knocked off and the broken toilet looked good to him after the air raid shelter. Putting a chair under the broken leg of the bed, he crawled under the blankets and went to sleep.

Within a short time the alert was sounded again, but this time Scheer refused to risk his life in the shelter. He decided that the Luftwaffe did not have enough planes to make him go back into the tunnel-like air raid shelter and stand shoulder to shoulder with the screaming Italians again. The hotel was deserted. Looking around the lobby, he saw that one wall was made of fieldstone, so he moved an overstuffed chair against the wall and sat down to await his fate. He did not have long to wait. There was a tremendous blast at the harbor and, to his horror, the fieldstone wall began to fall. Scheer was too scared to move. The wall crashed on him . . . and he stood upright and still alive! Like the "brick" wall that had hit

Oleman, the "fieldstone" wall was made of cardboard. The rest of the night was anticlimactic to Scheer.

A wall figured in the experiences of Ben Peralta, a supply officer with the Fifteenth Air Force at Bari, but this wall was for real. Peralta and a New Zealand officer were having an Italian dinner, complete with an ample supply of red wine, in a small restaurant near the waterfront when the bombs started to explode. As soon as the bombs landed near the eating place, the other diners, the owners, and everyone else left, leaving Peralta and his companion alone in the place. The bombing became more intense and the building shook, but the two officers kept on eating and drinking. Suddenly, as one bomb blasted a hole in the street less than a hundred yards from the restaurant, the New Zealand officer yelled, "Let's get out of here."

He promptly got up and crouched under a heavy Italian archway in the building, but Peralta refused to leave the table which was placed against a very strong-looking stone wall. The New Zealander would not take "no" for an answer, however, and grabbing Peralta by the arm, he pulled the American under the archway. A minute later another bomb exploded nearby and the stone wall collapsed, smashing the chair Peralta had been sitting on to splinters. All he received under the archway was a few scratches from the glass and mortar that was hurled around the restaurant by the blast. That was one wall that was not imitation.

Down the street at General Depot Number Five, John Kiser was still considering the sins of gambling, the question that was being kicked around in the day room when the antiaircraft guns suddenly began firing. Without a word the meeting broke up as the men scattered. When the chaplain regained his speech, he muttered that everyone should go to the air raid shelter, but he was too late. Much too late. Everyone had disappeared. Kiser went directly to the basement of the warehouse, feeling it was the safest spot, but as the explosions ripped away the windows, doors, and shutters of the building he wondered if he had made a mistake. Especially when he heard shrapnel hitting on the roof of the warehouse as many of the antiaircraft shells fell off target and exploded.

Finally the all clear sounded and Kiser left the basement. Outside he saw that the depot warehouse had taken a beating. There were no doors remaining, since the bombs

had either splintered them or ripped them entirely off the
hinges. The window glass was all shattered and most of the
frames had been blown inside the building. The roof had
gaping holes in it and the slate lay in piles inside the
building. From a distance the docks were a mass of flames
and, knowing there was nothing he could do to help, Kiser
went to his room. His bed was piled high with white powder,
since the mortar knocked loose from the ceiling had been
sifted by the mosquito netting and deposited on the blankets.
Cleaning the mortar from the bed, he crawled underneath his
blankets. He was still cold, so he put his heavy topcoat on top
of the blankets and as he got warm he began to doze.
Suddenly he heard nine short blasts on a ship's whistle
somewhere in the harbor and, although he did not know what
the signal meant, he recognized its urgency. Before he could
get out of bed, however, the entire sky was illuminated and
he saw a brilliant flash through the hole in the wall where the
window had been earlier in the evening.

Kiser ducked his head under the covers just as slate from
the roof of the building fell on his bed. The dust was so thick
he could barely breathe as he lay in the bed and listened to
the series of explosions and felt the warehouse tremble from
the concussion. Then, almost as suddenly as it began, the
bedlam was over and the quiet frightened him. Coughing,
shaking, Kiser lifted the blankets from his head and looked
toward the harbor. An enormous cloud of smoke was drifting
toward the warehouse and it seemed to be coming from a
ship that had just exploded in the harbor. He did not know it,
but he was staring at the remains of the *John Harvey*. He was
also watching the most deadly cloud he had ever seen in his
life. He did not know that, either.

10

"I CAN'T HEAR THE MUSIC!"

Kenneth Bixler, Richard Rodi, and Henry Philips, Jr., were delighted that they had traveled from San Severo to Bari. As members of the 315th Service Group, they were preparing a new headquarters in the city so that when their unit was transferred from the command of the British Desert Air Force, along with the Seventy-ninth Fighter Group, within a few days they would be ready to operate. The three officers had arrived in Bari on December 1 and spent most of that day looking over the city. After working at a temporary headquarters arranged for by the Fifteenth Air Force during the afternoon of December 2, they headed for the officers' club to have dinner. The officers' mess they visited was on the waterfront at the end of a quay protruding some seventy-five yards into the harbor. Before the war it was one of the better restaurants in Bari. The dining room, on the level of the quay, was enclosed in glass and diners could eat and look out across the water. Below the dining room, nearly on the water level, were a dance floor and bar, both of which were also enclosed by glass and lavishly decorated.

Bixler, Rodi, and Philips were in the dining room when a couple of antiaircraft guns opened up close by. None of the men were very concerned at the time.

"Probably some nervous Italian gunners," Rodi muttered, continuing to eat as though nothing had happened.

A few seconds later, however, they heard a distinct whine and knew that a bomb was dropping toward the building. They hit the floor. The first bomb exploded out in the water, close enough to take out all the windows of the officers' mess. Bixler saw the decorations that had been wrapped around one of the columns in a barber pole effect

105

start to unwrap like a snake and eventually it covered him as he lay on the floor. The young waitresses were screaming hysterically and were cowering in the corners. A few Italian civilians in the officers' mess were also panic-stricken and Rodi moved to try to calm them.

A second explosion splashed water from the harbor onto the floor of the room. The mirrors along the walls cracked, loosened, then fell headlong, missing people by inches. The waitresses howled louder and the young female vocalist stood wringing her hands and sobbing over and over, "I can't hear the music... I can't hear the music." Someone suggested evacuating the mess in favor of a shelter in the city, but Rodi knew that the streets, at the moment, were more dangerous than the building. Flak was falling along the road and sidewalk accounting for many casualties, and flying debris from nearby bomb explosions was injuring countless civilians and military personnel as they tried to get to the shelters. He decided to stay in the officers' mess. He was still there with his companions when the *John Harvey* exploded, doing still more damage to the building.

At about 8:30 P.M. there was a lull in the blasts and the three officers decided to try to reach their rooms in the city. Picking their way through the dining room past smashed tables, splintered chairs, and walking on broken glass, they reached the street that led away from the quay. They moved rapidly through the harbor area to their apartment, not stopping to check any of the destruction, determined to get into the comparative safety of their rooms. Rodi's room was damaged despite its distance from the harbor. The window was broken, a chair overturned, and his personal articles had been blown or knocked from the positions in which he had left them. While he was still trying to straighten the place up another alarm sounded.

This time the three Americans scampered into the underground air raid shelter across the street from the apartment and they discovered, just as Ralph Scheer did, that they had made a mistake. There were hundreds of men, women, and children jammed into the shelter. Some were crying, some were staring in petrified fright. For two hours they stood inside the shelter while the water rose continually higher and higher around their legs and the oxygen supply became lower and lower. Since they were two floors below the street, they could hear nothing at first, but later there was one deafening explosion. It sounded as though a bomb had hit at the shelter's entrance. Instinctively, everyone turned to face the noise and was met with a cloud of dust, obviously from the plaster walls and ceiling. For a horrible second Rodi feared the worst. He thought the shelter was caving in and the entrance—the only way in and out—was blocked. But when the dust cleared he was relieved to see that the shelter was still intact. The signs of panic were quickly calmed and nothing further occurred until the all clear sounded at 11:00 P.M.

Back in his apartment the three officers joined a medic occupying the room next to Rodi's for a drink of brandy and for two hours repeated their stories and listened to others. According to most of the men who joined the group in the medic's room, the military and civilian damage was great. Between ten and seventeen ammunition and gasoline ships were reported hit in the harbor. One soldier said that the projection booth in the Ensa Theater had fallen forward into the balcony injuring the audience, some seriously. A direct hit was made across from the Corona Hotel, killing many and rendering the hotel useless. Occupants of the hotel, mostly military, were hunting rooms for the night. Rodi did not know what was rumor and what was truth, but he was worried about the delay in setting up the headquarters for the 315th Service Group since the efficient operation of the Seventy-ninth Fighter Group depended on the services of ground units as well as its flying personnel. The Seventy-ninth Fighter Group had moved to the Middle East late in 1942 and had become part of the Ninth Air Force. The pilots of the group had flown ancient P-40s while moving westward in the wake of the British drive across Egypt and Libya to Tunisia. By escorting bombers, strafing and attacking enemy shipping, and supporting the ground forces, the Seventy-ninth Fighter Group played a prominent part in the Allied operations that defeated the Axis forces in North Africa, captured Pantelleria, and conquered Sicily. Now both General Clark and Field Marshal Montgomery were depending upon the group to help their armies in southern Italy. Any delay in its operational status could be serious.

Another American in the officers' mess that night was Donald D. Mossman, commanding officer of the Base Petroleum Laboratory of Petroleum Section, Allied Force Headquarters, which was situated in the Anic Refinery. He man-

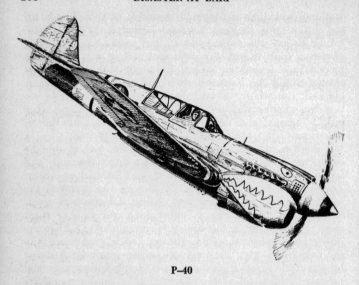

P–40

aged to escape the mess without serious injury and, as he stood outside where a British crew fifteen yards away was firing Bofors guns over his head, Mossman could see the flames along the fueling quay. It was obvious to him that the bombers had hit the fuel lines running along the quay and he wondered how much aviation gasoline would be lost. The Fifteenth Air Force planes at Foggia needed every drop of fuel available, were waiting for it. Now they would be grounded. Mossman sighed and turned his eyes away from the fueling quay. There was nothing he could do about the fires. He suddenly felt sick.

Walter Logan, the war correspondent attached to the British destroyers docked in Bari harbor, was nearly at the pier when the German bombers arrived and started attacking the ships. The first explosion knocked him down and he immediately lost consciousness. He did not wake up for three days. Meanwhile, a companion correspondent, Frank Fisher, was on the opposite side of the harbor and watched in horror as the bombs cascaded down from the Ju-88s. One of the initial string of bombs was off target and landed within fifty yards of his car, but did not damage it. Leaping into the car, Fisher and several friends drove through the middle of Bari to the other side of the harbor. A newspaperman, he felt he had to get the story of the bombing regardless of the danger.

Watching across a neck of sea a short distance from the docks, he saw a yellow flame spread out and then a cloud of smoke pour upward, its underside tinged with red. Without warning there was a terrible blast and the whole sky turned red.

"My God, they got the ammunition ship," a sailor near Fisher whispered.

There was a few seconds of silence and then a wind whipped through the town like a tornado. Houses in the old section of the city folded up like cardboard dollhouses and collapsed. There was a continuous crunch of breaking glass, punctuated by the heavier sound of doors, window frames, and Venetian blinds being ripped out. Scores of civilians were injured by flying glass. They walked about as if stunned, their faces like maps drawn with lines of blood. A naval officer, slightly wounded, stopped to talk with Fisher and said that he was standing within two hundred yards of the ammunition ship when it went up and was not even knocked down. Yet, ten miles inland, the concussion blew out windows. The force was felt at some points twenty miles or further from the harbor.

Everyone was talking about the force of the blast. None knew about the greater danger of the mustard.

At the Bari airport, several miles from the city, Lester Y. Murphy was sleeping in the C-47 that James Oleman had flown to Italy that day. Murphy was crew chief on the plane and had stayed behind at the field to check the aircraft prior to the return flight to North Africa. Before bedding down in his sleeping bag, he made certain that the rubber porthole plugs were in the windows of the C-47 so that no light could escape from the cabin during the night and to keep out the cold. He had been asleep only a few minutes when he felt the plane rock violently and an instant later everyone of the rubber plugs came flying out of the windows straight toward him. He ducked instinctively, realizing later that the plugs would not have hurt him even if they had hit him. He was so scared at the strange phenomenon of the flying plugs that he scrambled out of the C-47 as fast as he could move. Standing beside the plane, he saw the red glow hanging over the city and knew that there had been an explosion. He was still wondering what happened to cause the fire when a plane roared over the airfield at low altitude and he recognized its silhouette despite the darkness.

"A Ju-88! My God, the Luftwaffe!"

It was a sleepless night for the crew chief.

William Jones of the Fifteenth Army Group was still working in his office at Santo Spirito several minutes after the planes he had heard pass the village had disappeared to the south. He had a lot of work to do and was not paying any attention to the periodic noises from the direction of Bari. He did not even look through the large glass doors toward the city seven miles to the south. He did not, that is, until the glass doors suddenly blew into the office, knocking his papers in all directions and nearly upsetting his desk. A fraction of a second later there was a loud blast and the interior of the room turned bright red. Shocked, Jones stared through the opening where the doors had been and saw flames shooting high into the sky over the city of Bari. At that moment he knew who had been piloting the planes that had passed Santo Spirito a few minutes earlier.

"The Germans! They've bombed Bari!"

Jones recognized the overall importance of the air strike immediately, knowing full well that critical strategic decisions, both for future Allied bombing and for Allied ground attacks, were dependent upon the men and supplies coming into Italy through the port of Bari. The Cairo meetings between Churchill, Roosevelt, and Chiang Kai-shek from November 22 to 26; the following conference at Teheran between Churchill, Roosevelt, and Stalin on November 28; and the final discussion being held the next day, December 3, between Churchill and Roosevelt before each left for home undoubtedly concerned the future course of the war in all theaters.

The concern that Jones felt over the importance of the Bari bombing was justified. It was ironic that an Italian port that had shortly before December been in enemy hands was now a key to future operations in Italy and an important factor in the invasion of the Continent across the English Channel. The strategic situation as discussed by the Americans, British, Russians, and Chinese during "Sextant" (the code word for the Cairo meetings) and "Eureka" (code word for the Teheran conference) had drastically changed within the past few weeks. Italy had surrendered as expected, but the help she had given the Allies was disappointing. On the other side of the world, the tide was turning against Japan in the Pacific and the possibility for her decisive defeat increased the Pacific theater's need for American resources. In the ETO, Operation Overlord, the cross-channel invasion planned for the spring of 1944, demanded men, equipment, and supplies unequaled in the history of warfare. Consequently, every piece of equipment, every man, every round of ammunition, every bomb, and every gallon of aviation fuel lost at Bari could completely upset the delicate balance of the various plans decided upon at Cairo and Teheran.

During the meeting at Cairo, Roosevelt and Churchill decided on a tentative course of action to present to Stalin on November 28 at Teheran. Basically they agreed that Operation Overlord had top priority.

"Overlord remains top of the bill," Churchill stated, "but should not be such a tyrant as to rule out every other activity in the Mediterranean."

Still feeling that "he who holds Rome, holds the title deeds of Italy," Churchill wanted to keep the Mediterranean operations strong. Stalin, however, sided with the Americans during the Teheran conference by placing Operation Overlord at the top of the Allied operations priority. He did agree that the movement of Allied troops up the Italian Peninsula was important if, and this was a complete surprise to both Churchill and Roosevelt, the forces turned left into France instead of right into the Balkans and Austria. He firmly believed that this pincer movement would aid in making Operation Overlord a success. While some English and American leaders considered this as an attempt by Stalin to keep the Western Allies out of the postwar Balkans, there was enough evidence that it was sound advice since it would force the Germans to fight on two fronts. With this small piece of encouragement, Churchill, who desperately wanted to keep the British and American forces in Italy strong, immediately pressed for Operation Shingle.

Operation Shingle was designed as a knock-out blow to the German forces defending the Gustav Line by landing Allied troops on the beaches of Anzio, a little town thirty-three miles south of Rome on the Tyrrhenian Sea and sixty miles behind the German line of defense. By the time the Teheran conference ended, Churchill had convinced his companions that it was advisable to leave sixty-eight LSTs which

LST

were due to return from Italy to the United Kingdom on December 5 for Operation Overlord, in Italy until January 15, 1944. He planned to use these craft for Operation Shingle.

Unfortunately the Germans had no intention of cooperating with Churchill or any other Allied leader. Kesselring's Gustav Line, the scene of Garibaldi's triumph over the Neapolitans in 1860, was much stronger than either the British or American commanders had anticipated. Trying to move up the peninsula on schedule, the British Eighth Army and the Fifth Army, created out of three American and three British divisions, found the going rough and slow. Mud, dirt, slush, rain, and Germans were everywhere. Vehicles quit running, bridges were washed out or dynamited by the enemy, snipers were on every high ridge to pour fire down on the Allied soldiers. It soon became evident that neither the Eighth nor the Fifth Army would be in Rome by the end of December, 1943, as Churchill expected. It also became obvious that the Fifth Army could not reach the Anzio area in time to support the forces that would be landing there in Operation Shingle. The British prime minister refused to give up on his idea, however, deciding that, if the Fifth Army could not reach Anzio, the solution was to strengthen the Shingle force so it could stand on its own feet against the German troops that would be in the area. Two important problems had to be solved: more men and more supplies were needed! The success of Operation Shingle would depend initially on its shock effect, but overall only a fast buildup of men and supplies, faster than Kesselring would reinforce his own troops and supplies, would guarantee the operation. A large concentration of men, equipment, and supplies at Bari to be moved northward to Anzio as needed was imperative. Twenty-four hours before Roosevelt's and Churchill's meeting at Cairo on December 3, however, the Luftwaffe made their very successful raid on the ships in Bari harbor.

It was little wonder that, as Jones stood outside his office at Fifteenth Army Group Headquarters in Santo Spirito and watched the fires and explosions in Bari harbor, he felt frustrated. It was possible—even probable—that this disaster would have a serious effect on future Allied operations in both the Mediterranean and European theaters of war. Perhaps the Pacific, too.

11

"DID THEY HIT SANTA?"

Five-year-old Enzo Galanti was looking at a folder of pictures taken at Alberobello, the small town near Bari that had houses with roofs that looked like beehives, when there was a sudden roar over his parents' second-floor apartment on Abate Gimma. He raced to the window to see the airplanes, but, before he was halfway across the room, the floor dropped from under him. The boy tumbled down into the debris of the first floor of the building as the bombs from a Ju-88 ripped into the apartment house. Within a minute after he landed on the rubble below he was covered by falling litter. His father Giovanni, who had been in the kitchen of the apartment, was knocked out of a window and fell headlong to the street, splitting his skull open. He died instantly. Enzo's mother, Rose, was left standing in a large family room at the rear of the building, despite the fact that three of the walls had disappeared when the explosion occurred. The floor did not even sag and Rose Galanti teetered on the edge of a twenty-foot fall to the street below, staring at the spot where her son had been buried alive.

While she was still waiting for help, she saw the rubble below start to move and her five-year-old son suddenly stuck his head out of the debris. Looking upward, he saw his mother.

"Did they hit Santa?" were his first words.

Enzo, dazed and injured, was concerned about the tomb of Saint Nicholas that was located in the Basilica of San Nicola. With Christmas less than one month away, he was really worried. After his mother assured him that the tomb of Santa was untouched, a fact that she doubted at the moment, but told the boy because of the situation, Enzo smiled, dug his way out of the bomb damage and went out into the street to help a man who was putting a ladder against the remains of the building to help Rose Galanti down.

Miraculously the Basilica of San Nicola in the old section of the city was not badly damaged. Built between 1089 and 1197, the basilica possessed a magnificent facade with three portals and was considered the most famous of Apulian Romanesque monuments. To Americans, Saint Nicholas was Santa Claus, popular with all ages, but the real Saint Nicholas was archbishop of Myra in Asia Minor during the first part of the fourth century. A wealthy man, he was known as a dispenser of the good things of life, a giver of gifts, and traditions arising from stories of his generosity undoubtedly account for the legend of Santa Claus. But he was the patron saint of mariners, too, and it was this fact that led to the transfer of his bones from Asia Minor to the seaport town of Bari. In 1087 three ships sailed from Bari, apparently on a commercial voyage to Asia Minor, but really as an expedition to bring back the bones of the saint.

They landed at Myra, removed the remains of Saint Nicholas, and brought them back to Bari, arriving May 9, 1087. The relics were placed in a church dedicated to San Giovanni a Mare and the construction of the Basilica of San Nicola was begun. In 1089 Pope Urban II transferred the treasured bones to the crypt of the new basilica and designated the ninth of May as the fete of the saint. Each year a solemn procession recalled the transference to Bari of the bones of the patron saint. The day following this procession, pilgrims and sailors carried an effigy of the saint shoulder high to the Piazza Mercantile and, after a mass in the open air, the effigy was mounted on a sloop and taken out on the Adriatic Sea where it was visited by pilgrims and then brought back to land in the evening. It was little wonder that Enzo Galanti was worried about Santa, since he had grown up in awe of the memory of the saint.

Enzo and his mother survived the bombing, although the father died. So did many others. So many others that the number was never revealed if, in fact, it was never determined. The old part of the city, located as it was between the new and old harbors, took the brunt of the bombing and resulting explosions and fires. At the beginning of the air strike, the Luftwaffe was off target and several strings of bombs hit buildings in the new part of the city on Abate Gimma and

Via Sparano. Also, during the raid some of the bombers strayed off course and bombed the old part of the city, causing further damage and casualties. But by far the most deaths and injuries were in the old section and caused, not by German bombs, but by the resultant explosions of the Allied ships in the harbor. The citizens of Bari, having survived from the beginning of the war until late 1943 without serious damage to their city, were convinced that they were now safe. The Allies wanted the port intact so they could bring in their men and supplies and, just as they had not bombed it during preinvasion days, the Americans and British would protect the city now that it was in their control. Or so the Italians thought. Consequently, any mention of a possible Luftwaffe attack was considered ridiculous by the people of Bari. They knew better.

Little Enzo Galanti was completely fooled by the sound of the German planes, but Elio Dante was not. He heard the Ju-88s shortly after he and his sister Sophia entered the Basilica of San Nicola and recognized the sound immediately. Nudging his sister, he pointed toward the front entrance of the basilica.

"Let's go."

Sophia Dante hesitated. Her Catholic upbringing made her reluctant to leave the church in the middle of a mass, but her brother insisted, so she got up and quietly followed him outside. They had just reached the street when there was a loud explosion along Molo Foraneo west of the Basilica of San Nicola and Dante began running toward the harbor, yelling for his sister to go home. She did—and lived. Her brother did not—and died. He raced across the narrow finger of land sticking out into the water between the old and new harbors, the protruding finger of earth that held the old section of the city, and reached the fence around the docks just as a Ju-88 dipped low over the Stazione Marittima and released its bombs. Two of the bombs hung up in the bomb bay momentarily, just long enough that when they finally fell they hit within five feet of Elio Dante. He died instantly.

Sophia Dante reached her apartment on Via Venezia during the initial minor explosions at the harbor. A friend was parked in front of her building and motioned for her to get into the car. Once the automobile was loaded, the driver took his passengers into Bari to the railroad station at the west side of the city where they were safe. This act saved Sophia

Dante's life, because when the first ammunition ship exploded in the harbor many of the buildings along Via Venezia, including her apartment building, collapsed into heaps of rubble. The concussion leveled the eastern tip of the old city, knocking the old homes down like rows of colorful dominoes. Many of the inhabitants never knew what happened.

The law in Italy provided that passengers of all types of vehicles must dismount at the time of an air raid and enter a shelter. When the first Ju-88 dropped its bombs, an autobus carrying thirty-five dock workers, all Bari citizens, from Molo San Vito to Piazza Mercantile, on the southern tip of the old city, stopped immediately. The occupants leaped from the vehicle and began running toward a street shelter, but the same string of bombs, that killed Elio Dante also killed them. Another busload of Italians managed to reach the shelter safely, moments before the bombs landed, but the explosion broke a water pipe. As the level of the black water in the shelter rose, the townspeople in the shelter called out to each other in mutual comfort and to determine if they were still alive. A woman with a baby in her arms struggled to the stairs that led to the exit only to find her way blocked by impenetrable wreckage piled at the opening. The rescuers on the outside, separated from the victims inside the shelter, shouted encouragement as the responding voices inside became weaker and weaker. The woman with the baby had reached the top step and was straining against the debris covering the exit. For several minutes she tried to pick a path through the wreckage.

"Non voglio morire" (I don't want to die), she repeated over and over. Finally, vertigo, weakness, and confusion overcame her and those outside heard the splash of her body with that of her baby. Then all was quiet. Seventeen perished in the shelter.

Fortunately, the opera house on Victor Emmanuel was not hit by the bombers and citizens such as Ruderi Francesco and his wife Pier, old Carlo Abbati and his crippled spouse Rose, and hundreds of others escaped injury. Ironically, the man who was the happiest individual in the city of Bari because the Allies were in control of the city, Paola Bartole, the conniving restaurant owner who had closed a deal with an American supply officer that very afternoon, was not so fortunate. He had intended to go to the concert, but, when he reached Piazza Garibaldi, he suddenly changed his mind.

Remembering that he was supposed to check the apartment he had promised to turn over to the American officer, he turned and hurried back toward Abate Gimma. Bartole and the bombs from the off-target Ju-88 arrived on the street at the same time and the restaurant owner died in the blast.

Giacinto Iusco, the portrait painter, had started to put the American colonel seated before him on canvas when the Luftwaffe arrived. One second he was worrying about the light in the room, the next he was on the floor, his paints and brushes flying through the air. The American's chair went over backward and the palette 'landed on top of him, staining his uniform and his face. Both men remained flat on the floor for several moments, trying to understand what had happened. Finally Iusco got to his knees and looked out the opening in the wall where the window had been before the explosion. One look was enough.

"It's the harbor. The ships are on fire!"

The American nodded, got to his feet, and headed for the street. The Italian painter hesitated, undecided whether to stay in the apartment or not, then suddenly took off after the colonel. He had not liked the way the building shuddered. Another such blast and the entire apartment building might collapse.

Shortly before the Luftwaffe aircraft arrived at Bari on the night of December 2, a train slowed to a stop on the tracks behind the tents of the Forty-first Depot Supply Squadron and approximately three hundred German prisoners of war were permitted outside for a rest break. Under close guard, the prisoners were enjoying the fresh air and the cigarettes distributed to them by the Americans. When the first bomb exploded in the harbor area the prisoners, as one, leaped to their feet from where they had been sitting on the grass and began milling around in confusion. The American soldiers guarding the POWs attempted to get the Germans back on the train, but, before they could get them started up the steps, another blast sent Americans and Germans alike scurrying for cover. Some of the prisoners, unfamiliar with the area, began running toward the harbor, only to meet the men of the Forty-first Depot Supply Squadron running in the opposite direction. Allies and Axis soldiers intermixed and a few moments later they were all headed away from the harbor in unison, their enmity forgotten.

Other Germans recognized the air raid shelter on the harbor side of the railroad tracks and hurried to it, only to find that it was already knee-deep with water. Standing at the entrance and jabbering to each other in their own language, the prisoners tried to decide whether to go into the air raid shelter or not. One of the Germans seized a board lying on the ground nearby and ventured down the steps of the shelter far enough to measure the depth of the water. It was approximately three feet deep according to the high water mark on the board, but the Germans were worried that it might be getting deeper. While they were still arguing, an Italian woman hurried past them and went down the steps. The prisoners looked at each other, shrugged, and followed her. Five minutes later a bomb made a direct hit on the shelter. There were no survivors.

On the opposite side of the Forty-first Depot Supply Squadron area from the railroad tracks, "Bambino Stadium" was crowded with Italians and Americans watching the Yank teams go after each other in an intrasquadron game. The game was just about over when a terrific blast in the harbor sent the spectators rushing for the exits at full speed, much faster than any of the base runners had traveled the base lines during the game. Among those hurrying to get out of the stadium were Antonio Urbani, Giovanni Tomei, and Silvio Zugno, the three seventeen-year-old Italian youths who worked for the Americans at General Depot Number Five. They ran west until they reached Via Napoli and then turned south toward the city. At this point they were joined by several others and Urbani looked at the newcomers in amazement.

"Germans!" he told Tomei. "These guys are Germans."

The strangers who linked up with the three Italians on Via Napoli were more of the prisoners from the train who were running in circles. Once they saw others heading in a definite direction, such as Urbani, Tomei, and Zugno, they promptly decided they knew where they were going and the Germans followed.

At Via Brigata Regina, Urbani stopped and stared out the street toward the harbor. It was a fascinating sight to the young Italian. Several ships were directly in his line of sight, all burning. He saw some bomb explosions near the shore, wincing as the sound of the explosions reached his ears. The height of the waterspouts made by the bomb blasts amazed

him, since he had never seen a bomb explode before. Both
Tomei and Zugno urged him to hurry but Urbani refused to
move.

"In a minute...in a minute...," he muttered.

Finally, his two companions moved on down Via Napoli
toward an air raid shelter, leaving Urbani standing in the
middle of the street by himself. The Germans followed Tomei
and Zugno. Suddenly, an enemy plane appeared out of the
darkness to the south of the harbor, crossed over Molo
Foraneo and banked sharply to the left as the gunners on the
U.S.S. *Aroostook* fired their deck guns into its path. The
Ju-88 roared across the shoreline at an angle that took it
straight for the intersection of Via Napoli and Via Brigata
Regina, the spot where young Antonio Urbani was standing
watching the scene in the harbor. The plane was traveling so
fast that the sound of its engines was trailing it, so Urbani
never heard it approach. The German pilot was having
trouble maintaining altitude because of damage to the tail
section of the Ju-88, damage inflicted by the guns of the
U.S.S. *Aroostook*, and in desperation he salvoed his bomb
load. The bombs "walked" up Via Napoli as they exploded,
each bomb leaving a large crater. Urbani never had a chance.
At the last moment, after seeing the approaching plane, he
tried to run toward "Bambino Stadium," but he was too slow
and too late. The last bomb hit five feet behind him, exploded in a huge shower of dirt and cement, and when the debris
settled to the ground Antonio Urbani had disappeared. No
trace of him was ever found.

Tomei and Zugno, still trailed by their new-found companions, the confused German prisoners, forced their way
into an air raid shelter on Via Napoli. They stayed in the
shelter until the all clear sounded, then emerged immediately for some fresh air and to see if it was safe to try to reach
their homes. Despite the flames visible in the harbor area
and the minor explosions they heard, the two Italian youths
decided to go back to "Bambino Stadium" and get the
motorcycles they had left behind in their rush to get out of
the arena when the bombs first started dropping. They also
wanted to locate their friend Urbani. As they started back up
Via Napoli, the Germans went with them. Tomei motioned
them back to the shelter but the POWs refused. Finally the
Italian shrugged and hurried up the street toward the stadium, the Germans right behind him.

Fortunately, Tomei, Zugno, and the Germans were on the opposite side of "Bambino Stadium" when the *John Harvey* exploded. Even though they were protected by the forty-thousand spectator arena, the concussion, whipping around the oval exterior walls, knocked them to the ground. For several seconds the entire area around the stadium was as bright as day, even though they were approximately a mile and a half away from the East Jetty where the *John Harvey* had been anchored. None of the men were injured, however, and, after recovering from the shock of the terrific blast, Tomei and Zugno seized their motorcycles and started wheeling them toward Bari. The German prisoners once again began to follow them, but, before the perplexed and scared Tomei could yell at them again, an American military policeman appeared from the tent area of the Forty-first Depot Supply Squadron and called to the Germans. Evidently they recognized him as one of their guards on the train, because the prisoners immediately flocked around him, grabbing his hand and treating him as a long-lost comrade. The events of the night had made them completely forget that the American was their enemy, that he was taking them to a prison camp. They were delighted to see someone they knew, someone who would tell them what to do. The military policeman pointed toward the train that was still standing undamaged on the tracks across the road from the stadium, on the other side of the Forty-first Depot Supply Squadron tents, and the Germans hurried toward it gratefully.

As they started to climb aboard, a very heavy cloud of smoke drifted across the area from the harbor and one of the prisoners, after taking a deep breath, turned to the American military policeman and said in perfect English, "I smell mustard gas."

The military policeman looked startled. He took a deep breath and coughed, "Hell, that's garlic."

On the border of the old city, several hundred citizens of Bari had taken shelter in and around the famous Castello Svevo, a landmark of the area. This castle, built by Frederick II of Swabia on previous Norman fortifications, served as the Court of Isabella and Bona Sforza in the sixteenth century when great bulwarks were added with angular towers over the moat. It was a strongly built edifice, one that Bari citizens had confidence in when the Luftwaffe planes dropped their bombs. People streamed toward the castle from all directions immediately after the first explosion—down Via San Francesco D'Assisi, across Piazza Garibaldi, through the beautiful Piazza Massari with its many trees. Many of the inhabitants of the old section also hurried to the castle, recognizing in its thick stone walls a protective shield that would save them from the debris being hurled through the air by the exploding bombs and ships.

The centuries-old castle did not let the citizens of Bari down during the disaster. Those that stayed inside the landmark were not injured. Flying rubble slammed against the walls and bounced away leaving no more than a chip in the stone. Even when the *John Harvey* blew up, those inside the castle heard the muffled blast, but, unlike other buildings, Castello Svevo did not tremble. It remained as sturdy as it had during the Norman conquest—long before even the most imaginative dreamer thought flying was possible, let alone dropping bombs from a plane.

In *La Citta Vecchia*, however, the results of the air strike were entirely different. The old homes, jammed close together within the ancient city wall, were not as sturdy as the old castle. The narrow, winding streets contained the force of the blast, hemmed it in, and guided it down the "ravines" between the one-, two-, and three-story homes of various colors. There was no free path for the bomb concussion to follow. Consequently, the full strength of the explosions slammed against the old homes, tearing and ripping them apart as though they were cardboard dollhouses. Many of the inhabitants never had a chance to escape, never knew what happened.

Favilli Ernesto and his family were eating their evening meal in their home just north of Piazza Mercantile in the old section. His wife and six boys, the oldest ten years, were sitting at the table and Ernesto had just stepped outside into the narrow street to call their dog when the Ju-88s roared in from the sea. Despite the fact that he was within ten steps of his house, Ernesto never reached the door. A bomb landed nearly a block up the street from where he was calling his dog and exploded. The shock wave from the blast shot down the street and lifted the hapless Italian completely off his feet and carried him into an alley twenty-five feet away.

He was still lying on the ground when he saw his house collapse. The walls fell toward each other and the roof dropped straight down—straight down on Ernesto's wife and six boys. A piece of burning debris from the harbor explosions landed on the rubble of the house and, before the stunned Italian could get to his feet, the place was in flames. He heard his family scream, saw his wife momentarily in the burning house carrying the youngest boy in her arms. Her hair was on fire, her clothes were burned off, and her body was already turning black. Then, as the desperate husband attempted to reach her, she disappeared. Only the fact that several other residents arrived at the scene and grabbed Ernesto kept him from leaping into the flames. They pulled him back and dragged him down the street toward the opening in the wall that surrounded the old section of the city.

The wind off the sea helped spread the flames from the Ernesto home throughout the old city. The carnage of old Bari had begun. Within thirty minutes, two out of every four buildings on the finger of land stretching out into the Adriatic Sea between the old harbor and the new harbor had suffered damage. Many were burning, so many that the area inside the wall of the old city was turned into a huge crematory. Some buildings were cut open, their flammable insides exposed to the flames licking out from surrounding homes. There was little water to fight the fires and the nearby explosions of the ships in the harbor sent the fire fighters scurrying for an air raid shelter in an effort to save their own lives. Death was nearly certain for those who stayed at street level and probable even for those who went underground into the shelters. In addition, all communication had broken down. Confusion reigned throughout the entire ancient section of Bari, and it was everyone for himself.

Scores of inhabitants of the old city reasoned that if they could escape from the fiery hell inside the wall to the water they would stand a better chance to survive. They were not aware, of course, of the impending disaster of the ships moored in the harbor, believing that the ships might burn and sink, but not considering the fact that the vessels might explode. Their immediate concern was to escape the flames and the intense heat. The temperature in some parts of the old section was so high that it was suffocating. Instead of their lungs filling with life-sustaining air, they were filling with searing hot winds whipped up by the fire sweeping through the area. Death came fast, but not easily, under these conditions. Panic-stricken, the inhabitants raced for the water— straight toward the ships in the new harbor. They dashed wildly, running into each other, knocking children to the street in their headlong rush. Some of the men and women were on fire and screaming in pain and fright. Others were injured and blood was oozing down their faces or arms. Still others ran silently, paying no attention to anyone, keeping a straight and direct path toward the water. Across the main road, over the railroad tracks, up the stone breakwater blocks, and down the bank to the water.

Those that had their clothes on fire dove into the Adriatic Sea to douse the flames and had a momentary respite from death. Others leaned down and splashed water on their faces or hands to cool off, even drinking some of the water to wet their parched, scorched throats. The children had to be restrained from wading too deep in an attempt to escape the roaring flames of the old city which they could still see behind them. When military personnel tried to warn them away from the water, the Italians refused to budge. They knew that death awaited them where they had come from and wanted no part of it. Even a harbor full of burning ships seemed safer to the survivors of the old section of Bari. When they heard the horn on one of the ships shrieking steadily, they still would not move away. Swimming, drinking water, splashing themselves, the inhabitants of old Bari were taking their chances where they were.

The odds ran out when the *John Harvey* blew up. The explosions prior to the *John Harvey* blast had startled the people crowded along the water's edge, but only a small number had been injured by the resultant flying debris. The explosion of the *John Harvey*, however, not only wiped out Captain Knowles, his crew, and the military personnel on the ship, but it also killed most of the Italians huddled along the shore. There was no time to run, no time to hide, no time for anything. One moment the inhabitants of the old section were rejoicing in their good fortune for escaping from inside the wall, the next they were dead. The brilliant light of the blast clearly outlined the survivors as they lined the shore. It also attracted their attention and they turned to look out to sea just in time to face the unbearable concussion that swept out from the doomed ship in a 360-degree circle. For most of them it was their last look at anything on earth.

The mass of people along the water was ripped apart instantly. Some were blown upward, their broken bodies flying twenty-five to thirty feet high. Some were hurtled straight back the direction they had come from, straight back toward the old section. Many of the hapless victims were blown all the way back to the wall where their bodies were stacked on top of each other. The living and the dead were thrown together and those still breathing struggled desperately to free themselves of the corpses of their friends and neighbors, and, sometimes, their own family. Once free, they were not safe even then. The swirling winds of the explosion lifted rooftops and automobiles and trucks, depositing them all over the area. Flying fire missiles from the ships in the harbor penetrated the shoreline, forcing the survivors to retreat. There was no safe spot. Caught between the inferno of the old city and the explosions in the harbor, the citizens of old Bari suffered a high death rate. Fate selected some to live awhile longer, some to survive the entire ordeal, but the number was low. Even those who lived through the flames, survived the explosions, and avoided the flying debris faced a greater hazard, although they did not know it. The cloud of smoke carrying the mustard released from the hundred tons of chemical bombs aboard the *John Harvey* permeated the atmosphere over the old section and those that were still breathing filled their lungs with the lethal mixture.

12

"DOCTOR, WHAT'S WRONG
WITH THE LIGHTS?"

Medical planning for the invasion of Italy provided that the casualties would be evacuated to North Africa and the Middle East, using Sicily as a transit center in an emergency. Air evacuation routes included the Palermo-Catania-Bone-Bizerte-Tunis route, with between four and six flights a day average. Later the British Seventh Combat Casualty Station was moved to Bari and a line of evacuation was established from Potenza through Matera to Taranto and on to Bari. An alternate, directly from Gravina to the Seventh Combat Casualty Station at Bari, was also used at times. It had been planned that, as soon as the Fifth and Eighth armies had a firm foothold on the mainland of Italy, hospital bases would be established on a large scale at both Naples on the west coast and Bari on the east coast. But the general shortage of shipping necessitated considerable delay in these plans and the above routes were used to get most of the wounded to North Africa.

Several steps were taken to upgrade the medical arrangements in Italy, to help get the casualties from the front to well-equipped hospitals as soon as possible and save lives. In an effort to alleviate the space available for shipping medical supplies to Italy from North Africa, the H.S. *Dorsetshire* was gutted and used exclusively for this purpose. As temporary facilities at Foggia, Barletta, and Reggio became overloaded, ordinary railroad rolling stock was converted into ambulance trains to move the wounded to Bari. On October 25, 1943, a new district—the Second District—was formed to coordinate the evacuation and treatment of casualties; its headquarters was established at Bari. It controlled, among other things, all the general hospitals on the eastern side of Allied occupied Italy that were receiving Eighth Army patients.

Six days after the new Second District was established at Bari, the Three New Zealand General Hospital personnel began arriving in the city and started setting up their equipment in the Bari Polyclinic three miles south of the city. Also situated at the huge building were the Ninety-eight British General Hospital, and the Fourteen Combined General Hospital, the Thirty Indian General Hospital, and the Four Base Depot Medical Stores. One block of the structure was also used for a time by the medical services of the Italian Army. In addition to these medical facilities at the Bari Polyclinic, others were established around the city and its outskirts. At the end of November, 1943, the Fifty-four British General Hospital, the Forty-two West African Section, the Sixteen Indian Field Laboratory, the Five Venereal Disease Treatment Center, the Three Field Transfusion Unit, the Thirty-four Field Hygiene Section, and the Thirty-five Antimalaria Control Unit were all in the vicinity of Bari. Yet facilities were always overloaded, the medical personnel overworked. The Allied medical planning was still far behind schedule at the beginning of December, but, with more ships becoming available to carry supplies, equipment, and personnel from the North African theater to Italy, it seemed that the worst of the ordeal was over. With the arrival of Three New Zealand General Hospital and the establishment of the American Twenty-six General Hospital near the end of November at Bari, the outlook was bright. Allied leaders estimated that within thirty more days the medical facilities in Italy, and especially at the important center of Bari, would be completely adequate.

The most fascinating medical facility in the city was the Bari Polyclinic that housed the Three New Zealand General Hospital. If Mussolini had completed the plans he had for the medical center, it would have been an ideal place for the Allies to establish their casualty centers. Unfortunately for the British, New Zealanders, and Americans, he did not and this created confusion and hardship for the medical personnel trying to work at the Polyclinic. The nurses and doctors learned to treat patients under conditions never described in their textbooks, but, by the end of November, Three New Zealand General Hospital alone had treated 656 patients at the Bari Polyclinic. The newer Ninety-eight British General

Hospital, despite a shortage of nurses that required "borrowing" sixty-four New Zealand sisters and nurses, was also in full operation. The personnel at this unit was also learning new tactics, some very enlightening to conservative British morals. Being on the east coast of Italy, many of the guerrillas fighting in Yugoslavia who were wounded were brought to Bari. The Ninety-eight British General Hospital received a shipload of these troops early in November. Some were women, some were men, and all were wearing tattered, decrepit uniforms that made it difficult to tell which were which when they were admitted. Consequently it was discovered later that many of the women were in the same section as the men, so it was decided to move them to an all female area. It sounded easy, but it was not. Everytime the nurses or doctors attempted to move the women, the feminine Yugoslav guerrillas pulled long knives from under their pillows and refused to budge. They wanted to stay beside the men—and they did.

Just behind the Bari Polyclinic was the site of the master antiaircraft gun emplacement for that part of the city and, when an occasional German plane was sighted, the guns blazed away long before the alert was sounded. When the Three New Zealand General Hospital personnel first arrived, the noise of the guns scared the nurses every time they fired and many humorous incidents occurred. One nurse, taking a bath when the antiaircraft battery let go, grabbed her hat and raced for cover, wearing it and nothing else. Another time a sedate and reserved sister dove under a table when the guns fired—and found herself sitting on the lap of a young sergeant! As the days passed, however, and no enemy bombs were dropped, despite the fact that the guns behind the Bari Polyclinic blazed away every day, the medical personnel began to ignore the sound and rarely took cover.

On the night of December 2, Three New Zealand General Hospital was functioning in a routine manner. A stretcher party had left for the railroad station at Piazza Roma to meet an incoming ambulance train from the front carrying a load of wounded soldiers. Up-patients and the staff on duty, including Sergeant Major Robson and Sergeant Major McCauley who had been arguing about the respective merits of soccer and rugby football, were in the patients' recreation room watching a movie. At 7:30 P.M., just as the stretcher party arrived with approximately one hundred casualties to be admitted to the hospital, the bofors guns behind the building began firing. The busy nurses, sisters, and doctors hardly looked up at the sound of the guns, having heard them so often that the noise was routine. They knew that, as soon as the gunners shot a few rounds at some imaginary target in the sky overhead, they would quit for the night and quiet would return to the hospital. Or so they believed. When the barrage intensified instead of letting up, however, Colonel Gower, the commanding officer of the hospital, decided to investigate.

Gower, J. D. Cottrell, L. A. Bennett, and several other officers went outside of the Bari Polyclinic to determine, if they could, what the gunners were firing at so steadily. E. M. Somers Cocks, a sister assigned to the hospital, leaned down and looked out a window. She could see red and yellow tracer shells streaking skyward, but was unable to see any aircraft near the hospital. At that moment the movie was halted in the patient's recreation room and the loudspeaker crackled.

"Everyone will disperse to the shelters, please."

Miss Cocks shrugged as she looked at the blank screen. It was an irritating interruption, but she was confident that it would not last long. There had been many barrages over the hospital before and the alerts had never lasted more than half an hour. It was not until later that she recalled that the wail of the sirens had come after, not before, the firing of the guns.

Outside, Gower and his companions saw the flares hanging in the sky over the city, outlining the buildings in sharp silhouette. The ferocity of the guns increased while he was staring at the flares until the whole heavens seemed streaked and pierced with criss-crossing lines of red and yellow and green. The noise of the guns hurt his ears and made his head ache. Looking into the sky, the commanding officer shook his head.

"I can't see any aircraft. They must be in the clouds if there are any Germans up there."

There were a few low-hanging clouds in the sky, but not really enough to hide fast-flying planes. Suddenly, Gower noticed a fog uncoiling itself skyward and recognized it as man-made. It was obvious that the British defense forces were attempting to hide the city and the harbor from attackers. Before he could call to his companions, a succession of equally spaced flashes, followed seconds later by a series of dull explosions, told him that this was no fake alert. The flashes and blasts were from a string of bombs dropped from enemy planes!

"Air raid! Take cover!" he yelled.

M. E. Jackson, the matron of the hospital, heard the muffled blasts in the ward where she was checking on some patients and momentarily wondered where they came from. She, too, hurried to the entrance and looked outside at the sky which was now a multicolored ceiling over the city and harbor. There was a terrible beauty about the whole scene, a beauty that kept her watching in fascination as more bombs were dropped. It reminded Miss Jackson of a vivid fireworks display.

Without warning, a vast fountain of flame with jets of various shades of green, red, and yellow streaming from its top arose in the air about a mile away from the hospital. Matron Jackson, Gower, Bennet, and several others gaped at the mysterious fountain. There had been no loud blast reaching their ears, no indication of what had caused the unusual geyser, and none of the observers realized at that second that light traveled faster than sound. Not until they were flung flat by the mighty blast of the ammunition ship in the harbor did Gower and the others understand what had happened. Fortunately, Matron Jackson had stepped back inside the hospital a fraction of a minute before the concussion reached her and was not knocked down. She immediately hurried to the main light switch and pulled it to the off positon.

The blast had shattered all the windows of Three New Zealand General Hospital quarters in the Bari Polyclinic, throwing pieces of broken glass onto the beds of the patients. Several window spaces that had been bricked up temporarily because no replacement glass was available caved in and several nurses were injured by the hurtling bricks. In the wards the beds were hastily dragged into the center of the rooms, away from the more vulnerable walls. All work on the seriously wounded soldiers was halted and the hundred battle casualties that had just arrived from the railroad station lay on the floor of the reception room awaiting the end of the raid. Among the casualties were several German POWs. They looked pleased at the explosions and the resultant damage to the hospital, gabbing and pointing excitedly at each new blast. Finally a burly sergeant walked over to the Germans and in no uncertain terms told them that if he heard one more word or laugh from them he was going to hit them across the mouth. The Germans quieted down.

The raid went on. Leaping flames and billowing clouds of smoke indicated where the bombs were finding their mark. When the *John Harvey* exploded, window frames and more bricks from the walls of the building were knocked into the wards. One sister was hit on the nose by a piece of a brick, a senior medical officer was knocked down, and another officer's pipe was blown out of his mouth as he stood in the middle of the dispensary smoking. In the center of the hospital wing there was an elevator shaft that had never been put to use. Since the arrival of the Three New Zealand General Hospital personnel, doors had been installed on the entrances to the shaft at each floor and these doors were securely bolted so that no nurse, sister, or doctor could step into the empty shaft accidentally and fall to the bottom. When the *John Harvey* exploded these heavy doors were blown off the shaft entrances and in the darkness several of the hospital staff narrowly escaped falling to their deaths by inadvertently walking into the void. When the lights went back on one sister was stretched out on the floor with both her legs dangling through the open passageway to the unused elevator shaft. Two more feet and she would have been killed.

When the all clear sounded at 11:00 P.M., Gower and his staff took stock of the damage to the hospital. It was considerable. Complete panes of glass were nonexistent and most windowframes were sagging, if they remained in the opening at all. Doors were wrenched from their frames or split completely in two. Broken glass was everywhere. The staff immediately went into operation again as well as they could under the existing conditions. Some were assigned the duty of cleaning up as much of the debris as possible and preparing beds for the hundred battle casualties that had arrived just prior to the air raid and were still lying on the floor of the reception room. Gower knew that it would not be long until the casualties from the bombing would be arriving.

Kathryn Salo, the U.S. Army nurse assigned to the American Twenty-six General Hospital, a short distance from the Bari Polyclinic that housed the Three New Zealand General Hospital, had just walked a short distance with her friend when she heard the guns start firing. She thought that it was just another alert, a practice operation, and did not quicken her pace. The officer with her knew better. Grabbing her arm as the first string of bombs exploded in the harbor area, he hurried her into a nearby Italian home.

At the Twenty-six General Hospital, John Shifflet, the baker, was busy in the huge kitchen when he heard the rumble of the antiaircraft guns. Then came the thunderous roar of the bombs, and immediately the hospital lights went out. Running to a window, Shifflet looked outside and, as others all over the city who were looking toward the harbor at the time, was completely fascinated by the dazzling bluish light of the enemy flares that lighted the area. He finally turned away from the window and felt his way through the dark kitchen toward a hospital shelter, but it took him too long. Before he had reached the corridor leading to the shelter, there was a mushroom of flame, sparks, and smoke at the harbor and a few seconds later the force of the blast of the first ship exploding reached the Twenty-six General Hospital. Casements were blown in, glass shattered, doors knocked off their hinges, and those of the hospital staff in the direct line of the concussion were flattened. The screams of the injured coming out of the darkness added to the horror. Some of the casualties were not injured by the explosion, but the tremendous noise of the blast had rubbed nerves already raw from the shock of the raid. Others, badly cut and bleeding, were in terrible pain.

"Doctor... doctor... doctor."

Working by the light of flashlights and with a minimum of instruments, bandages, and medicine found in the blackness of the hospital interior, the doctors dressed wounds, extricated fine slivers of glass from flesh, set broken bones. They worked on the injured even as the air raid continued, even during the blast of the *John Harvey* that shook the entire building. As the huge cloud of smoke, mustard, and debris drifted toward the city, George S. Bergh watched it glumly.

"Our equipment? What about our equipment?"

Everyone in the Twenty-six General Hospital was aware that the equipment to operate the hospital was on the *Samuel J. Tilden*, one of the merchant ships in the harbor. Without the long-awaited equipment, the hospital could not function and it was now obvious that there were going to be a great many casualties as a result of the Luftwaffe air strike.

"Where is the manifest of the *Tilden*?" a voice said out of the darkness. "Who was on the ship?"

By the light of a flashlight the Twenty-six General Hospital survivors studied the names of the personnel aboard the merchant ship carrying their supplies:

Leo S. Kaczmarczyk	Charles W. Moore
John H. Adamson, Jr.	Raymond A. Arsenault
Buster Long	Stephen Corey
Ralph J. Taylor	Leo A. Drake
Lawrence H. Buys	Delbert L. Hall
Byron A. Bell	Clare E. Lash
Peter N. Gasparich	Donald P. Merrill
Edmund T. Podlewski	Robert W. Robinson
Peter Minichello	William T. Steinberg
Lewis R. Bowden	James L. Stewart
Harold J. Gadbaw	Charles W. Woods

In addition, the manifest listed five hospital units and an unestimated amount of Army cargo, much of which was medical supplies. Bergh knew, as he looked toward the harbor, that the Twenty-six General Hospital would be very fortunate if it received a fraction of the equipment shipped to it on the *Samuel J. Tilden*. In fact, it was doubtful if any of the men aboard the ship survived the holocaust at the harbor.

Miraculously, the men of the Twenty-six General Hospital who had been on the *Samuel J. Tilden* had all managed to get away from the burning merchant ship except Leo Kaczmarczyk. He was lost as a result of the bombing. The other Twenty-six General Hospital personnel escaped, although some of the men suffered very serious injuries. One of the last men to leave the ship was John Adamson of the medical group who was painfully injured, but stayed until the last to take part in the rescue work. The survivors, however, were in no condition to immediately join the staff at the Twenty-six General Hospital and take up their assigned duties, consequently the already short-handed medical staff at the facility was reduced further. At a time when hospital care was critically needed at Bari because of the German raid, there was less available than ever.

Clifford Price of the Fifth Medical Supply Depot was still cleaning up a warehouse in preparation for storing the medical supplies to be delivered by the *Samuel J. Tilden* when Oberleutnant Teuber and the other Ju-88 pilots roared across the harbor at Bari. As soon as he heard the warning sirens, Price rushed to the door of the warehouse to see what was happening. He reached the doorway at the same instant the first bomb exploded and the concussion of the blast staggered the surprised soldier. When he saw the bright glare of the flares that the German bombers had dropped over the harbor, he did not hesitate. His long months in North Africa had taught him to move fast when the enemy attacked and Price did just that. He headed for his billet on the street running along the harbor. It was a good try, but, unfortunately, the German planes stopped his flight halfway to his destination. There was a loud explosion in front of him and, while he was still trying to determine where that bomb hit, another bomb exploded behind him. Price froze against a wall along the street, where he stayed until the Ju-88 disappeared to the north. Uninjured, despite the closeness of the exploding bombs, he hurried to his billet reaching it just in time to get inside before the *John Harvey* blew up. Once again Price was lucky. He was not even cut by the flying glass from the shattered windows of the building that were knocked out by the force of the blast. It was a night of confusion for the soldier from West Virginia, but he was certain of one fact— the warehouse he had cleaned out earlier that day would never contain the expected medical supplies from the *Samuel J. Tilden*. There no longer was such a ship afloat.

At the Hotel Miramar, Walter Anderson of the Fourth Medical Supply Depot was still discussing details of the organization of his new facility at Bari with Don McGregor and John DeLuca when the bombing took place. None of the men in the room heard any warning siren or antiaircraft guns firing. The first indication they had that an air raid was in progress was when the first string of bombs began dropping. They did not even have time to get to a bomb shelter and had to "sweat out" the air strike in the hotel. The concussion from the bombs and the exploding ships made the hotel sway as though it were going to collapse. The windows and shutters of Anderson's room blew in. The chandelier came down and much of the plaster from the ceilings and walls came off. When things finally quieted down and the trio determined the havoc that had been caused at the harbor by the German aircraft, they knew that the medical supplies en route to their organization would never arrive either.

Anderson shook his head. "We'll have to request more equipment and supplies from North Africa," he said, "and they'll have to fly it in. We're going to need it and soon."

He was already picturing in his mind the influx of casualties that would be swarming to the Bari hospital facilities within a short time, the wounded, shocked victims from the harbor and the city. At that time neither Anderson nor anyone else at Bari considered the fact that the casualties would also be suffering from exposure to mustard.

Unfortunately, neither the Allied military personnel nor the Italian civilians were prepared for an adequate defense against a chemical agent on the night of December 2, 1943. During four previous years of combat the Axis powers had not used toxic agents, as either an offensive weapon or a defensive weapon, and there was no reason to believe that they would use it during the winter of 1943 in Italy. Brigadier General Charles S. Shadle, chief chemical officer, Allied Force Headquarters, had confidently predicted that there was little threat of the Axis using gas warfare during the Allied landings on the coast of North Africa, and he had been proven correct by subsequent events. However, during the Sicilian landings, small stores of enemy toxics had been discovered but Shadle was still convinced that Hitler did not plan to use them. He based his prediction on the way the agents were stored and their placements. Many Allied intelligence agents protested Shadle's theory and tried to convince Washington that toxics would be used by the enemy during the Italian landings. Once again, Shadle was correct in his prediction, and from then on it was assumed by Allied military leaders that gas warfare was no problem. They did not even consider the possibility of Allied troops—and Italian civilians—being gassed by their own chemical agents!

Chemical warfare training was given every American military man and woman in World War II, but, because the likelihood of an enemy gas attack was so remote, few of the trainees took the schooling very seriously. It was a phase of training that was required, that everyone experienced, more as an unusual interlude in the more conventional aspects of their combat training, and then promptly forgot. The Chemical Warfare Service of the AAF had the mission of providing for defense against chemical attack; advising and making recommendations for both offensive and defensive measures; and to supply the necessary equipment. The CWS assigned chemical officers to headquarters staff positions from air force down to wing level and, below that echelon, either officers or NCOs were given additional duty as unit gas officers. At best, the chemical warfare defense preparations at the lower levels of the AAF organization were only fair. Other technical services that were required nearly every day in a combat theater received much more attention than chemical warfare defense techniques that might never be needed; so, by December, 1943, the American military personnel at Bari were definitely not ready for a gas attack.

Neither were the medical facilities in the Bari area ready to treat gas casualties. The hospital staffs were so busy treating soldiers wounded in combat, men injured in non-combat accidents, those who were ill, or military personnel suffering nervous disorders that they had little time to keep abreast of the latest recommended treatments for victims of toxic agents. Most of the medical facilities and many of the field first aid stations had an ample supply of gas masks to use to protect themselves or their patients who did not have their own gas masks with them in case of a chemical attack. There was a supply of protective ointment, some protective clothing, and impregnites. In March, 1942, the CWS's Medical Division drew up a list of equipment and materials that it felt should be included in a gas casualty medical kit to be distributed in the field. They recommended that the kits contain, among other items, petrolatum and amyl salicylate for removal of mustard from the skin, sodium sulamyd to prevent blister gas eye infection, BAL ointment for any liquid blister gas contamination of eyes, eye and nose drops, a floating white soap for decontamination, calamine concentrate for relief of mustard burn itching, and a screening water testing kit to detect toxic agents in water supplies.

The kit was of an unwieldy trunk type of construction and weighed almost three hundred pounds. Shortly after the appearance of this large kit, a smaller gas casualty chest evolved and was issued on the basis of one to each twenty-five individuals and as an accessory to vehicular equipment. It contained some of the items included in the larger kit, but was not nearly as complete, of course. There was only one trouble, however. The ships carrying these vital kits, large and small, were the same ships that Anderson, Price, Gower, and the other survivors of the German air strike watched burn, explode, and sink in the harbor at Bari that tragic night.

13

"LET'S GET OUT OF BARI!"

Leroy Eure, the dock specialist with the 1095 Dock Operating Company, survived the bombing and the exploding ships, although he had only been halfway to the Hotel Spa when the Ju-88s arrived overhead and began their attack. He was standing in the lobby of the hotel just before midnight when several U.S. Navy Armed Guardsmen, accompanied by merchant seamen from ships in the harbor, arrived. They were covered with oil, burned, and were suffering from exposure and shock. The survivors told Eure that they had leaped from their ships and swum underwater as much as possible to the pier, then made their way to the street where they were picked up and brought to the hotel. Eure knew immediately that the men needed medical help and arranged transportation for the casualties to a dispensary located on the outskirts of Bari.

After he had made certain that all the casualties had been directed to the medical facility, he went upstairs to his room and, for the remainder of the night, watched the burning ships in the harbor. He knew that the damage inflicted by the enemy planes had been serious, but it was not until dawn the next morning that Eure discovered the tragic proportions of the German air strike. The ship he had finished unloading the night before was gone. A Norwegian coal ship had its stern section blown out of the water and was on the breakwater. A tanker was on the bottom of the dock area, with only the superstructure showing. Small ships were scattered all over the harbor. Eure saw two piles of bombs on the dock and walked over to inspect them. He was horrified to see that the one pile had taken a direct hit from the German planes, yet not a single bomb in the pile had exploded! There were M-43 five-hundred-pound bombs scattered all over the place. After an inspection of the dock, Eure knew that it would be immobilized for at least a week, perhaps more.

At approximately the same time that the casualties reached the Hotel Spa on the night of December 2 and Eure directed them to the dispensary, Coxswain A. M. Nikkila and Ship's Cook H. K. Olsen, both of the U.S.S. *Pumper*, reached the trapped crew of the *John Bascom* at the tip of the East Jetty. It was a dangerous trip for the two men. They dodged burning ships, maneuvered away from a broken petroleum line that threatened to burst into flames at any second, and avoided huge chunks of debris in the water to reach Captain Heitmann and his crew. Nikkila and Cook loaded their launch with as many of the trapped men as possible and started for shore. A British minesweeper, on its way out of the harbor, spotted the survivors on the East Jetty and altered its course to pick up some of the men. Others had to wait for the launch to return.

The wounded were sent ashore first and, because they required stretchers, the motor launch could only accommodate a few during the first trips. It was not until nearly 2:00 A.M. that Heitmann, Rudolph, and Lesesne, the last persons taken off the East Jetty, boarded the launch for the perilous trip to the dock area. They were evacuated just in time. The fire, by this late hour, had reached the torpedo nets that bordered the East Jetty and the three men were caught between these flames and the flames of the burning ships along the East Jetty. When Heitmann and his companions got ashore, the British Army personnel working along the dock gave them each a blanket to wrap around themselves and directed them to a waiting truck. They were driven to a nearby sport club building that was being used as an evacuation station. The gymnasium was filled with people lying on blankets. There was no heat in the building and most of the windows were broken. Since the survivors were wet and the night was cold, everyone in the room was shaking. It was not until five hours later that a tub of hot water arrived with some tea in it for the shivering survivors to drink; this helped warm them somewhat. Heitmann inquired about medical aid for those who were in serious condition and was told that the available medical facilities were overcrowded at the moment, but that efforts were being made to find a place for the casualties in the gymnasium. Rubbing his irritated, bloodshot eyes, the captain nodded.

"I hope it doesn't take too long."

James Oleman, the Fifty-second Troop Carrier wing pilot who had been at the movies when the Ju-88s arrived over Bari, caught a few hours sleep in his hotel room at the Grande Albergo delle Nazioni after the all clear sounded. Early the next morning he and Jens Lerback, his roommate, walked down to the harbor. The damage was tremendous. Buildings along the street bordering the water, despite the fact that they were constructed out of reinforced concrete, were mere shells. Trees were stripped bare of limbs and leaves. Ships were burning all over the harbor. Finally Oleman turned to his companion and muttered, "Let's get out of here."

They caught a truck back out to the airfield and, as they passed a row of barracks he had noticed earlier, Oleman was amazed to see that they were demolished. It appeared that the concussion had lifted the roof off the barracks long enough for the walls to collapse inward part way and then the roof settled back down. This made a structure about ten feet high, a weird, twisted structure that was a clear indication of the force of the blasts that had been experienced in the area.

At the airport he was relieved to learn that his C-47 had not been damaged. A short time later Oleman took off and, on his way home to his base at Trapani, Sicily, he flew directly over the top of Mount Etna. Looking into the cone of the volcano, he told Lerback, "This volcano has nothing on Bari harbor when it comes to destruction."

He was absolutely correct.

The toll in dead and wounded among the military personnel on ships in Bari harbor was high, very high. So high that it became known as the "Second Pearl Harbor" in military circles. Seventeen merchant ships carrying thirty-eight thousand tons of cargo were sunk and eight others badly damaged that night. Those sunk were:

U.S.—*John Bascom, John L. Motley, Joseph Wheeler, John Harvey, Samuel J. Tilden*
British—*Testbank, Lars Kruse, Fort Athabaska, Devon Coast*
Norwegian—*Lom, Bollsta, Norlom*

Italian—*Barletta, Frosinone, Cassala*
Polish—*Puck, Lwow*

Statistics revealed by the U.S. Coast Guard report on "U.S. Merchant Vessel War Action Casualty" filed on the American vessels lost at Bari indicate not only the effectiveness of the German bombers during the air strike, but also the extremely high loss of life. For example, the report on the loss of the *Joseph Wheeler* given to the commandant, U.S. Coast Guard, Washington, D.C., on January 5, 1944, includes the following information:

Time of attack	1930 hours
Did ship break in two	Yes; exploded
Was SOS sent	No
Time sunk	2000 hours
Lifeboats carried	4
Lifeboats lost	4; 3 by explosions, 1 by heavy weather
Life rafts carried	4
Life rafts lost	4; bomb explosions
Life floats carried	2
Life floats lost	2 bomb explosions
Lifesaving suits carried	50
Lifesaving suits used	None
Total on board (at time of action)	41
Total casualties (lost)	41
Total rescued	None

The report on the *John L. Motley* was filed on October 31, 1944, nearly a year later:

Time of attack	1940 hours
Time sunk	1945 hours (within five minutes)
Lifeboats carried	4
Lifeboats lost	4
Life rafts carried	4
Life rafts lost	4
Life floats carried	2
Life floats lost	2

Lifesaving suits carried	75
Lifesaving suits used	None
Total on board (at time of action)	75
Total casualties (lost)	64
Total rescued	11

The report filed by Joseph L. Blair, captain of the *Samuel J. Tilden,* to the commandant, U.S. Coast Guard, Washington, D.C., was dated January 4, 1944:

Time of attack	1910
Time sunk	Abandoned at 2045 hours; sunk at 0200 hours by Allied torpedo
Lifeboats carried	4; 3 used
Lifeboats lost	4; 1 by bomb explosion
Life rafts carried	4
Life rafts lost	4
Life floats carried	32
Life floats lost	32
Lifesaving suits carried	72
Lifesaving suits used	None
Total on board (at time of action)	28 gun crew; 41 ship crew, 209 passengers
Total casualties (lost)	27
Total rescued	251
By boat	56
By raft	80
By floats	115

On January 24, Captain Otto Heitmann of the *John Bascom* filed his report from a hospital bed:

Time of attack	2000 hours
Time sunk	Abandoned at 2045 hours; sunk at 2130 hours
Lifeboats carried	4; 1 used
Lifeboats lost	4; 3 by bomb explosions
Life rafts carried	4; 1 used
Life rafts lost	3 by bomb explosions
Life floats carried	2
Life floats lost	2

Lifesaving suits carried	70
Lifesaving suits used	None
Total on board (at time of action)	73
Total casualties	11
Total rescued	62

There was little to report on the fate of the *John Harvey* except that the merchant ship had completely disappeared. On January 10, 1944, a statement was taken from Deck Cadet James L. Cahill by the district cadet-midshipman supervisor in New York City concerning the loss of the *John Harvey*. Paragraphs two and three of the report state:

> 2. On December, 1943, at 1930, while subject vessel was anchored just inside the jetty with a full cargo of ammunition, the harbor and port were attacked by German bombers. Subject vessel was alongside two other vessels also loaded with ammunition. During the attack, one of the three ships was hit by a large aerial bomb, which exploded and the concussion caused the other two ships to explode.
>
> 3. The writer was ashore at the time of the attack and consequently does not know the exact details of the sinking. It was presumed that all hands aboard the ship at the time were lost.

The last paragraph of the report by Cahill explains further about the casualties:

> 5. To the best of the writer's knowledge the only survivors were the seven men ashore at the same time as the writer. The other three Cadet-Midshipmen assigned to subject vessel, namely; Cadet-Midshipman Richard B. Glauche, Cadet-Midshipman Alvin H. Justis, Cadet-Midshipman Marvin H. Brodie were aboard at the time of the attack, and it is presumed that all were lost. As far as the writer was able to learn, there was no trace found of the Cadet-Midshipmen and subject vessel was demolished.

No mention was made, even at this late date, that the *John Harvey* carried one hundred tons of mustard!

The other ships in the harbor suffered heavy loss of life and severe damage. The *Lyman Abbott* had three men killed and sixty-seven survivors; the British ship *Fort Lajoie*, with a complement of fifty-five, including eight naval and four military gunners, had one killed and eight injured; the British freighter *Fort Athabaska* had fifty-six on board and lost two killed and forty-four missing, while only ten survived; the British tanker *Devon Coast* had twenty-three on board when it was sunk by the German bombers and one was killed; and the *Testbank*, another British freighter that was blasted to pieces, had seventy-five on board and seventy were listed as missing on the official report.

Those that miraculously made it ashore alive, such as Captain Heitmann, Rudolph, the personnel of the Twenty-six General Hospital, Vesole of the Armed Guard, and Bloomberg of the *John L. Motley*, were in a state of shock even if they were not seriously wounded. They stretched out on the ground, the street, the sidewalk in their wet, oil-covered clothes, many of them more unconscious than conscious, Michael Musmanno, the American officer who was the military governor of the Sorrentine Peninsula and whose converted Italian schooner, the *Inaffondabile*, had been sunk by the German bombers, also reached solid ground. Increasing the tempo of his paddling aboard his makeshift raft as the ships in the harbor continued to explode, Musmanno reached a point where he could wade ashore. He landed at Marcella Vecchio, just beyond the end of the sidewalk that bordered the Lungomare. A British guard quickly confronted the U.S. Navy officer and his Italian crewmen who landed a few seconds after he did, but, as soon as Musmanno identified himself, the sentinel summoned the corporal of the guard. The corporal of the guard immediately took the men from the *Inaffondabile* to a large tent where they had an opportunity to dry their clothes in front of a potbellied stove. A friend of Musmanno's, Lieutenant B. Ashton, offered the U.S. Navy officer one of his uniforms to wear until Musmanno's was fit to use again and, fortunately, Musmanno accepted it. He stripped, taking off his oil-covered uniform, and put on the one given him by the lieutenant. He did not know it, but he had just saved his own life.

As soon as he had changed his clothes, Musmanno went into the city. To him it looked like a medieval city conducting a mass midnight burial. Roman torches dotted the blackness of the city. Wailing and weeping could be heard from the shadows and, in the distance, he heard survivors chanting. The electric power system had been crippled, requiring the use of the torches to furnish enough light for rescuers to dig for buried victims. Firemen, carabinieri, home guard, and Allied soldiers worked furiously all night digging out survivors and dead from the wreckage of Bari. Slowly, those in shock, those wounded, those injured were moved to the various medical facilities in the area. Musmanno helped load several of the victims into ambulances and onto the back of trucks during the long night and, by morning, he was near exhaustion. The sinking of his schooner, the period in the waters of Bari harbor, and several hours of rescue work had sapped all energy from him. He went to a hotel and stretched out on a bed. Five minutes later, just as the sun came up, he fell asleep.

It was a dawn to chill the soul of those still alive in Bari. Fires were burning in the harbor and a huge pall of smoke hovered over the port and the city, hiding the sun and making the entire area much darker than normal. Flames still flickered in various sections of Bari, too, especially in the badly damaged old section. Dogs, hungry, homeless, and lost, roamed the streets hunting their masters—or something to eat. Drinking water was difficult to find, food nonexistent at the regular markets that had been demolished by the German planes. Children ran through the streets, some wearing bloody clothes, screaming for one of their parents. A few blocks away a mother crawled along a narrow, debris-covered road of the old city, her ankle broken, searching desperately for the same children. Communications were entirely broken down. Families hunting each other had to depend upon their own eyes. Even friends and neighbors were too busy with their own personal tragedies to help. Those who could salvage any of their belongings from their homes packed the goods on their backs or in carts they managed to scrounge and headed out of the city. Others did not even wait to try to salvage anything. They walked, caught a train, or hitched a ride on a horse-drawn cart and hurried away from Bari. It was as though the city had a plague. Everyone that could move under his own power, or could get anyone to help him if he could not, tried to get as many miles away from the city on the Adriatic Sea as possible—and as fast as possible.

By midmorning the ships that were still seaworthy were also leaving. Captain McCammond took the U.S.S. *Pumper* out of Bari harbor at 10:00 A.M. on verbal orders from the British port director. The director came on board and ordered McCammond to leave immediately.

"Move out at reduced speed," he said "and form up with the other ships that will be leaving as soon as possible."

The *Hadley F. Brown* left a few hours later and, as she sailed past the sunken hulks of the other merchant ships, Gunner Robert Kirchhoff noticed some odd marks on his arms. Looking more closely, he saw that they were watery little sores. He promptly forgot about the mysterious sores, however, as the movement of the ship made him aware of the soreness around his kidneys from the concussion of the blasts. He did not know that the watery sores were from the mustard released from the *John Harvey*.

The Allied ship *Bistera* had a strange experience the morning after the disaster. The ship had come through the German air strike without any damage and immediately took part in rescue operations as soon as the enemy bombers left the scene. After picking up thirty survivors from the slime-covered harbor, however, the port director ordered the *Bistera* to clear the harbor; she headed for Taranto. Four to six hours later the entire crew began having trouble with their eyes—a gritty sensation, followed by burning and pain. The commanding officer ordered all hands to use an eye wash, but this seemed to have no effect and the eye problems continued to increase in severity. The ship reached Taranto harbor eighteen hours after the raid; her crew, now almost completely blind, had great difficulty in mooring her. The toxic chemical from the *John Harvey* was taking effect, but as yet no one understood what caused the mysterious ailments among the Bari disaster survivors.

At about 1:00 P.M. on December 3 the *Francis Drake*, a merchant ship that had sustained only minor damage, made its way out of the harbor. The crew had been lucky during the air strike. The radioman had been slightly wounded and an ordinary seaman had fallen overboard. He had been recovered quickly, however, without apparent injury; but, as the *Francis Drake* passed through the opening that led to the Adriatic Sea from the harbor, Bill Colp, another crewman, saw some burns on the rescued sailor's arm.

"Where did you get burned?"

The sailor shrugged. "I didn't see any fire around me while I was in the water. Lots of oil but no flames."

Colp remembered that shortly after the German air strike he had heard a rumor about a ship in the harbor that was carrying mustard gas bombs, but he had been unable to find out anything about such a ship. As he looked at the sailor's arm he wondered if the burn might have come from contact with a toxic chemical, but, since the sailor dismissed the burn as "not amounting to anything," Colp promptly forgot his suspicions.

During the early hours of the next morning, someone aboard the *Lyman Abbott* called, "Gas." The individual who shouted the warning has never been identified. Many of the crew put on their gas masks for about half an hour, but, when they saw that none of the other men in the harbor area were wearing masks, they took their own masks off.

Meanwhile, as the ships were leaving Bari, the hospitals began getting an influx of patients from the dock area, the harbor, and the city. Heitmann, who had been taken to the sport club building after his rescue from the East Jetty, was finally moved to the Three New Zealand General Hospital for medical treatment. Here he received a cup of hot tea, his wounds were bandaged, his eyes were treated, since they were completely bloodshot by this time, and a piece of shrapnel was removed from the back of his left hand. It was at this time that he felt a sharp pain in his back, along his spine, but he did not mention it to the hospital personnel since he could see they were very busy.

As soon as he was treated at the hospital, Heitmann went to the War Shipping Administration office in Bari, reaching it at about 1:00 P.M. Here he learned from Agent Holmes that all of his crew who had made it ashore were assembled at an army depot near the harbor under the supervision of the British Ministry of Shipping, so he immediately went to the depot. At 3:00 P.M., approximately fifteen hours after his rescue from the East Jetty, he finally got out of his wet clothes. Standing in the street outside a British Army Supply Barracks, Heitmann undressed and a couple of his crewmen helped him don a British Army battle-dress outfit.

One hour later he and several of his crew boarded the British ship S.S. *Defender* for evacuation to Taranto, Italy. The eighteen crew members of the *John Bascom* who had been on the ship during the bombing, were aboard the

Defender when she left the dock. The survivors in addition to Heitmann were:

> W. Rudolph, second officer
> W. Lesesne, purser
> A. Bergman, deck cadet
> G. Stevens, able-bodied seaman
> G. Casavant, fireman-water tender
> Ng Chung, saloon messman
> J. Borges, gun crew

Ensign Vesole, Third Officer Collins, and others of the *John Bascom* crew who were too badly injured to travel were left behind in area hospitals for treatment.

In addition to the *John Bascom* survivors, the *Defender* carried about 350 survivors from the various ships lost during the German air attack. The *Defender* was one of the very few ships in Bari harbor during the raid that was not bombed, although she was at a dock in the inner harbor. Her decks were holed from beams and parts of other ships' structures that landed on her during the explosions and most of her gun turrets were damaged and some even blown away, however.

"One time during the night," the captain of the *Defender* told Heitmann, "it rained fuel oil for ten minutes after an explosion. That is why my ship is covered with dirt and oil."

At 5:00 P.M. on the third of December the *Defender* sailed from Bari. The water along the East Jetty where Heitmann and his crew had been trapped was still burning fiercely, making the captain of the *John Bascom* more appreciative than ever of the efforts made by his rescuers to get him and his men off the jetty. Many vessels in the harbor were ablaze from stem to stern and the surface of the water was dotted with mangled steel protruding from sunken ships. The *Defender* had to pick her way through the obstacles to the open sea. As she steamed past the *John Bascom*, Heitmann saw that his ship was sunk from stern to amidships in about forty feet of water and was belching flames at least fifty feet high from bow to stern. The dense black smoke rolling across the harbor made it difficult to see clearly, but Heitmann was certain the flaming hulk was his *John Bascom*.

Just north of Brindisi, the *Defender* ran ashore and the escort vessels left the hapless ship to fend for herself. After tank and bilge soundings were taken, it was discovered that the vessel was not leaking anywhere and that she was on a flat sandy beach. The fuel oil and water on board the *Defender* were transferred to another section of the ship, the water ballast was discharged, and within a few hours the *Defender* came off the beach under her own power and the Bari survivors were once again on their way to Taranto. Heitmann's back was paining him badly by this time, so when the second officer of the *Defender* offered him and Lesesne the use of his room, the captain of the *John Bascom* quickly accepted. Heitmann slept on the blankets on the deck while Lesesne used the settee, because, for a reason still unknown to them, he commenced blistering all over his body. Neither Heitmann or Lesesne could look into light without wearing sunglasses because of a severe burning sensation in their eyes. Lesesne grew progressively worse as the time passed and Heitmann tried everyway possible to help him. Finally the blisters got so bad that he could neither sit nor lie down. The next day, when the *Defender* anchored in the harbor of Taranto, Lesesne was one of the first casualties taken ashore to a British hospital.

Back in Bari other survivors were showing signs of the mysterious burns as they arrived at the various hospitals, the same type of burns and blisters suffered by Lesesne.

14

"WE HAVEN'T ANY MORE BEDS"

At Three New Zealand General Hospital the battle casualties from the hospital train that had arrived a few minutes before the German bombers and had been placed on the floor during the raid were moved to the wards as soon as relative peace returned to Bari. Gower and his staff had just managed to get them safely into beds when casualties from the harbor raid began pouring into the hospital. The majority of the wounded and injured were from the dock area, seamen and workers on the wharves who had been unable to escape the area in time when Richtofen's Ju-88s roared in from the Adriatic Sea. They were all nationalities—English, Indian, Italian, Norwegian, American, Polish—but they all had one thing in common. They were covered with oil, badly burned, and in a state of shock. Some were suffering from exposure, having been in the sea for hours before being rescued.

The official war diary of Three New Zealand General Hospital and the December, 1943, monthly report to the DMS by Aubrey Watson, a company officer assigned to the hospital, both indicate the extent of the tragedy. The war diary, a summary of events and information filed daily, states (in part):

December 2   Admissions 128   Discharges 58

At 1930 hours, following an alert, enemy action over the harbor and city area commenced. Antiaircraft fire was continuous. Two terrific explosions from the harbor, with large glare, were felt and seen. Casualties within the hospital were of a minor nature but all window glass was shattered.

December 3   Admissions 26   Discharges 85

The large proportion of the admissions are from the docks, casualty cases due to enemy action and explosions. They comprise several services and a number are of a serious nature. An immense pall of smoke is today visible over the harbor where several ships are burning. One at least is an oil tanker. At least five direct hits on buildings in both the old city and the modern part are seen. Practically all glass in windows is shattered and large doors and shuttered entrances are bulged or broken. The two large churches in the old city (Duomo-Cathedral and 11th Century Basilica of San Nicola) are not materially damaged, though a direct hit has wrecked a building adjacent to the former. 1330 hours, the trail of an enemy reconnaissance plane at considerable altitude is visible. A sunny day is considerably assisting the morale of all and civilians appear to be well controlled.

This brief information was entered into the war diary from the vantage point of the Three New Zealand General Hospital. Neither Gower nor any of his staff had time to go to the city or the harbor area to investigate conditions further. If they had checked further, they would have discovered that every street leading out of Bari was crowded with an unending stream of refugees fleeing from the city. Some moved along on high-wheeled carts piled with household furniture and personal effects. Others carried their burdens on their backs. There were bicycles and toy wagons, motorcycles and a few midget automobiles. Many of the women balanced bundles on their heads and some of the refugees led a goat or a sheep on a leash. Everyone was scared. Where they were headed, few knew or cared. They just wanted to be out of Bari before there were any more bombings, any more explosions. Even the train heading northward toward Foggia was overloaded on December 3, with Italians hanging on the sides of the cars and many sitting on the roof. The engineer found his cab so crowded that he barely had room to operate his controls.

Watson's short monthly report included the following information on the German air strike:

. . . . General: a heavy air raid early in the month caused some setback. Blast from big explosions in the port area broke hundreds of windows and caused some structural damage. This caused a setback in the building program. Quite a number of casualties due to the air raid were brought to this hospital, which added to the difficulties. However, the entire staff made an extra effort and things were soon restored to normal. Apart from a few cuts and abrasions, there were no casualties among staff members of the hospital.

Gower had nineteen officers on his hospital staff, plus five attached officers. The attached officers were Dental Officer N. M. Gleeson, chaplains A. Macfarlane and J. D. W. Raine, and New Zealand Red Cross Commissioner G. W. Tweedle. There were also 162 other ranks of the unit or the nursing staff and WAACs. Every member of the staff worked feverishly as the casualties from the harbor kept coming to the Three New Zealand General Hospital during the early morning hours. Because of the heavy influx of patients, limited staff, and the general confusion resulting from the surprise German air raid, the officers of Three New Zealand General Hospital, as did all the medical units receiving the casualties that morning, waived all army regulations pertaining to admittance procedures and sent them straight to the wards and available beds without bothering to fill out the normal information forms. Many who arrived at Three New Zealand General Hospital were so badly injured that they died soon after they were admitted and before the hospital staff had time to learn who they were. This was especially true of Italian civilians; thus, no accurate records of the number of casualties were possible.

It soon became evident to Gower that there was not nearly enough room available at Three New Zealand General Hospital for all the casualties from the harbor and city being sent to his facility. After consultation with his staff, he decided to put some of the stretcher patients in an unfinished part of the building. There was no light in this section, no water, no sanitary arrangements, but he had to find a spot for the casualties, so he ordered them placed in the unused wing. Matron Jackson made the patients as comfortable as possible and she and her staff devised makeshift facilities to take the place of normal facilities that were not available.

Unfortunately, at Three New Zealand General Hospital there was no time to take the oil-soaked wet clothes from each of the patients as they arrived, wash their bodies clean of the scum clinging to their skin, and give them each dry hospital gowns or new uniforms, even if such clothing had been in sufficient supply, which it was not. The medical regulations were ignored due to the onrush of patients. The doctors noticed immediately that many of those admitted to the hospital were suffering from burns, and as was normal practice, gave their first attention to shock. Eighty percent of the deaths from burns result from secondary shock, so the medical staff started giving plasma to the most seriously injured in an effort to prevent shock. They also took other steps to aid the patients. They placed most of the stretchers in such a position that the patient's head was lower than his feet, halting the possible loss of blood from the brain. They kept the wounded wrapped in blankets, knowing that a patient in shock had to be made comfortably warm.

When Cottrell walked through the wards it was obvious to him that the men had all the symptoms of bad shock. They were pale, weak, and exhausted. Many were complaining of thirst, while others were cold and clammy with perspiration. Most of the patients had rapid, unsteady pulses, breathed rapidly and shallowly, and their blood pressure was abnormally low. By prescribing the normal treatment for shock, the medical staff of the Three New Zealand General Hospital felt that they were making the right move. They had no idea that the toxic chemical mustard was involved in the situation.

More than eight hundred casualties were hospitalized immediately following the air raid—the exact number will never be known. Later it was discovered that 628 of the injured were suffering from mustard exposure. Empty bomb casings discovered during an investigation days after the air strike revealed that at least two to three thousand pounds of the hundred tons of mustard were released just above the mole. Thousands more pounds of the chemical were scattered throughout the harbor when the *John Henry* exploded. Some burned and the vapor drifted toward land with the billowing smoke from the burning ships. Such mustard as was not burned either sank to the bottom of the harbor or was mixed and dissolved in the oil on the surface of the harbor. It was this mixture of mustard in oil that affected the survivors the most. The amounts of mustard in oil varied considerably from one part of the harbor to another and, consequently, the area where a merchant ship crewman or ship passenger abandoned the vessel by leaping into the harbor was important. If he was fortunate enough to abandon ship where the mustard concentration was light, his chances for survival were much better. Those on board vessels that had been docked near the *John Henry* were not so lucky. They became seriously contaminated by swimming through the waters in that section of the harbor. Still others who had not been in the water throughout the disaster, inhaled the mustard fumes as they blew across the city. On the morning of December 3, however, it was still not known that mustard exposure was a factor to contend with, so the normal medical treatment for victims of shock and burns or injuries progressed with no thought to any other measure being necessary.

At the American Twenty-six General Hospital it was learned that what the staff had expected was true. All the equipment and supplies that had been on the *Samuel J. Tilden* and destined for the hospital were lost in the German attack. At the same time it was apparent that the need for medical facilities to care for the victims of the disaster was urgent. Therefore, immediate action was taken to set up an emergency hospital to operate on a limited basis in order to provide an expansion of the existing medical facilities which were furnished by the British and New Zealanders.

It was not easy. Equipment and supplies were in short supply in Bari, hoarded as though they were pure gold. A message was sent to Major James Hicks, the officer in charge of medical services at the Foggia airfield complex, explaining the serious situation. Hicks did all he could to help, sending small amounts of dressings and bandages and a few surgical instruments obtained from the Air Force General Depot Number Five and the Adriatic Medical Depot. Later, additional supplies were obtained from Naples. For immediate use, however, it was the Italians who furnished one hundred hospital beds, bedding, pajamas, bedside tables, and two dressing carts.

On December 4 the first patients were admitted to the Twenty-six General Hospital, all casualties from the German raid. The treatment at the American hospital was similar to that at the Three New Zealand General Hospital and at the British Ninety-eight General Hospital. Blankets and hot tea to keep the patients warm, plasma for the most serious, stretchers placed so that the patient's head was lower than his feet. In addition to operating the hastily assembled emergency hospital, the staff of the Twenty-six General Hospital made other contributions to the care of the casualties of the disaster. Anesthetists, technicians, and nurses were sent on detached service to assist in the care of patients at the Ninety-eight British General Hospital. That service was continued for sixteen days, covering the critical period following the attack.

Other officers and Red Cross workers attached to the Twenty-six General Hospital, who did not have specific duties at their own or the British hospital, made a search for missing American army, navy, and merchant marine personnel. The search covered the entire surrounding district as far as Brindisi and Taranto and it resulted in the location of 65 U.S. Army men and 120 members of the U.S. Navy and Merchant Marine.

Many of the cases at the Bari hospitals, after several hours, appeared in good condition and were permitted to be sent to an Auxiliary Seaman's Home, still in their oil-contaminated clothing. Others, tired of waiting for aid at the medical facilities and feeling improved, just walked out of the hospitals and went looking for a place to sleep. Most of these men still had on their contaminated clothing. A few individuals, on their own initiative, cleaned all the oil from themselves promptly, but this number was much too small. While it was an extremely hectic period for the doctors and nurses, everything went as expected until the evening of December 3. The first indication of trouble was in the resuscitation wards where the men brought in supposedly suffering from shock, immersions, and exposure were bedded.

A very noticeable variation from normal response to the treatment given was that many cases began having eye trouble. Patients in the hospital, and even those cases not yet admitted, noted burning of the eyes and an excessive secretion of tears. Weeping became very marked and was associated with spasms of the eyelids and a morbid fear of light. Within twenty-four hours the eyes were swollen and the patients complained that they were blind. There really was no lack of vision, but the eyelid spasms were so bad that the victims would not open their eyes. Another puzzling factor to the doctors was the pulse and blood pressure readings of the men supposedly in shock or suffering from immersion and exposure. The pulse beat was barely evident and blood pressure was down in the range of 40–60 mm Hg. and yet the patients did not appear to be in what the doctors considered clinical shock. There was no worried or anxious expression or restlessness, no shallow breathing, and the heart action was only a moderately rapid 110–120, considering the condition of the pulse and blood pressure. The patients did not complain of chest pain, have altered respiration, injured eardrums, or blood tinged sputum as in typical blast injuries. They were rather apathetic. Upon being spoken to they could sit up in bed and would state that they felt rather well at a time when their pulse was barely perceptible and their blood pressure perhaps 50.

"I don't understand it," a young New Zealand doctor told Gower. "These men don't respond to the usual measures. Even plasma infusions, at best, give only a small, temporary rise of blood pressure. Most cases don't show any response to plasma, warmth, stimulants and morphia. I just don't understand it."

The young doctor was not the only person in Bari who did not understand the action, or lack of action, of the patients. British medical staffs at the Ninety-eighth General Hospital, American doctors and nurses at the partially open Twenty-six General Hospital, the staff at the Fourteen Combined General Hospital (Indian), and the Italian civilian doctors were all puzzled. In each of the various hospitals, the general apathy of the men was quite consistent and impressive. They could be roused, but when the external stimulus was removed they immediately returned to their apathetic state. Since the casualties included men of at least twelve nationalities or races, some of the doctors tried to determine if there was any difference between the physical or mental condition of the men from one country compared to those from other parts of the world. There was none. The apathy was as striking in one as in the other.

However, the war in Italy did not stop because of the tragedy at Bari on the night of December 2 and, as the wounded came to the city from the front, the survivors of the German air strike had to share the medical staff of the hospitals with them. Montgomery and his Eighth Army were assaulting the German positions along the Sangro River and

"The Battle of the Sangro," as it came to be known, was expected to be another masterpiece of strategy for the British field marshal. Unfortunately for Montgomery, the weather, the Italian topography, and a determined Nazi stand foiled his plan.

The Sangro River had a wide gravel bed and normally was only a few feet deep, so it did not present much of a problem to the Eighth Army. The fields on each side of it, however, did present a problem to the Allied troops since they were soft, muddy, and a soggy trap. The Germans decided that instead of defending the river they would set up a line of defense on high ground three miles north of the Sangro. It was there that the four divisions of Germans waited for Montgomery's five divisions, knowing full well that the Allies had only four routes to their line of defense. One was the main coast road, the only highway capable of carrying the Eighth Army's supplies; the second was Route 81 which was fifteen miles inland and ran parallel to the coast road; the third path to Li Colli Ridge where the panzer divisions were positioned was Route 17 from Castel di Sangro to Popoli; and the last road available was the narrow Alfredena–Pescina route. These last two were so narrow that they could carry only one-way traffic and ran through the mountains. Consequently, Montgomery had little chance of using deception to aid his attack. The Germans knew he was coming and they knew what roads he would use!

Initially, the Battle of the Sangro was supposed to start on the night of November 20–21, 1943, with British and Indian troops moving up the main coast road while the New Zealand Division would attack along the inland Route 81. On November 9 it started to rain and, by the date of the planned attack, the Sangro River was too deep for patrols to wade across and the fields on either side much too soggy to withstand the weight of the tanks and trucks. Rather than attack on November 20, Montgomery tried to ferry heavy weapons across the river and, for the next few days, all that was accomplished was the task of getting a few antitank weapons and tanks to the north side of the Sangro. On the twenty-third of November flood waters swept down from the mountains and completely submerged the three temporary bridges the British had managed to stretch across the water, causing more delay.

Finally on November 27, one hundred tanks were moved

across the river and the attack began up the main coast road. The following day the New Zealanders started north along Route 81, but by now the timing was off and Montgomery's well-planned attack was a shambles. To make matters worse, the Ninety Panzer Division that had been in Sardinia was sent to reinforce the German troops on Li Colli Ridge and the British troops ran directly into them as they moved up the main coast road. The New Zealanders had their troubles, too. Their tanks and trucks bogged down in the fields north of the river and the bridges they built over the Sangro were damaged by German shelling and, despite the same air superiority of the Allies that was also depended upon to protect Bari, by an accurate Luftwaffe air strike. This German Air Force raid was made on November 28, only four days before the disastrous mission against the Allied ships in Bari harbor but, as usual, the lesson was ignored. The following days were better for the New Zealanders and they forced the German ground troops back. Pressing on, they attacked Orsogna, the only block in their path to Chieti, but the Twenty-six Panzer Division launched a vicious counterattack and forced the New Zealanders back out of the town. This was the furthest point north any Allied troops penetrated for the next five months. The date was December 3, 1943, and the casualty rate was high. The wounded were immediately loaded on the nearest available transportation for removal to the hospitals in Bari—hospitals already overcrowded with survivors of the harbor bombing the previous night.

Some critics of Montgomery have stated that he should have pushed on further along the main coast road that day, since he definitely had the German troops in that area retreating fast. These critics said that he showed "logistic timidity." But Montgomery had heard about the Luftwaffe air strike against the ships in Bari harbor and he knew the importance of the harbor as a supply depot for his Eighth Army. While he still did not have the details about the disaster at Bari, it is certain that he took the situation into consideration when he planned his next move against the German positions to the north. It was fortunate that he did because Bari harbor would not be open to the merchant ships carrying the supplies he needed for several weeks.

On the opposite side of the Italian Peninsula, Mark Clark's Fifth Army moved north to destroy the Bernhardt Line on December 2, the date of the tragedy at Bari. His first attack, called Operation Raincoat, was on Monte Camino and was directed against the Fifteen Panzer Grenadier Division. Unfortunately, neither the preliminary bombardment against the German positions on the mountain by Allied artillery, during which more than four thousand tons of shell were fired, nor the air strikes which were too inaccurate, were effective. The fighting was hard, the casualties high. Many of the wounded went to Naples, but a large number of the Fifth Army casualties ended up in Bari and added to the already crowded hospital wards. Operation Raincoat lasted from December 2 to 10 and these same days were the crucial ones for the survivors of the German bombing at Bari harbor. To the nearly exhausted hospital staffs it seemed that the flow of incoming wounded and injured would never cease. It was impossible to concentrate on any one group of patients. Everyone had to be treated as well as possible in the time available. Consequently, the Bari survivors were treated for shock, immersion, and exposure during these initial days after the tragedy and expected to recover more or less of their own accord within a short time.

A few did recover. The majority did not respond to the treatment. Captain Otto Heitmann, who had been evacuated on the *Defender* to Taranto, felt somewhat better after a couple of days and decided he wanted to go back to Bari and check on his former vessel, the *John Bascom*. He went to the Royal Navy building in Taranto and talked to the liaison officer, Captain H. W. Ziroly.

"I think the bridge of the *John Bascom* is still above water," he told the Britisher. "If it is, I want to try to board her and empty the safe."

When Heitmann abandoned the bombed ship during the bombardment, he had only turned the dial a quarter of a turn.

Ziroly looked at Heitmann and shook his head. "Captain, there is only one place for you and that is the hospital. I'll call the..."

Heitmann, his voice failing rapidly because of his immersion in the mustard-saturated water of Bari harbor, swore quietly. "I'm going to Bari one way or another. If you won't help me, I'll go somewhere else."

He started out of the Royal Navy building, but Ziroly stopped him. "Just a minute. If you're so bloody determined, I'll get you a ride, Captain."

Within a few minutes a British officer arrived in a jeep with several blankets. Wrapping Heitmann in the blankets, the officer headed for Bari, covering the sixty miles in approximately two hours and fifteen minutes. Heitmann said later that if he had not already lost his voice, the driving of the Britisher would have scared it out of him anyway.

At Bari the port authorities provided Heitmann with a launch and two British sailors to take him to the *John Bascom*. The ship was sunk from stern to number three hatch, he discovered, and the hatch was full of water. Number one hatch was still smoldering from the flames which had partially destroyed it. The decks and steel house structure were caved in and torn up, masts had buckled in half. There was nothing left of the top bridge except the steel bulkheads and the platform of the starboard wing of the bridge. Searching the wreckage, he discovered the safe resting above water against an iron framework. The iron straps that had held it in place prior to the attack were completely melted away.

"I won't be long," he whispered hoarsely to the two nervous British sailors watching him. His voice was barely audible.

He tried to turn the dial, but it would not move no matter how hard he tired to twist it. Picking up an iron strap lying nearby, Heitmann tapped the dial several times and managed to twist it to zero. He was as surprised as the British sailors when the handle moved easily, but when he tried to pull the door open he discovered that the heat had welded it shut at the top edge.

"Give me a hand," he whispered to the nearest British officer.

The two men put a piece of angle iron into a small opening between the side of the safe and the door and pried the door all the way open. Heitmann discovered that the papers and money inside the safe were charred but intact so he took the entire contents with him. Before he left the *John Bascom*, however, he walked out on the starboard wing of the bridge and near the ladder he found what he was hunting. The charred remains of Nicholas Elin, the crewman who had been killed during the German air strike and left aboard the ship when it was abandoned. Feeling lonely and sick, Heitmann left his ship for the last time.

He returned the money from the safe—$1,268—to the Finance Section, Sixtieth Service Group, U.S. Army, in Bari and obtained a receipt for it. The secret code and documents he had taken from the safe were wrapped in stiff cardboard for him and Heitmann carried them personally until he was finally evacuated back to the United States. After leaving the Finance Section office, he and the British driver went to the Miramar Hotel in Bari where Heitmann slept in a bed for the first time since the ordeal on the night of December 2 when his ship was sunk by the Luftwaffe. It was only the second time he had taken his clothes off since that fateful night. The first time had been when he was given a British battledress uniform shortly after he was rescued from the East Jetty, an action that probably saved his life, since his captain's uniform had been soaked with the oil-mustard mixture.

The morning after he salvaged the money and papers from the safe, Heitmann felt so much better that he decided to go to the various hospitals in the area to try to visit with his wounded and injured crewmen who had been left behind when he went to Taranto on the *Defender*. The British driver took him to Three New Zealand General Hospital and the Ninety-eight British General Hospital, but at both places, when he inquired about his crewmen, he discovered that the staffs had been so overworked that no records of patients had been kept. Realizing that it was useless to ask the nurses or doctors any further questions that they could not answer, the captain started walking through the wards hunting his crew. Finally, a navy gunner who knew him showed Heitmann where Ensign Vesole was bedded down. Vesole, who had fought so gallantly against the Luftwaffe planes and had helped to get his men and the crew of the *John Bascom* to the East Jetty where they were ultimately rescued, was in serious condition. He asked the captain to write his wife and Heitmann promised to do so, thinking that the ensign, though badly injured, would recover. Vesole died shortly after Heitmann left the hospital.

Collins, the third officer of the *John Bascom*, was isolated in the hospital and the doctors would not permit Heitmann to see him. He, too, died before the captain left Bari. Although wounded himself, barely able to speak, his back tormenting him, Heitmann made one more stop before he left Bari to return to Taranto. He went to the War Shipping Administration office and asked the port representative to see that the body of Elin was properly taken off the ship and buried ashore. He was assured that this would be done.

Heitmann and his driver then left for Taranto. All the way back to the city, however, one fact kept puzzling the captain. Why had Ensign Vesole, Third Officer Collins, and so many of the other Bari harbor survivors died so abruptly despite the excellent treatment they had received for shock, burns, and their other injuries? It seemed strange.

15

"DOCTOR, WHAT CAN WE DO?"

On December 5, 1943, three days after the disastrous raid by the Ju-88s on the ships in Bari harbor, the following report was sent to the commanding officer of the Ninety-eight British General Hospital:

Subject: N.Y.D. Dermatitis Cases received from Local Air Raid on night 2nd-3rd December 1943.

To: Officer Commanding, Ninety-eight General Hospital

Sir:

I respectfully submit the following report written at your request and at short notice. It should be regarded as an interim report.

1. About 430 casualties were received from the incident.

2. No official notification was received till the following morning that N.Y.D. (D) cases might be amongst the casualties.

3. As a result I was considerably puzzled by the extremely shocked condition of the patients with negligible surgical injuries.

4. Many of these patients were treated as "Immersion" cases and were wrapped in blankets to warm them up. This naturally aggravated the subsequent development of the dermatitis.

5. The complaint, rarely seriously made, of "smarting eyes" was considered to be due to oil fuel and not regarded as of any importance.

6. I have in the Surgical Division 140 cases of this condition. The remainder are in the Medical Division.

7. There have been ten deaths in my Division due to this condition. I expect this number will probably be more than doubled.

8. 70 percent of the cases are severe. I expect there will be a high incidence of severe sepsis. This will raise nursing problems of the utmost gravity in a Forward Field Hospital.

9. The local condition of the skin lesions conforms with the description given in the official manual.

10. The general condition is marked by a serious cardiocirculatory failure that shows no response to plasma infusion or other resuscitation measures. This does not conform with official description of the disease.

11. Expert advice on this condition is requested.

12. Advice as to the evacuability of these cases is requested—at the moment of writing few are fit for evacuation since it must be stated that deaths are occurring quite unexpectedly in patients with minimal lesions

> I have the honor to be, Sir,
> Your obedient Servant
> (Sgd.) A. L. d'Abreu,
> O. i/c Surg. Division
> Ninety-eighth General Hospital

SECRET

As the report indicates, there was considerable confusion among the medical personnel charged with the care of the Bari harbor survivors. They had done their best to deal with the rapidly deteriorating condition of the mustard casualties— but the damage had been done. The failure to take simple measures such as washing the oil from their bodies resulted in many deaths that need not have occurred. Some of those who bathed on their own initiative had only minor burns. The remainder, already saturated with the oil-mustard mixture, continued to inhale the toxic fumes, since the vapor pressure of liquid mustard is fairly high and gaseous mustard is given off at normal temperatures. Thus, those who still had the deadly mixture on their clothing and skin were continuously inhaling mustard gas. In many cases, blast damage to the lungs that would not otherwise have been lethal, when combined with the mustard vapor, produced death.

It was the eyes that first made many of the doctors suspicious that they were dealing with an "unusual" situation. Patients began complaining as early as an hour or two after being admitted to the hospital that their eyes "felt as though they had sand in them." This irritating feeling was followed by a burning sensation and pain sufficient to awaken any of those who had fallen asleep. The ophthalmic specialist at the Ninety-eight British General Hospital, Major Leonard Gluck, was not particularly worried when one of his aides came to him early on the morning of December 3 and told him that a large number of the patients were complaining about the pain in their eyes.

"I understand," Gluck said. "They will have pain for awhile. That flying glass caused severe injuries to many of the patients' eyes."

"But it isn't cuts from the glass, Sir," the aide said. "They are complaining about a gritty feeling. I can't find anything in their eyes but the pain seems to be severe."

"I'll take a look" Gluck said, walking quickly toward the ward.

The Ophthalmic Department of the Ninety-eight British General Hospital had one surgeon, two sisters, one orderly, and twenty-three beds, ten of which were scattered elsewhere in the hospital. By the time Gluck was summoned to check on the patients again on December 3, several hundred men were jammed into the department, all in pain, all requiring urgent treatment. The wards and corridors were full of cases and all available space in the hospital was urgently needed for the eye cases. The general ward sisters first began the treatment of new arrivals, but, as the number of cases increased and their condition became worse and worse, Gluck requested four extra sisters to help him. They were formed into four teams of one sister plus one assistant (patient or orderly) each. These teams, under the supervision of Gluck, toured the general wards and did all the eye treatments, using their own judgment in many of the cases. It was one of the assistants who had summoned the major to examine some of the patients when their eyes seemed to be getting worse instead of better.

Gluck checked several of the survivors. He discovered

that their eyelids were badly inflamed, their faces red as though they were suffering from early sunburn. Some of the cases that had been admitted early during the night of December 2–3 had blisters on their faces and their skin was peeling in some instances. When the lids were opened water literally gushed out and their eyes were turned up so far that often only the cornea could be seen. Most of the men were in pain but were relieved temporarily as soon as their eyes were washed out. Gluck decided not to use cocaine or any other surface anesthetics that were available. The worst part of the situation was that the eyes pained so much that many of the patients believed they were permanently blind. The effect on the morale was dramatic. No matter how often Gluck or the sisters told the men that the condition appeared to be only temporary, based on the symptoms, none believed them.

Finally Gluck ordered a different treatment, suspicious that some irritant, probably a chemical, had caused the eye conditions.

"Let's start with a saline washout followed by .05 percent atropine, one drop of albucid, and then use a flap of lint as an eyeshade," he instructed his staff.

"There is only a very small quantity of albucid available, Major," a sister said.

Gluck nodded. "Use it all. Discontinue the atropine as soon as the pupil dilates."

It was also during the morning of the day after the German air raid that the first skin lesions were noticed on the survivors. At first there was no pain associated with the skin changes, despite the fact that the blistering was extensive on some of the patients. In others the skin was thickened and not of normal texture. A few of the men had pitted burn areas, but most of them did not, although the areas were extremely tender to pressure. Later, these whole areas of skin were to strip off their superficial layers, covering, in some cases, up to 80–90 percent of the body surface. The coloration that developed was most striking; bronze, reddish brown, or tan in some, red in others. The distribution of the burns was quite varied, but certain patterns were present, depending upon how the individual had been exposed. Burns were found where the slime from the surface of the harbor had been in contact with the skin. Some that were immersed were burned in all areas. Those individuals who had only their feet or arms in the water were burned only in those areas. Individuals in patrol boats that were showered by oil and water from the harbor were burned where the deadly oil-mustard mixture landed. Vapor burns were more marked on the exposed areas and in the armpits and groin. The soles of the feet and the palms of the hands were remarkably free from burns for some strange reason.

The chemical-oil mixture was especially severe and distressing in the genital region. The penis in some cases was swollen to three or four times its normal size and the scrotum was greatly enlarged. The skin there, and in the fold of the groin, was very vulnerable. These lesions were quite painful and, in addition, caused much mental anguish. For a man to have trouble in the genital region and also believe that he was going blind was enough to drive him insane—and some came very close to reaching this stage during the first forty-eight hours after the air strike.

The doctors did everything they could under the circumstances to help the patients. Keeping the lesions of the skin clean in itself was a prodigious nursing problem. Vaseline-gauze dressings or bland ointment dressings were very satisfactory, but, if the vaseline gauze was used, the nurses had to be careful to use an adequate amount of vaseline to keep the gauze from sticking. A few cases were treated with amyl salicylate, but these cases did not seem to dry up any faster than those with no treatment. Most cases were cleaned and then simply dusted with sulfanilamide powder or a bland powder. Sometimes they were just cleaned and no local therapy used. It soon became apparent that none of the treatments were any better than the simple cleaning of the lesions. In one hospital, tannic acid tanning was tried, with some cases tanned with a triple dye, but these cases did even more poorly, if anything. They definitely were not benefited.

As Captain H. M. Denfeld, a doctor stationed with the Fourteen Combined General Hospital on temporary duty, checked the survivors at noon on December 3, he definitely felt that a chemical of some type or other was involved in the condition of the patients. This feeling was spreading among the medical staffs of the hospitals in the Bari area, but no one could definitely define the chemical agent. Denfeld visited the British Port Authority Headquarters building, but the officer in charge could not—or would not—give him any information.

"Do you know whether any of the Allied ships that were sunk last night was carrying chemicals?" he asked.

There was a long hesitation before the British Royal Navy officer answered the captain. Finally he said, "The cargoes carried on the ships were all war materials and, as you know, the manifests are secret. Top secret."

Denfeld was in no mood to listen to such bureaucratic talk, especially since the cargo was at the bottom of the harbor and there were patients dying in every hospital in Bari.

"I don't give a bloody damn about your secrets," he bellowed. "We have men dropping dead for no apparent reason and we have to find the reason. Some of us suspect a chemical agent is causing the trouble. Is it?"

The Britisher shrugged. "I'll contact the Royal Navy in England. If such cargo was carried I'll notify you."

"How long will this take?" Denfeld demanded.

"Several days, perhaps."

The captain swore and walked out of the office. Several days! Even several hours was too long. Lost in thought, Denfeld walked along the dock area, staring at the sunken ships, some still smoking, in the harbor, wondering what the vessels might have been carrying in their holds. It was not a pleasant sight. Bodies were floating between the wreckage and the ships, dotting the still oil-covered surface and resembling black logs. Already the stench was beginning to permeate the air, so strongly that Denfeld covered his mouth and nose with a handkerchief several times. The British were taking bodies from the harbor using two bedsprings wired together. They attached the bedsprings to the hook on the end of a crane boom and the crane operator then lowered them into the water. Men in boats pushed the bodies onto the springs and the bodies were hoisted onto the dock and dumped into trucks. Denfeld thought that the procedure resembled that used by fishermen who pulled in their nets filled with lobsters and dumped them into large containers. The victims' arms and legs stuck out in grotesque positions just like the claws of lobsters. It was a horrible scene and the captain hurried on down the dock.

Seeing an American soldier standing along a pier staring at the wreckage of a ship a few hundred feet out into the harbor, Denfeld stopped to talk with him.

"Your ship?" he asked.

The American shook his head. "No. I was supposed to oversee the unloading of the ship, but it never made it to the unloading area. Those damn Germans sunk it just as the captain was moving toward the dock."

"What was the ship carrying?"

The American—Denfeld never thought to ask the man his name—shrugged. "Same old items, I guess. Guns, ammunition, fuel for the bombers up at Foggia. I don't know exactly. My job was to unload whatever it was carrying and deliver it to the depot."

As he talked, the American reached into his back pocket and pulled out his handkerchief. He then took off his glasses and wiped the tears from his eyes and for the first time Denfeld noted that the man's eyes were very red and looked sore. The captain noticed something else, too. His own eyes were bothering him.

"Are your eyes irritated?" he asked the American.

"They sure as hell are, Captain. They've been watering all morning."

"When did they start bothering you?"

"After I came down to the dock to check on the ships," he said. "I think it is that oil on the top of the water that causes it."

Denfeld looked down at the water from where he was standing on the dock. He estimated the distance at about six feet straight down, give or take a foot, and, just as the American had said, the surface was completely black with oil. The wind was blowing off the water toward the land and the smell of the oil was very strong. Now and then, as a small boat passed nearby, Denfeld could feel a fine spray hit him as the wind whipped the churned-up water inland. Yet, he had been around oil many, many times and it had never bothered his eyes before today.

"Why do you think it is the oil?" he asked the American who was still wiping his eyes

"I was out in a motor launch earlier today, trying to help recover some bodies, and I accidently fell overboard. I was only in the water a few minutes, maybe five at the most, before my buddies pulled me back into the launch, but my eyes have been bothering me ever since."

"Did you get the oil into them?"

The American nodded. "Yeah, I can't swim very well and I was floundering around, splashing the water and oil all over the place. I got the oil in my eyes, in my mouth, and up my nose. I had a hell of a time staying afloat."

Denfeld looked at the man's uniform. It was spotless. "Did you change clothes afterwards?"

"Sure did. Washed myself off and put on a clean uniform. I was a mess."

It was possible, Denfeld realized, that a large quantity of oil in the eyes could irritate them temporarily, but, remembering the symptoms of the patients back at the Fourteen Combined General Hospital, he knew that their trouble was caused by more than oil.

"Did you ever unload a ship that carried chemicals of any type?" he asked the American.

The soldier turned and faced the captain. "You sure are asking a lot of questions. Maybe you better get the answers down at British headquarters. I'm only a sergeant with a strong back and husky arms who uses them to unload ships." He started to walk away.

"Wait a minute, sergeant. Wait." Denfeld got his identification pass from his wallet in his pocket and showed it to the American. "I'm a medical doctor stationed with the Fourteen Combined General Hospital."

The sergeant still was not convinced. "You don't look as though you come from India to me. That hospital is operated by the Indians."

Denfeld grinned. "You're bloody sharp. No, I'm not from India. I'm from Ipswich, England, stationed at the hospital on temporary duty because of the shortage of medical personnel. I'm only trying to determine what is bothering the patients we have received from the harbor last night after the Luftwaffe raid. There is something mysterious about their reaction to our treatment but I can't figure out what it is."

The sergeant handed the identification pass back to Denfeld. "I know what you mean. I was over to the Three New Zealand General Hospital an hour ago, just after I changed my uniform, to see a friend of mine and he is in a hell of a shape. Can't see and his . . . He is all swollen between his legs."

Denfeld nodded. "We have hundreds of cases just like him and so far we can't discover what is causing these symptoms. Acts like it might be the result of some type of toxic agent, some chemical."

4.2″ Chemical Mortar

The American was silent for several seconds as he stared toward the ship lying on the bottom of the harbor, the ship he had been assigned to unload. "Sometimes the ships bring in such things as chemical mortars, flame throwers, white phosphorous for smoke and smoke pots, if that's what you mean."

The captain scratched his head. "I don't really know whether that is what I mean or not. Could be something like that." Mentally he went over the weapons mentioned by the sergeant one by one, as well as he could without any reference material to help him to try and determine a clue to the condition of his patients at the Fourteen Combined General Hospital. He was especially interested in the chemical mortars, since he was well aware that the 4.2 inch mortar had been used in the taking of Sicily early in the summer. Mortar squads were among the first waves of troops to hit the beach, and they went into action a few minutes after landing. The mortar had made an excellent impression on commanders in infantry, ranger, armored, and airborne units. Yet he knew that the 4.2 inch chemical mortar, in this instance, had been delivering high explosives, not toxic agents. Had any change in procedure been made in the planning for the conquest of Italy, he wondered?

"What did the troops plan to deliver with the chemical mortars?" Denfeld asked the American sergeant.

"High explosives fragmentation shells and smoke shells."

"What kind of smoke shells?"

"White phosphorus," the sergeant said.

Denfeld was familiar with the white phosphorus used by the American troops. It was a solution of sulphur trioxide, in chlorosulfonic acid, and titanium tetrachloride. The shells threw up a large volume of dense, white smoke that was useful as a marker or as a smoke screen. burning pieces of phosphorus flying through the air also frightened enemy soldiers and could ignite underbrush, hay, paper, or other combustible material. It could burn a man, too, but Denfeld knew that the survivors of the Bari harbor bombing were not suffering from white phosphorous burns. He was certain of that. He knew a white phosphorous burn on sight.

Flame throwers were a possibility. All medical personnel, including Denfeld at the Fourteen Combined General Hospital, had been briefed on the new M1 A1 flame thrower that had just been developed. Fourteen thousand of the new weapons had been delivered to the Mediterranean theater in June, 1943, and it was entirely possible that some of the ships in the harbor the night of December 2 had been carrying another shipment of them. Yet, as he remembered the appearance of the burns on the faces and bodies of the survivors in the Fourteen Combined General Hospital, he refused to believe that they were caused by the flame throwers. The new M1 A1 used napalm, and the victims of the ship explosions in Bari harbor had no burns of this type.

Shaking his head, Denfeld said, "Guess I must be on the wrong trail, Sergeant. None of these items that you mentioned would cause the symptoms most of the men in the hospital have right now. If a ship loaded with flame throwers had been bombed or had caught on fire during the air strike, those flame throwers would probably have ignited and burned the men to a crisp." He looked at the American and grinned. "Thanks anyway. I better get back to the hospital."

As he started down the sidewalk, the sergeant called him back. "There is one more thing you should know, Captain."

"What?"

The American looked around the area carefully to make certain that no one else was within hearing distance. "Sometimes the ships bring in mustard bombs!"

For the first time since the casualties had begun to jam the Fourteen Combined General Hospital, Denfeld felt as though he was learning something vital about their condition. "Are you sure?"

The sergeant nodded. "Of course. We're stockpiling the mustard bomb in various locations outside Bari and other cities and airfields in southern Italy in case we need it."

Denfeld was still skeptical, however. There had been no toxic agents used during the long years of the war, despite the fact that at one time or another both the Allies and the Axis powers had been in very serious situations that required every weapon at their disposal. Perhaps the sergeant was exaggerating, intentionally or unintentionally. He had to find out.

"Have you ever unloaded a ship carrying mustard bombs?"

"Yes."

"How do you know they are mustard bombs and not high explosive bombs?" Denfeld asked.

The sergeant smiled. "There are several ways to discover the difference, but the best method is to listen to the briefing the chemical warfare officer in charge of the shipment gives all the men involved in unloading the bombs. We always handle them with care, real careful like, and we always have our masks handy in case the bombs' casings might be leaking."

"You're certain about this information."

"Yeah, I'm sure. However, I'm not saying there was any mustard bombs on any of the ships in the harbor last night when the Luftwaffe sunk them because I don't know."

"Where are the mustard bombs usually carried on the ships?"

The sergeant pointed toward the bow of a boat nearby. "Anytime I was ever involved with unloading them, the mustard bombs were in the number one hold in the bow where the water tanks lined the bottom. Usually there was a large steel top on the hold that could be bolted tight to make the hold airtight and watertight. The only way that I know that mustard could escape would be for a bomb to make a direct hit on the bow of the ship and blow the number one hold."

Denfeld nodded. "Could be... could be... I got to get back to the hospital."

As he hurried along the street toward the Fourteen Combined General Hospital, Captain Denfeld wondered if he had finally solved the mystery of the NYD burns he had been reporting. Was the term *not yet diagnosed* now answerable? Was it mustard?

If the trained medical staffs of the overcrowded Allied hospitals in the Bari area were puzzled by the physical condition of the harbor casualties, the civilian population of the city was completely bewildered. Some of the injured civilians had managed to get admitted to the hospitals in the area, but most were fortunate if they received any treatment at all. A few went to the nearest military first aid station and stood in line to get examined and have their injuries treated, but the majority of the Italian casualties were left to their own suffering. There were just too many wounded and injured to take care of and the military personnel got the preference because, as a British major declared haughtily as he blocked the doorway of a hospital, "There is a war on, you know."

Those civilians who had obvious injuries or wounds such as broken bones, bullet wounds, or bad lacerations had less trouble finding someone to help them than those who were covered with oil and suffering "merely" from shock and exhaustion. Many former Italian Army medics were in Bari and helped as much as they could by setting bones or stitching wounds when an American, British, or other Allied doctor was not available. Those who complained during the early hours of December 3 that they were having trouble breathing did not receive much sympathy and, at first, little or no help.

Alessandro Raucci, a sixty-year-old resident of the old section, had rushed from the burning holocaust of old Bari once it caught on fire and headed for the high bank and stone breakers along the west side of the harbor. He was still there watching the ships in the harbor burn when a merchant vessel at the south end of the East Jetty exploded and the resulting concussion formed a tidal wave that soaked Raucci. Grabbing a lightpost, the old man managed to keep from being washed into the harbor, but not before his clothing, face, arms, and feet were saturated with the oily waters.

Raucci considered himself fortunate to be alive and ignored the oil-soaked clothing. He did not change the tattered pants or shirt, nor did he bathe his exposed skin that was also covered with the oil slime from the harbor. The following morning, just before 11:00 A.M., he noticed a few blisters on his arms and at the same time his eyes began burning. At this time he was sitting on the steps of the scarred but still standing Basilica of San Nicola, the burial place of Santa Claus, talking with a friend, Pietro Sbordini. His eyes began to pain him badly and finally Raucci could barely see because of the flood of tears coming from them.

"What's wrong, Alessandro?"

"I can't see," the old man muttered. "My eyes hurt."

Sbordini, twenty years the junior of Raucci, had been at Taranto when the German bombers struck Bari, so he had not been injured or subjected to the mustard. One look into Raucci's eyes, however, and he realized that the old man needed medical help. But where could he get it?

Sbordini tried two different hospitals—Three New Zealand General Hospital and the Ninety-eight British General Hospital—but both were overflowing with military casualties and refused to admit the old Italian. Finally he took Raucci to a first aid station at the south end of Molo Foraneo which had been set up early on the morning of December 3 to help the injured and wounded civilians. It was operated by Italian and British personnel, mostly medics with an occasional doctor stopping in to help. A British sergeant washed the old man's eyes with clean water several times and put some ointment on the eyelids.

"Now, go home, take a bath, and put on clean clothes," the Britisher told Raucci.

The old man did not understand English, but Sbordini did and he tried to explain to the sergeant that Raucci could not possibly follow the instructions.

"He can't..."

The sergeant gently pushed the pair toward the door without permitting Sbordini to finish his explanation. "There are too many in line waiting to be treated to talk any longer. Please move on."

Sbordini wanted to tell the sergeant that the old man had no home to go to, no place to bathe, no clean clothes to wear. Raucci, just like hundreds of other citizens of the old section, had little or no choice but to keep wearing his oil-mustard saturated clothes. By the evening of the third, the old man was in bad shape. His eyes were swollen shut and he was in a near coma as he lay on the ground just a block from the Basilica of San Nicola in a lean-to Sbordini had constructed from some partially burned fish nets and sail canvas.

"Alessandro, wake up."

The old man would move his arms and legs every time Sbordini yelled at him and once or twice he muttered a few words, but a moment later he was back in the coma. The younger man watched him all night and just before dawn he could tell that Raucci was having serious difficulty breathing. Also, his skin was brownish looking and pealing in various spots. Scared, Sbordini ran back to the first aid station for help, but there was no one at the temporary medical facility. After looking around the area, thinking that the first aid station might have been moved to a new location but not finding it, he returned to the lean-to.

"I can't find anyone now but I..."

Despite the fact that Sbordini was speaking in a loud tone of voice, the old man did not stir.

"Alessandro!"

Still Raucci did not move a leg or an arm or mutter as he had done previously.

Dropping to his knees, the younger man put his ear to Raucci's chest and listened for his heart beat. There was none! He checked his pulse. There was none!

Alessandro Raucci was dead.

Similar situations were common all over old Bari during the days immediately after the German air strike. With very little medical aid, the Italians suffered alone, died alone. Many of the residents of the old section did not even know which direction to turn to try to get help and many of those who did were turned away at the jammed hospitals of the Allies. During such a tragedy it was only natural that the various Allied forces in Bari took care of their own before they treated those few who a few weeks before had been their enemies. It was not that the British, American, and New Zealand doctors, nurses or sisters were not willing to treat the Italians. It was just that there was not enough time, not enough room, not enough medicine, not enough equipment. Someone had to suffer and, in this case, it was the Italians, especially those from old Bari whose homes had been in the direct line of the exploding ships in the harbor.

How many civilians died during the aftermath of the German air strike will never be known. Even the records at the hospitals pertaining to the military and merchant marine casualties admitted were sketchy because of the nature of the disaster and the need for quick treatment. There were no records kept whatsoever on the number of civilian casualties, so the estimate of citizens who survived the holocaust that one thousand, at least, died during and after the German air strike is regarded as fairly accurate. It is known that huge clouds of smoke rolled inland from the harbor after the *John Harvey* exploded, and mixed with this smoke was the mustard. The smoke covered the entire old section, mixing with the billowing smoke from the burning homes, and the Italians undoubtedly breathed some of this deadly vapor into their lungs. For weeks afterward, citizens who had previously been in good health, were bedfast, had difficulty breathing, and, in many cases, died unexpectedly. Add these victims to those whose clothes and bodies were saturated with the oil-mustard mixture, those who died because of direct bomb hits or those trapped in the flames, and the estimate of one thousand deaths among the civilians is probably too conservative.

By the end of the second day after the Bari disaster, it was apparent that outside help was needed, that the mystery deaths were continuing in large numbers among both the military and civilian casualties.

16

"TELL IKE'S HEADQUARTERS THEY ARE ALL DYING!"

Allied Force Headquarters in Algiers, under the command of General Dwight D. Eisenhower, was well aware of the disastrous air strike made by the Luftwaffe on the night of December 2, 1943, on the shipping in Bari harbor. Eisenhower had been notified within hours after the raid and immediately recognized the importance of the loss of the vital supplies that he had been depending upon to aid the Allied forces fighting desperately in Italy against a very determined German Army. Yet, his was the overall picture of the tragic results of the German air strike and how it could affect the Allied advance. As commander in chief of the Allied Forces, Eisenhower could not know all the small details of the bombing; consequently he was unaware of the mustard shipment aboard the *John Harvey*. He always made certain that a quantity of the mustard was available in a theater of combat for reprisal use only, since he was uncertain of German intentions in the use of toxic agents, but he never made it his business to know exactly what ship carried the mustard or the location of each storage depot.

Major James Hicks, the officer in charge of medical services for the Americans at the Foggia airfield complex in Italy, had notified Lieutenant Colonel Ryle Radke at Allied Force Headquarters that the medical supplies that he had depended upon to set up improved facilities in Italy had been lost when the Allied merchant ships were sunk in Bari harbor by the German bombers. The messages passing back and forth between Algiers and Italy during the first two days after the Luftwaffe air strike dealt entirely with the loss of supplies, equipment, ships, and men. Not a word was mentioned about the mustard. It was taken for granted by Allied Force Headquarters in Algiers that there were many seriously wounded and injured men in the hospitals at Bari, but that was to be expected when the effectiveness of the surprise enemy air action was considered. This situation only emphasized the need for replacements for the supplies, especially the medical supplies, lost at Bari and, in this regard, Colonel Earl Standlee, the executive officer at Algiers, cabled Washington in an effort to obtain the needed materials.

Consequently, it was a shock to General Fred Blesse, deputy surgeon for Allied Force Headquarters, when he suddenly received a "red light" call from Italy informing him that the survivors of the Bari harbor bombing were afflicted with a mysterious malady. By this time many of the medical experts in Bari were suspicious that a toxic agent of some sort was causing the mysterious deaths and they were convinced that the German aircraft had probably used chemical bombs as well as high explosive bombs during the raid. When this information was relayed to Blesse he immediately summoned the one man he felt could solve the mystery.

"Tell Colonel Alexander to come to my office at once," he ordered an aide.

Lieutenant Colonel Stewart Francis Alexander was well known throughout military medical and chemical corps personnel as an expert consultant on chemical warfare medicine. Standing about five foot eight inches, stocky, and wearing glasses, the twenty-nine-year-old Alexander looked more like a laboratory assistant than the veteran combat doctor that he actually was. He had graduated from Columbia University College of Physicians and Surgeons in 1937 and was commissioned as a first lieutenant in the Medical Corps Reserve, U.S. Army, that same year. Called to active duty on November 14, 1940, he was immediately assigned as battalion surgeon for the Sixteenth Infantry Division, but this assignment was short-lived. In the fall of 1941 he was transferred to the Medical Research Division, Edgewood Arsenal, Maryland, where he conducted research into the various effects of mustard and nitrogen mustard agents, not realizing at the time that this knowledge would be invaluable two years later at Bari, Italy.

In the summer of 1942 General Eisenhower wired General George C. Marshall, chief of staff of the U.S. Army, that he needed a medical officer skilled in chemical warfare

medicine on his staff. Because of his background, Alexander
was chosen for the job and immediately left for Indiantown
Gap, near Harrisburg, Pennsylvania, where Colonel Charles
Van Way was getting personnel together for Eisenhower's
staff. Suddenly, however, his assignment to join the general in
North Africa was canceled and Alexander was sent to join
General George S. Patton, Jr., and stayed with Patton throughout Operation Torch, the invasion of North Africa. Later he
was one of the medical officers present at the Casablanca
conference between the president of the United States, Franklin D. Roosevelt, and the prime minister of Great Britain,
Winston L. S. Churchill. Leaving that conference, Alexander
joined General Mark W. Clark's Fifth Army and, finally, after
a period of several months from the time he was originally
selected to join Eisenhower, he moved to the general's headquarters at Algiers as consultant, chemical warfare medicine,
Allied Force Headquarters.

Blesse was not able to brief Alexander in detail because
he knew very little about the Bari tragedy himself. "There
seems to be some concern over the number of unexplained
deaths at Bari as a result of the German air strike," he told
Alexander. "You better get over there immediately and see
what you can learn. There is a possibility that a toxic agent is
involved."

Alexander left Algiers on a transport plane, having been
given a top priority by Eisenhower, and arrived in Bari to
discover that he had already been considered "dead." The
waiting British officials had been told that he was flying to
Bari on an earlier plane and as they congregated at the field
to meet him, they were horrified to see the aircraft crash as it
attempted to land. Everyone aboard the plane was killed.
However, before the Britishers left the airport, Alexander
arrived on a second plane—much to their relief.

He was taken directly to the nearest hospital so that he
could examine the patients. As Alexander stepped into the
hospital, one fact bothered him immediately. Turning to the
British medical officer accompanying him, he asked, "What's
that odor?"

"It's from the oil that most of the survivors had on their
bodies and clothes when they were brought here. We haven't
had time to disinfect the wards as yet."

Alexander remembered his long hours of research at the
Edgewood Arsenal in Maryland and the odor that had perme-

ated his laboratory there while he was working with mustard. This was the same odor! Saying no more, he began examining the patients in the wards. The first thing he noticed was the unusual and extremely varied skin lesions. "Were the lesions noticeable as soon as the patients arrived?"

"No. They weren't evident during the first twelve hours. We didn't notice any unusual-looking patches of skin until the morning after the bombing," Colonel W. J. A. Laird, commanding officer, Ninety-eight British General Hospital said. "Within twenty-four to thirty-six hours after exposure the lesions were widespread, however."

"Were the skin irritations always this reddish-brown color?"

Laird shook his head. "They deepened in color from day to day and as the color changes occurred in the superficial layers of the skin it developed into a bronze hue. At first, the patches of damaged skin would fade on pressure, but later they would only partially fade."

Alexander nodded. So far everything was fitting into a pattern. Even the small blisters on the skin of the patients were not of the textbook variety. In many cases it was difficult to determine where the edges of the blisters were located. There was one fact that bothered him. The fluid accumulations of the blisters in the superficial layers of the skin were diffused, not like those that he would have expected had the victim been splashed with liquid mustard. In fact, in many cases, large areas of superficial layers of the epidermis were separated from their deeper layers and torn loose, rather than forming definite blisters. This was puzzling and tended to make Alexander think his theory that the victims were suffering from exposure to mustard was wrong.

On the whole the skin burns were remarkably mild in degree. Most of the burns Alexander classified as first and second degree, with only rarely an area of third-degree damage. He was well aware that mustard first acts as a cell irritant and finally as a cell poison on all tissue surfaces contacted. The initial symptoms of mustard poisoning usually appear in from four to six hours; the higher the concentration, the shorter the interval between the exposure to the agent and the first symptoms. According to Laird, the symptoms did not show up until after twelve hours. What was the significance of this fact? Did it mean that if the men had been exposed to mustard that it was not a direct exposure?

"I feel that these men may have been exposed to mustard in some manner, Colonel," Alexander explained. "Do you have any idea how this might have been possible?"

"None."

"Have you checked with the port authorities whether the ships in the harbor might have been carrying mustard?"

"I have and they tell me they have no such information available."

Alexander knew that this could mean many things. Perhaps the British authorities who controlled the port of Bari might not have manifests of all Allied ships crowded into the harbor on the night of December 2, 1943, and were completely ignorant of the fact that one or more of the vessels were carrying toxic agents. There was also the possibility that the port officials did know that poison gas was on a ship or ships in the harbor that night, but, because of security, propaganda, and political reasons, would not admit it. He knew that the burden of proof was on his own investigation and, if the men were to be given the proper medical treatment, he had to act fast.

Lifting the blanket from another patient, Alexander noted an unusual sight. The burns exactly followed the pattern of the type of exposure the man had suffered. The area that had been subjected to the oil on the top of the harbor surface was outlined clearly by burns. He could tell that the oil had landed on this patient's neck and run down the chest and back. Alexander immediately checked other nearby patients and discovered the same distribution of burns. If the victim had been immersed in or covered with the oil solution and then wrapped in a blanket, practically his entire body was covered with surface burns. If only his legs or arms had come into contact with the oil solution, then only these parts of the body were burned. He realized that this was an important clue, but at the moment he could not relate it to the other facts he had so far determined since his arrival at Bari. So far, according to Alexander's personal evaluation, he had learned:

(1) The lesions were not severe enough in their local damage to have been caused by liquid mustard.

(2) The distribution of the large majority of the lesions was impossible to explain by mustard vapor.

(3) The almost absolute correlation was between the men who were covered with oil from the harbor and lesions sustained by these individuals.

Leaning down closer to the patient he had just examined, Alexander asked him where he had been during the bombing. "Were you aboard one of the merchant ships?"

The patient shook his head. "I was on a PT boat in the harbor when the German bombers arrived."

"How were you burned?"

The patient shook his head. "I'm not sure how it happened. There was a loud explosion when one of the ships blew up and I felt oil land on my neck and then run down my chest and back. We headed for shore as fast as we could."

Alexander nodded. "I don't doubt that you did. How about first aid? Did you receive any treatment as soon as you reached a hospital?"

"No. I kept my clothes on and I didn't get to wash the oil off until after forty-eight hours."

Alexander was thoroughly convinced that, if the contaminating agent had been liquid mustard, the burns would have been much worse. Could it have been a dilute solution of mustard, he wondered? Mustard could form a true solution in crude oil up to 20 percent, yet even this amount of mustard seemed high when the burns received by the victims were considered. In addition, why would some of the victims have much more serious burns than others? Was it possible that the concentrations in the different areas of the harbor varied considerably?

Another clue could be the effect of the mysterious agent on the victim's nose, throat, and lungs. Alexander investigated these symptoms next, trying to be completely objective but still suspecting that mustard was the culprit, despite the denial of the British port authorities that they were aware of any ship in the harbor that night carrying such a chemical agent. He soon discovered that there were no symptoms of any respiratory tract irritation during the first thirty-six hours after exposure. The doctors at the military hospitals had very carefully watched the victims for any indication of blast injury to the lungs, so they were certain that there were no complaints by the patients about their respiratory tracts during these initial hours. During the second day, however, the casualties began to cough and complain of congestion in the head. The cough progressed in severity, the doctors told Alexander, and became associated with mucus in the sputum. By the time Alexander arrived from Algiers, most of the victims were complaining of sore throats and a huskiness of the voice. There was no spitting of blood initially, no chest pain, and no pain felt when breathing, nor were the mucus membranes tinged with blue as was usual if the respiratory tract was severely irritated.

"Just prior to your arrival, Colonel, we noticed symptoms of lower respiratory tract infection," Laird told Alexander.

Alexander had already noticed the symptoms in several of the patients he examined while the commanding officer of the Ninety-eight British General Hospital had been explaining about the initial irritation directly after the exposure. He noticed that several of the casualties had a marked rise in temperature and pulse rate, that their breathing was labored, and that their sputum was now blood tinged. The question in Alexander's mind was whether these victims had been injured by concussion from the blasts and these symptoms were the result or, as he suspected, were the symptoms from exposure to a toxic agent?

"I want X-rays taken immediately of some of these patients who definitely have lower respiratory tract infection symptoms," he said.

The X-rays indicated that very few of the victims had actually suffered blast damage to their lungs or lower respiratory tracts. However, the most seriously ill had been burned on both the front and back of their chest walls by the mysterious toxic agent, a fact that clearly indicated that it was the burns sustained during the exposure to the harbor waters that were causing the respiratory tract symptoms.

"How soon after the bombing did the first death occur, a death that was not the result of the victim being hit by an object or otherwise killed as a direct result of the explosions?"

Laird did not have to refer to his notes. He had gone over the case so many times in his own mind that every fact was crystal clear.

"The first death occurred eighteen hours after exposure," he said, "and it was very unusual. None who witnessed it will ever forget the experience."

The patient had appeared to be in marked shock, but was remarkably clear mentally. He died abruptly, seconds after speaking with a nurse and seemingly feeling much better. There was no indication of distress at the time of death. One moment he was talking, the next he was dead.

"Are you certain that he was not a victim of blast injury?"

"Certain. There were blast injuries in Bari that night and

there were blast deaths, but these cases were separated insofar as possible from the group of casualties suffering from the NYD burns."

Alexander knew that much more research was necessary to definitely determine the nature of the toxic agent he suspected was causing the mysterious deaths. Autopsies, microscopic pathology, and the entire detailed routine common in such situations. But he also knew that if he was to help save the lives of the hundreds of victims in the military hospitals and the countless hundreds—perhaps thousands—of civilians suffering the same symptoms all over Bari and the surrounding area, he did not have time for all the additional research at the moment. He had to determine the toxic agent to which the victims, military and civilian, had been exposed and prescribe the proper treatment.

Because of his extensive work with mustard at the Edgewood Arsenal in Maryland prior to his overseas assignment, Alexander knew the background of this particular toxic agent. He knew that when the German Army brought out mustard gas for the first time in April, 1915, the agent had caused havoc among Allied troops. The mustard not only attacked the respiratory system, but also the skin, soaked through clothes, shoes, leggings, and resulted in painful blisters. It was proven at that early date that it was impossible to protect soldiers completely from mustard. At that time the crude mustard used was a mixture of approximately 70 percent dichloroethyl sulfide and 30 percent sulphur and other sulphur compounds. An oily, brown liquid that evaporated slowly, giving off a vapor five times heavier than air, the toxic agent smelled like garlic or mustard in high concentration. It irritated and poisoned body cells, but generally many hours passed before the symptoms appeared.

After the Armistice the Chemical Warfare Service closed down the mustard plants at Cleveland, Ohio; Buffalo, New York; Midland, Michigan; Hastings-on-Hudson, New York; it did not do any additional research at Edgewood until the early 1930s. Not until 1940, however, was the Edgewood Arsenal opened for large-scale production again. After the mustard was in production, a number of purification methods were examined including distillation under low pressure, distillation using steam and organic liquids, extraction with solvents, treatment with ammonia, flash distillation, steam distillation, and crystal fractionation. The only processes that proved practical for large-scale production were vacuum distillation, steam distillation, and solvent extraction.

All this information was known to Alexander, but actually was of little use to him during his investigation at Bari. What he had to know was whether mustard in one form or another had been dispersed over or in the harbor. He knew that mustard was the predominant toxic agent stockpiled by the American military forces to use in retaliation in case the Axis powers used chemicals, that production lines at Edgewood Arsenal and the Rocky Mountain Arsenal were delivering millions of pounds of the agent to the military. Since mustard evaporated slowly and remained effective from several hours to several days, largely depending upon the weather and the ground terrain, it was considered a valuable asset to stockpile in case it was needed. It was planned to use it in retaliation by sealing off an enemy area into which American troops were advancing and to hamper enemy lines of communications, airfield, landing beaches, artillery emplacements, and observation points. If Allied troops had to withdraw from a position, the mustard could be used to contaminate the routes of the enemy advance. The mustard was in production, was stored at various depots in combat areas around the globe, but was it at Bari?

While Alexander was still sitting at his desk trying to decide on his next move, he reviewed the methods he was aware of in which the mustard could be used, hoping that he could then determine if any of the equipment or weapons used in dispersing the agent were on the manifests of any of the ships in the harbor on the night of December 2. For ground delivery, he was familiar with the 4.2-inch mortar that had also interested Captain Denfeld, the British doctor who was temporarily stationed at the Fourteen Combined General Hospital and had suspected mustard as the possible culprit the day after the air raid, but had not been able to prove it. However, it was the method of aerial delivery of the mustard that interested Alexander because of the nearness of the Foggia airfield complex and the availability of the new Fifteenth Air Force aircraft and crews, commanded by Doolittle, to make a reprisal attack if one were required.

For such aerial mustard attacks the Chemical Warfare Service had bombs and spray tanks both. The M70 and M70A1 bombs weighed 115 pounds and were developed by the Ordnance Department in the 1930s while the M47A1 and

M47A2 100-pound bombs had been developed by the Chemical Warfare Service. The bombs were approximately four feet long, about eight inches in diameter and contained a cylindrical burster. There were from 60 to 70 pounds of mustard in each casing and each bomb contaminated an area of from fifteen to forty yards in diameter when dropped, depending upon the thickness of the vegetation, altitude of the aircraft, and the weather.

The four M10 thirty-gallon spray tanks carried on a plane could cover an area of seventy-five to eighty yards wide; and six hundred to seven hundred yards long if the mustard were sprayed from an altitude of one hundred feet. The larger M33 or M33A1 tanks held twice as much mustard and an airplane carrying two of these tanks could contaminate approximately the same area as four of the smaller tanks. Mustard was not easy to spray successfully, however, and Alexander was convinced that, if mustard was aboard any of the ships in Bari harbor the night of the German air strike, it probably was in bomb casings and not spray tanks. The Chemical Warfare Service had expended much effort in an attempt to improve the spraying properties of mustard, especially when it became evident after the beginning of World War II that planes flying at low altitude and moderate speeds would probably be shot down before they could complete their mission. When it became standard operating procedure for the spray planes to fly at least a mile high and at speeds well over 300 mph, the mustard droplets were carried away from the target area by the winds or evaporated so quickly that they either did not reach the ground at all or were so small that they did no contaminating. To make the droplets larger, scientists and chemists searched for a material to thicken them. Later, it was determined that there was no advantage in having thicker droplets so the idea was abandoned.

To Alexander, the possibility of mustard bombs being aboard one or more of the merchant ships was much greater than the mustard, if that actually was the toxic agent causing the deaths, being present in any other form. And, if mustard was the troublemaker, then it evidently had been diluted by the oil and water of the harbor, thus causing symptoms that differed from those that would have been evident if the victims had been exposed to concentrated liquid mustard. This, of course, added to the puzzle.

"Have you had a sample of the oil from the harbor

chemically analyzed?" he asked a staff member of the Ninety-eight British General Hospital.

"No. We know that it is oil from a tanker and from the fuel line along the quay so . . ."

"Get some analyzed immediately."

He also decided that it was imperative that autopsies be performed on the men who had already died from the "Burns, NYD" to see if his diagnosis of exposure to mustard could be verified.

"I want tissue samples and an autopsy performed on every patient who dies," he told Laird.

The Britisher shook his head. "I don't think we have either the personnel or the equipment to handle that many autopsies."

"Then do the best you can," Alexander said. "I will contact Major Hicks at Foggia. He hasn't much equipment but perhaps he can help out with some medical personnel."

Next, Alexander decided to try to get a sketch made of the harbor as it was on the night of December 2, a sketch that would locate the anchorage of as many of the ships in the harbor that night as possible. This was a very difficult, complex task and he knew that it would require the complete cooperation of the British port authorities. Fortunately the necessary cooperation was promised and the sketch was begun that very day. Alexander hoped that once he knew the location of the ships that were in the harbor that night, he could correlate the deaths in hospitals that were attributed to the unknown toxic agent with the ship positions. If such a chart showed that a predominant number of these deaths occurred near one certain ship, then the cargo that was on that ship could be investigated thoroughly and perhaps the toxic agent giving the trouble could be identified for certain. It was a gamble, but one that offered a slight chance of success and the Bari situation was so desperate that no possibility of determining the source of the mysterious deaths could be ignored.

Hicks and the British hospital personnel began the autopsies that Alexander requested immediately, concentrating only on the bodies of those victims who had died from unknown causes. By the day following Alexander's arrival at Bari from Algiers, the first of the pathology reports were available. As he studied these preliminary reports, he was more certain than ever that the culprit was mustard. One report stated, in part:

> (a) Skin
> There were varying extents of first and second degree burns covering in many bodies almost the entire skin surface. The burns were quite superficial on the whole, and there was relatively little whole skin destruction. Third degree burns were quite uncommon and were confined for the most part to the buttocks and neck regions. In many areas the surface layers of the skin could easily be rubbed loose, as though its attachment to the next deeper layers had been destroyed. These surface layers could be stripped loose in large patches. When the superficial skin layers were removed in this manner a normal pinkish skin appeared beneath. The pathologists repeatedly noted that these layers of the skin were dislodged upon handling of the body and commented upon the "living" appearance of the deeper layers. As the superficial skin layers were stripped loose they often took the surface hair with them.
> *Thermal burns were readily distinguished from the chemical burns.*

It was obvious to Alexander that he had been right all along in his diagnosis that the victims definitely had chemical burns as well as burns caused by the fires in the harbor that night.

The same autopsy report reviewed the respiratory tract investigation pertaining to the deaths that occurred during the three days immediately after the German air strike.

> In the deaths of the first three days the findings in the lungs varied from normal lungs to varying stages of congestion. Some of the lungs were mottled mauve brown on the surface and had a mottled congestion throughout. In several, distinct rib markings were noted on the surface. The congestion was the most consistent and striking observation in the lungs and was far more impressive than the relative-

ly small hemorrhages. Cases showing definite and
significant blast injuries that were interpretable as
such were deleted from the study. Any case where
blast injury of the lung was of a degree sufficient to
have been considered a major factor was classed as a
blast death.

In the summation of the findings in the lungs it
would appear that there were two definite types of
pathology. There were the irritative surface damag-
ing effects of the inhaled toxic agent which followed
bronchial congestion and was followed later by secondary pulmonary infection. At the same time there
were present in the lungs the results of wounds or
injuries sustained the night of the explosions. Many
of these victims of blast injuries died within 48
hours. However, the wounds or injuries seen in
many of these cases were of a type and degree that
would not, in itself, have killed the individual. Were
it not for other factors, the individuals would have
recovered from the small hemorrhages and larger
bruises sustained by their lungs. Actual knowledge
of such lung bruises were not known at the time of
death and were only examined pathologically because the individual died of other factors. The serious consequences of imposing a toxic agent vapor
injury upon a lung partially damaged or bruised by
blast is at once apparent.

The gastrointestinal tract, stomach, liver, gall bladder,
pancreas, spleen, lymph nodes, bone marrow, kidneys, heart,
and other organs had all been examined, but it was difficult to
tell from the preliminary report whether the suspected toxic
agent had affected them or not. Alexander had seen enough,
however. He was completely convinced that the agent was
mustard. There was now no doubt in his mind.

While he was still trying to decide on his next step now
that he had made his decision, he received a telephone call
from a British officer at the dock.

"Colonel Alexander, we have just recovered a bomb
casing from the floor of the harbor. It definitely contained
mustard. It is evident that the German planes dropped
chemical bombs during the air strike."

Alexander was stunned! He had not considered the fact that the mustard might have been used by the Luftwaffe, that the German bombers had used poison gas during the raid on Bari harbor!

17

"COLONEL, WHERE DID THE MUSTARD COME FROM?"

Had Hitler, in desperation, decided to use poison gas to try and stop the Allied drive up the Italian peninsula? Had Washington made an error in its evaluation of the possibility of the Germans resorting to gas warfare? After all, it had been Germany who introduced poison gas on a large scale to the art of warfare on April 22, 1915, on the Western Front during World War I. Why should they not use it in World War II? Yet, Alexander and other officers who had been associated with the Chemical Warfare Service for an extended period of time knew that Allied military authorities did not think Hitler would use poison gas. There were several reasons for this line of reasoning.

It had been learned that Hitler definitely had a personal antipathy to gas warfare and military intelligence personnel in Washington were convinced that he would never order the use of poison gas on the battlefield. A study of documents and plans obtained from underground sources that the German high command had drawn up for pursuing the war against the Allies indicated that these high-ranking German officers and their field commanders had devoted their attention to strategy, tactics, and weapons that excluded gas warfare. In addition, it was known that the German high command believed that world opinion would be outraged if Germany became the aggressor in gas warfare, although some of their other actions during the war made it doubtful that the public opinion factor was of primary importance to them.

Brigadier General Charles S. Shadle, chemical warfare officer, Allied Forces Headquarters, summed it up when he said, "The Axis powers, in my opinion, neither have the necessary supply of toxic munitions in the Mediterranean area nor are in a position to use them if they did."

These were comforting words—until it was recalled that on the afternoon preceding the attack on Bari, Air Marshal Sir Arthur Coningham, commander of the British air forces supporting the Eighth Army, had said during a press conference, "I would regard it as a personal affront and insult if the Luftwaffe should attempt any significant action in this area."

If the air marshal had been so tragically mistaken, was it possible that Shadle too had underestimated the capabilities of the Germans to wage gas warfare and their decision to do so? Shadle, as so many other offices who had studied the possibility of an Axis gas warfare offensive, believed that during the early part of the war when both the ground and aerial tactics of the Germans were so successful, gas warfare would either have hampered the German advance or would have posed technical and logistical problems that Germany, at that time, was not prepared to handle. Later, when Germany was forced on the defensive as she was during the Italian campaign, the use of gas would have been decidedly to her advantage, but by this time the Allies supposedly had air superiority and Shadle was convinced that the German leaders would fear retaliation in kind, especially against the homeland. Germany had no large stock of protective clothing for civilians and there was a shortage of gas masks.

The question in the mind of Alexander and many other Allied officers at Bari, however, was whether the Germans had decided to disregard the odds and use poison gas. The rumor that they had used mustard during the air strike on the ships in the harbor spread across the city very rapidly once it started. Gas masks were prepared for immediate use, as many of the Allied soldiers believed that the Germans would return and drop more chemical bombs on the city and the harbor; civilians refused to return to Bari, preferring to stay in the countryside until it was definitely ascertained whether poison gas was being used by the Germans. Allied commanders at Bari were confused, but decided not to take any chances. They gave orders to prepare chemical bombs stored in depots outside of the city for a retaliatory attack if it was required. For several hours the entire military situation was delicately balanced on the question of whether a new phase of the war—a chemical warfare phase—had begun or not.

Meanwhile, more practical steps were being taken to

determine whether the bomb casing recovered from the harbor floor had actually contained mustard or not, whether it was a German bomb or an Allied bomb. It did not take very long to discover that the casing most definitely had contained liquid mustard and ordnance officers of the Fifteenth Air Force identified the casing as an American type, an M47A1 hundred-pound bomb that was often used as a vehicle for carrying liquid mustard. This settled the question of whether the Germans had used poison gas bombs on the night of December 2 or not, but, unfortunately, it did not stop the rumor. Communications in the city were still not completely restored and this added to the confusion and lack of reliable information. Poor cooperation between British port authorities and American military forces also aided and abetted the rumor. Doolittle had no intention of scheduling his Fifteenth Air Force bombers to drop chemical bombs on German troops, but it was generally believed in the Bari area by many Allied soldiers and Italian civilians that a huge retaliatory raid by American bombers was being planned. The rumor went far beyond the Allied use of mustard. Such toxic agents as phosgene, hydrogen cyanide, cyanogen chloride, lewisite, and adamsite were all supposedly going to be used and nerve gases and biological warfare were often mentioned. The one predominant fear among responsible Allied commanders during this period was that a retaliatory raid might be made by mistake before the rumor was discounted. Consequently heavy guard was placed around all dumps containing chemical warfare supplies.

Now that his suspicions had been confirmed and Alexander was certain that medically he was dealing with patients that had been exposed to mustard mixed with water and fuel oil and patients exposed to mustard vapor, he advised the various military hospitals of the fact.

"These patients should have been treated immediately after exposure to the mustard for the best results," he told the military medical staffs, "but since you were unaware that this agent was involved I certainly don't blame you. We must now do the best we can to save these victims."

Knowing that the skin blisters were not caused by ordinary burns but from chemical burns, the conventional procedure of preserving them was abandoned. The blisters were punctured and drained, but the doctors and nurses attempted to save the outer "roof" of the blister as a protection under

the sterile dressing that had to be applied. The problem of
maintaining cleanliness of the skin was tremendous, since so
many of the casualties had extensive burn areas. A casualty
with burns covering nearly the entire body area required the
full attention of one nurse or corpsman, and this was impossible because of the number of victims and lack of medical
personnel. The hospital staffs did their best, but, in many
cases, their best was not enough and death resulted. In a
desperate attempt to save the victims, the following types of
treatments were used in the various hospitals and upon
different patients within the same hospital:

> No dressing—covered with protecting cradle but no
>   local therapy used
> Starch or talc powder dressing only
> Vaseline dressing over acriflavine
> Acriflavine 1–10,000 dressing
> Sulfanilamide powder dressing
> Calamine lotion painting
> Dry sterile dressing
> Sulfadiazine ointment
> Tannic acid locally
> Vaseline gauze dressing
> Wet saline dressing
> Warm saline baths
> Vaseline dressings
> Ensol dressings
> Triple dye

The medical staffs tried to compare the effectiveness of
the various treatments, but there was not enough time to
really control the procedures to such an extent that important
data could be obtained. There was no local treatment sufficiently
outstanding over the others to merit specific approval. The
simplest treatments were the most satisfactory in that they
demanded the least attention. The more comfortable treatments were more satisfactory in that they disturbed the
patient less.

Prophylactic sulfonamide therapy was prescribed for all
the victims with irritated respiratory tracts, but, unfortunately,
this treatment was not begun soon enough in many cases.
Distinct symptoms of the upper respiratory tract were taken
by the doctors to mean that there was also the possibility of

exposure of the lower respiratory system to the mustard. Alexander emphasized that medical personnel should not wait for a rise of temperature or definite indication of pneumonia before giving the patient oral sulfonamide. When pneumonia did develop, nursing care became extremely difficult because of the extensive chemical burns of the victims on their bodies and their painful throats. Forced fluids were a necessity, but, when the nurses attempted to follow this procedure, the patients would scream as the skin peeled from their bodies and the fluids trickled down their raw throats. This made the giving of adequate nourishment a considerable problem.

Nose drops relieved the victims' nasal congestion to a small degree. Gargles and mouthwashes were used. Inhalations of steam and compound tincture of benzoin had relatively little effect upon the irritations in the upper respiratory tract, however. On the whole, the treatment used on the respiratory tract following the inhalation of mustard vapor by those casualties who had been trapped in the billowing smoke containing the toxic agent was very discouraging. While no accurate records or surveys were made at the time, it is assumed that a large number of civilians died from inhaling the mustard vapor, since large sections of the city, including all of the old city, were completely covered with the clouds of smoke that rolled inland from the burning holocaust in Bari harbor.

As Alexander discovered on his arrival at Bari, the first death had occurred eighteen hours after exposure to the mustard. This record did not, of course, refer to the hundreds of deaths which occurred during the air strike from blast injury, normal burns, drowning, or other causes that could be definitely determined—only cases due to mustard exposure. As far as he could learn, there were four deaths altogether the first day after the bombing. After the initial twenty-four hours the deaths in the local military hospitals classified as due to mustard exposure were:

2d day	9 deaths
3d day	11 deaths
4th day	8 deaths
5th day	4 deaths
6th day	4 deaths
7th day	5 deaths

| 8th day | 9 deaths |
| 9th day | 9 deaths |

This did not include the unknown number of civilians who died in the city or in the outlying countryside, never understanding what was wrong with them, never knowing that they had been exposed to mustard.

Alexander noted that there were two peak points in the death curve chart, one on the third day and the second on the ninth day. He related the first peak to the acute systemic effects of the burns plus acute systemic effects of the mustard. The second peak was reached because of the effects of secondary pneumonia imposed upon patients already weakened by the toxic agent. The greatest worry among hospital personnel in Bari was the fact that the number of deaths was increasing despite the treatment that was now being given in the hospitals for mustard exposure. The delay in starting the proper treatment because the doctors had been unaware that the victims had been subjected to a toxic agent was the main reason for the increase in fatalities. In addition, many of the military survivors of the bombing had been evacuated from Bari to hospitals in Brindisi, Taranto, North Africa, and other areas and each of these installations had to be notified that these men had been exposed to mustard. Communication was a problem and sometimes the warning about the mustard came too late for those most seriously affected. Sometimes the message never reached these hospitals at all.

Captain Heitmann of the *John Bascom* returned to Taranto on December 7, five days after his ship was sunk in Bari harbor by the German bombers, still not feeling well but trying to avoid going to a hospital. A veteran of the fighting, Heitmann thought that time would heal his aches and pains, that being bedded down in a hospital was for those men on the critical list only. Unfortunately, there were many hundreds of other military men who felt the same way and did not receive the proper treatment for their mustard exposure. Most of them, of course, were not aware that they had been exposed to mustard. By the time Heitmann got back to Taranto, his voice was failing rapidly, and Ziroly, the liaison officer at the Royal Navy building, insisted that he go directly to the nearest hospital for treatment.

The captain shrugged and whispered, "I want to go over to the Seventy and see my purser anyway."

At the Seventy British General Hospital in Taranto he visited with William Lesesne, the purser of the *John Bascom* who had been severely burned over the face and body during the air strike. Lesesne was in so much pain that Heitmann could not speak with him, so he queried the doctor on duty about the man's condition.

"He's not good, Captain. It will be several weeks before he will even be well enough to transfer to the American Naval Hospital at Palermo." Staring at Heitmann, the doctor said, "I want to examine you, Captain. You look as though you are in damned bad shape."

The examination proved what Ziroly had advised earlier in the day—Heitmann needed hospital care immediately. When the doctor at the Seventy General Hospital called a nurse to take the captain to a bed, however, Heitmann interrupted quickly.

"Not right now, Doc. I have some business to take care of and I'll be back in an hour."

"Make certain it is no longer."

Heitmann walked out of the hospital and kept going. If he was going to be confined to a hospital he wanted to go to an American installation, not a British facility. Later, he was grateful that he made the decision he did. When he met Lesesne in New York months later, the purser told him that the British doctors did not seem to understand his case and could not get his burns to heal. It was not until he was shipped to an American hospital that an American doctor cut and removed the scabby skin and treated him properly that he improved. The British, from top-level politicians and high-ranking officers down to the Bari port authorities, refused to concede that the victims were suffering from mustard exposure for a long time. Much too long. This complicated the treatment of the patients and caused unneeded delay in communications to medical facilities regarding the true condition of the casualties.

The following day, Heitmann left Taranto by train for Naples and arrived there at 6:00 P.M. on December 10—still without having the proper medical treatment. He was quartered at the United Seaman's Service Club and promptly went to sleep in the warm bed provided. The next morning he could not speak. His voice was gone entirely. At the War Shipping Administration office in Naples he conducted his business by writing, knowing that he could no longer delay his admittance to a hospital. At 2:00 P.M. he was admitted to the Seventy Station Hospital, eight days after his exposure to the mustard in Bari harbor, still not knowing what was wrong with him except for the shrapnel wound in his hand and his injured back.

Before nightfall he experienced great difficulty in breathing and began coughing continuously. Doctors and nurses kept him in a sitting position in an effort to ease his coughing spells, but this did little good. He did not know it but he had inhaled mustard vapor and his respiratory tract was badly irritated. During the following ten days he was given the best of treatment, many of the ones recommended by Alexander in Bari, and gradually his voice returned and his breathing became easier. By the end of the month he was improved enough to be evacuated to North Africa for further hospitalization. He was one of the lucky ones who received late medical care but recovered because of the excellent quality of the treatment he finally did get. There were many others, in and out of uniform, who were not so lucky—and died.

As far as Alexander was concerned, the cause of the mysterious deaths at Bari had been solved. It was mustard. There was no question about it. The sketch that he had asked be made, in cooperation with the British port authorities, U.S. military officials, dockworkers, and anyone else who could help, was further verification that the culprit was mustard.* The sketch indicated the location of the various ships in Bari harbor on the evening of the raid. By questioning the victims concerning what ship they had been aboard and identifying the dead and investigating what ship they came from, a great deal of information was obtained that was not known previously. Designating the ships by numbers the sketch revealed:

Ship 1	no survivors
Ship 2	18 deaths
Ship 3	9 deaths
Ship 4	11 deaths
Ship 5	3 deaths
Ship 6	10 deaths
Ship 7	2 deaths
Ship 8	0 deaths

*A copy of this sketch appears in the Appendix.

Ship 9	0 deaths
Ship 10	11 deaths
Ship 11	2 deaths
Ship 12	4 deaths
Ship 13	1 deaths
Ship 14	1 deaths

The sketch also showed that the greatest number of mustard-induced deaths occurred among the personnel closest to the Liberty ship 1. Investigation revealed that ship 1 was the *John Harvey* and reluctantly the British port officials finally admitted that the *John Harvey* was carrying a hundred tons of mustard bombs!

Now that he knew what the toxic agent had been and where it had come from, Alexander felt that his assignment in Bari had been accomplished satisfactorily and he could return to his headquarters in North Africa. Soon after arriving at the Office of the Surgeon, Headquarters, North African Theater of Operations, Algiers, he began issuing the reports on the medical aspects of the tragedy, notifying various units of his experiences at Bari so that if the situation ever occurred in their areas they would be prepared. One of his first papers was a preliminary report entitled "Toxic Gas Burns Sustained in the Bari Harbor Catastrophe," dated December 27, 1943. This twelve-page document, classified secret, was for the director, Medical Service, Allied Force Headquarters, and copies were sent to appropriate individuals and organizations as was customary. The report included a short résumé of the air raid, casualties, first aid treatment, general observations from a medical viewpoint, clinical observations, eye treatments given, skin reaction to the agent, treatment of the skin, systemic effects, pathological findings, a discussion, and a summary. It was a routine medical report—except for the findings that the mysterious toxic agent was mustard from one of the American merchant ships.

One copy was sent to Commander George M. Lyon, Medical Corps officer stationed in London, with the following letter accompanying it:

U.S. Secret
Equals British Secret

Headquarters
North African Theatre of Operations
Office of the Surgeon
APO 534

27 December 1943

Commander George M. Lyon, M.C.
U.S.N.R.
Office of Naval Attaché
American Embassy, London

Dear Commander:

I am enclosing a copy of a preliminary report of a group of mustard casualties that I recently had the opportunity to see. I am particularly anxious that you have such information as I have already gathered, as this type of picture I feel the Navy is more likely to see again than the Army.

As you well gathered from the report, the systemic effects were far more severe than I had ever anticipated as being possible. While these effects will probably never be of this degree following the use of mustard in the field, I think the possibility of their recurrence in Naval accidents might be possible. It is also worth bearing in mind that, if they may be of this degree in some cases, in many others they will be present to a milder but still perhaps significant degree.

It is still too early to properly appraise the various features in this group of casualties, but I did want you to see this preliminary report.

With kindest regards, I am
Sincerely yours,
Stewart F. Alexander
Lt. Colonel, M.C.

Two days later, Alexander sent a copy of the preliminary report and tissue blocks from about forty cases that had been prepared by British hospitals to the Edgewood Arsenal, Maryland, with a letter that stated:

U.S. Secret
Equals British Secret

Headquarters
North American Theatre of Operations
Office of the Surgeon
APO 534

29 December 1943

Colonel John R. Wood
Medical Research Laboratories
Chemical Warfare Center
Edgewood Arsenal, Maryland

Dear Colonel Wood:

I am enclosing a preliminary report of a group of mustard casualties I recently had the opportunity to see. The report is somewhat sketchy in places but I believe it will give you a general picture of the problem as I saw it.

The point I am most anxious that you and Dr. Winternitz's group consider is the picture I have tentatively described as systemic effects. The blood changes and the liver changes I think are very definite. The blood pressure changes might be explained, as I have alluded in the report by the subtotal body area burns even though of relatively mild degree. Many of the cases also had some degree of lung trauma from the blast, but they did not die respiratory deaths. We may grant that blast effects accounted for some of the later deaths, but it still leaves many cases that died with neither of these factors being significant. As you will gather, it was a most interesting group of cases, and left plenty of room for mental gymnastics.

I am sending you under separate cover tissue blocks from about forty cases, prepared by the British Hospitals. They were fixed in Zenker's Solution, washed and then brought up to 50 percent alcohol for shipment. I am afraid the volume of alcohol for the amount of tissue is rather small, and they should be changed as soon as they arrive. I am also sending you under separate cover the gross pathological findings on all these cases.

I should like you to:

1. Acquaint Dr. Winternitz with the features of this group of cases.

2. Send me your microscopic findings.

3. Send me your comments on the medical aspects of the episode.

With kindest personal regards,

Stewart F. Alexander
Lt. Colonel, M.C.

In addition to other U.S. units to which Alexander sent the preliminary report, he also sent copies and accompanying letters to Porton, England, which was the British equivalent of Edgewood Arsenal with respect to chemical warfare research; Colonel W. Bailey, RAMC, British commander of Number Two District in Italy; Colonel Laird at the Ninety-eight General Hospital; and Lieutenant Colonel P. T. L. Day of the Eighty-four General Hospital. Supposedly, this was merely a polite but routine routing of the report and Alexander expected no reply. Consequently, he was shocked when he was told a short time later that Prime Minister Churchill did not believe there were any mustard gas casualties at Bari, Italy, on the night of December 2, 1943!

"But I have proof," Alexander insisted when he was informed about the message from Churchill. "There is absolutely no doubt that many of the casualties were victims of mustard exposure. None whatsoever." Colonel Perrin Long, senior medical consultant, North African Theater of Operations, backed Alexander in the diagnosis of the mustard exposure and, after Eisenhower's headquarters was informed that no other conclusion was possible, the medical report was once again forwarded to the British prime minister.

Churchill's reply was immediate. "The symptoms do not sound like mustard gas."

At Allied headquarters it was suggested that, for the sake of cooperation between the British and the Americans, perhaps the cause of the chemical burns should just be stated as, "NYD"—"not yet diagnosed." The medical officers, especially Alexander, refused to change the report, saying that their professional integrity was at stake. Since the report was secret there was no danger of it being used as propaganda by the Axis, they insisted. Just because the prime minister of Great Britain did not want to admit that any seaport con-

trolled by the British had experienced the war's worst poison
gas tragedy was no reason to falsify the medical report on the
victims.

The argument continued for several days, with messages
being relayed back and forth between Americans and British
at a furious pace. Neither side backed down from its position
in the controversy. Eisenhower, convinced that Alexander's
diagnosis was correct, approved the report and it was entered
into the official records. Churchill, on the other hand, directed that all British records be purged of any mention of
mustard and refer to the burns as "due to enemy action."
Many of the British doctors openly supported Alexander, but
officially they could do nothing.

Despite Churchill's edict to the British Medical Corps,
some reports had already been filed concerning the tragedy.
One such paper was the "confidential" report of the Three
New Zealand General Hospital which stated, in part:

> 99 cases were taken in 3 NZGH on 2/3 Decem-
> ber 43 following an air raid. As previously stated
> these persons had been immersed in the sea (follow-
> ing destruction of ships in the harbour). They were
> extremely cold and wet; suffering from severe de-
> gree of shock; in some cases from very severe
> injuries and almost all were covered to a greater or
> lesser extent with a thick deposit of fuel oil. They
> were divided up at first into two groups:
>
> (a) Those suffering from physical injuries and
> "flash" burns of the face and hands—admitted
> to Surgical wards.
>
> (b) Those suffering from shock consequent on
> immersion, and as was thought at that time,
> from the effects of "blast"—admitted to Med-
> ical wards.
>
> In the first few hours there were several deaths.
> After resuscitation, operations were performed on
> the most seriously injured, including two craniotomies
> for depressed fracture of the skull, and one amputa-
> tion through the lower third of the tibia.
>
> At the end of twelve hours a number of patients
> began to complain of pain in the eyes and blistering
> about the face and the neck. The signs in these

cases were different from those diagnosed as "flash" burns in that there was no singeing of the eyebrows or hair. Rapid degeneration of general condition occurred in a number of cases and coincidentally extensive areas of blistering of covered parts of the body, notably axillary, perineal and scrotal regions appeared. These were diagnosed as "chemical" burns. Information was received that the water and oil in which they had been immersed was contaminated with a concentration of mustard gas. Thereupon those cases showing blistering and a severe degree of conjunctivitis were transferred to one ward.

Post Mortem examinations were carried out on 10 cases. Certain findings were similar in all cases and in one group there were additional abnormal pathological appearances. Briefly described these were:

Group A. (5 cases):

(1) Very extensive loss of superficial skin over face, hands, arms, buttocks, lateral wall of chest and scrotal regions.

(2) Brownish pigmentation of remaining skin.

(3) Marked chemosis of conjunctivae.

(4) Intense congestion and oedema of larynx, severe degree of tracheitis (in two cases showing minute areas of actual ulceration). Similar congestion of upper end of oesophagus with pallor of the remainder of the oesophagus beyond the cricoid cartilage.

Group B. (5 cases):

Similar findings as (1) to (4) above.

(5) Signs of "blast" injury to lungs in all cases— also in one case in heart and kidneys.

These signs were subserous hemorrhages plus other characteristic areas of hemorrhage deeper in the organs concerned.

Owing to transfer of most of these patients to other hospitals, their subsequent history is incomplete. Three patients, however, remained till 23 December, 1943, and they, as well as two still under treatment in Ward 13, show no after effects of

conjunctivitis and are healing satisfactorily without
scar formation of "burnt" area.

                    L. A. Bennett
                    Lt. Col., NZMC
                    O. i/c Surgical Division

The war diary of Ninety-eight British General Hospital
records on the Bari air raid noted: "Casualties continue to
arrive from bombed area. Figures total 444 excluding 19
admitted dead. Of this number 331 are mustard gas burns
which are being diagnosed 'Dermatitis N.Y.D.' later called
'Burns Enemy Action.'"

In the hospital's quarterly report there was additional
reference made to the Bari victims as follows: "... an unusual
episode has been the case of over 200 cases of mustard gas
lesions. This followed an accidental explosion due to an air
raid. The outstanding features were the high death rate from
systemic disturbances in the first 48 hours when 17 patients
died—all without respiratory complications and all with a
well-developed picture of cardio-circulatory failure which failed
to respond to the usual resuscitation measures—plasma infusions and oxygen administrations."

Another statement was made later that pertained to the
German air strike against the Italian port: "During the War of
1939–45 fortunately the only series of cases (casualties from
war gases) that had to be dealt with came from the successful
German air attack on shipping in Bari harbor."

As though to settle the argument once and for all, the
U.S. Army report on casualties aboard the Liberty ship *John
Harvey* referred to the lethal cargo aboard the vessel, the
mustard that Alexander had diagnosed as the cause of the
mysterious deaths. Dated 20 April 1944, it stated:

MEMORANDUM TO: Chief, Casualty Branch,
                    A.G.O.
          SUBJECT: Review and Determination
                    of Status of Persons Miss-
                    ing in Action as the Result
                    of the Sinking of the S.S.
                    John Harvey.

1. Facts: a. The following officers and enlisted men
have been carried on the records of this office as
missing in action since 2 December 1943 in the

North African area following an attack by enemy airplanes on the S.S. *John Harvey* on which they were passengers:

Beckstrom, Howard D.	0-1035557	First Lieutenant
Hines, Aubrey A.	0-392885	First Lieutenant
Tucker, Arthur B.	0-1012701	First Lieutenant
Richardson, Thomas H.	0-1945468	Second Lieutenant
Jamerson, Broadus J.	34,387,714	Sergeant
Taylor, Bennie G.	34,280,849	Private First Class
Thompson, Charles N.	16,111,728	Private First Class
Wilson, Fred	34,424,654	Private First Class
Bodie, Wilson	34,425,224	Private
Tensley, Willie	32,235,802	Private

b. Item 22 attached to the proceedings of a board of officers appointed by the 15th Air Force pursuant to a cable from the North African Theater of Operations, Special Orders 14, Headquarters, 15th Air Force, to investigate the air raid on the harbor at Bari, Italy, 2 December 1943, consists of a casualty report from the Adriatic Base section, Bari, Italy. According to this report all of the personnel listed in paragraph 1a above were passengers aboard the S.S. *John Harvey* and have been missing in action since the raid. It also contains the information that Lieutenant Beckstrom and the six enlisted men were on detached services with the 701st Chemical Maintenance Company and were detailed aboard the ship due to the presence of chemical supplies in the cargo. Lieutenants Tucker and Hines were assigned to the 1st and 13th Armored Regiments respectively; Lieutenant Richardson, Transportation Corps, was serving as Cargo Security Officer.

If further proof was needed, Axis Sally broadcast the news to the world on her nightly program. "I see you boys are getting gassed by your own poison gas," she announced sarcastically over the radio!

Naturally, none of the news releases relating to the bombing of the ships in Bari harbor referred to the mustard. A short North African communiqué was given newsmen on December 4 stating only that "damage was done. There were a number of casualties." A fortnight later the Washington *Post* broke the story of just how devastating the German air strike had been—still with no mention of the mustard. "Bari" according to the *Post* "was the costliest sneak attack since Pearl Harbor. Of the thirty-odd ships in the harbor, at least seventeen had been sunk— among them five U.S. Merchantmen. Casualties totaled at least one thousand."

A high administration official made a very accurate forecast when he said, "You're going to hear more about that raid before you hear less. Somebody at Bari underestimated the Nazis."

Secretary of War Henry L. Stimson was extremely angry by the news leak since he had intended to have another news conference that same day and release further official details. He held the news conference as scheduled, but was brusque, stiff, and curt to the reporters. When a reporter asked if the Allies had actually been caught napping at Bari, Stimson snapped, "No! I will not comment on this thing."

In all probability, Stimson was fearful that the world might learn conclusively that many of the casualties at Bari had died from exposure to poison gas—poison gas from one of the Allied ships. The news from Bari was bad enough. If the world had learned about the mustard it would have been worse, much worse.

18

"THEY DIE SO SUDDENLY, DOCTOR!"

There were 617 known mustard casualty cases among the military and merchant marine personnel at Bari on the night of December 2, 1943, and 13.6 percent of these casualties proved fatal. The true number will never be known, nor will the number of civilians who died from the mustard ever be learned. When it is considered that of the 70,752 men hospitalized for gas in World War I only 2 percent died, as against the more than 13 percent in Bari, the tragedy is magnified. In Alexander's summary to his "Final Report of Bari Mustard Casualties," dated June 29, 1944, he stated:

Summary.
1. There were 617 known mustard casualties from the Bari harbor episode and 13.6 percent of these casualties proved fatal.
2. The fatal casualties were due primarily to exposure to a mustard in oil solution for prolonged periods of time.
3. Unusual hemodynamic changes and shock were the dominant initial picture. This was related to the extent of sub-total surface burns and to the mustard agent.
4. Blast injuries of sub-lethal severity were an important pulmonary complication, upon which the superimposition of exposure to realitively mild vapor inhalation proved serious and fatal.
5. Systemic effects were severe and of greater significance than has been associated with mustard burns in the past.
6. Many questions referable to the changes in the

liver, kidney, and hematopoetic system remain
not explained, and solutions, if desired, must be
found by experimental work.

7. The type casualty described is not likely to be
reproduced to this degree in any tactical employment of mustard if the opportunity for prolonged
absorption is obviated.

8. The definitive treatment of mustard casualties
proved discouraging.

The last statement was uttered again and again by the
medical staffs of all nations at Bari during the period that
the mustard victims were being treated. Some of the patients
were not seriously affected and recovered within a few days,
but many of the casualties completely puzzled the nurses and
doctors, primarily because there never had been a similar
episode in any war. As far as is known, there was never
another situation where the casualties were immersed bodily
in a solution containing mustard. In World War I the gas was
usually delivered in vapor form by the Germans and the
inhalation of the agent caused the casualties. A few handling
accidents in World War II hospitalized a small number of
men, either because they inhaled the mustard vapor or were
burned by the liquid mustard. Bari, however, was the first
and only time on record where the toxic agent mixed with
fuel oil and the men were saturated with the lethal solution.
Consequently the treatment for such victims was not known
but was improvised as each hour passed. Many of the cases
documented in Alexander's final report on the incident indicated the medical problems encountered and give an eyewitness account of the suffering and death that resulted from the
mustard exposure.

Case 1

1. Clinical Sheet on Lt. _____, R.M. Officer, 86
General Hospital.

> 3 Dec. 43 Was on deck of a motor torpedo
> boat during air raid on Dec. 2, 1943.
> He was splashed with water and oil.
> Five or six hours later he developed
> soreness of his face and irritation of
> his eyes. Ship remained in harbor
> all night.
>
> 4 Dec. 43 Admitted 1200 hours. Mild conjunc-

tivitis with some mild fear of light.
No blistering of forehead or face.
Atropine to eyes. Saline wash outs,
calamine to face.

5 Dec. 43 Small blisters appeared on chin,
deep in beard. Dust with sulfonamide powder.

6 Dec. 43 Eyes normal. Skin of face pigmented
but not sore. Beard area satisfactory.
Fit to return to Transient Camp.
Discharged.

Comment: A very mild eye casualty from mustard in
oil solution.

Case 2

1. Clinical Sheet on C.P.O. _____, 86 General
Hospital.

5 Dec. 43 Arrived 2330 hours. Exposed to irritant vapor during air raid on Bari,
2 Dec. 43 at 2000 hours. Was on
duty barefooted in engine room at
time. Was sprayed with contaminated oily water. Had no treatment
until arrival.

6 Dec. 43 1. Conjunctivitis—Eyes irrigated
with boric acid. 2. Left ear, left
side of neck, scalp 2nd degree burns.
Blisters opened and amyl salicylate
applied. 3. Both feet blistered—
opened.

8 Dec. 43 Eyes well. Neck and feet—vaseline
gauze. Scrotum sore—calamine.

11 Dec. 43 Left ear discharging—clean with boric. Neck—improving. Feet—
vaseline gauze.

17 Dec. 43 Ear much better. Neck—healed.
Right foot—healed. Left foot septic—
vaseline sulfanilamide. Scrotum—
sore.

19 Dec. 43 Penis slightly infected. Clean with
Eusol. Vaseline gauze.

21 Dec. 43 Penis satisfactory. Foot comfortable.
Ear slight discharge.

22 Dec. 43 Foot healing well. Ear dry. Penis healing.

24 Dec. 43 Good progress. Feet almost healed. Penis healed. Ear slight watery discharge.

29 Dec. 43 Healed dry. Tender pink skin both feet.

4 Jan. 44 Return to unit.

Comment: This record is typical of many of the moderately severe skin lesions.

Despite the fact that this was only a typical case, the patient was hospitalized for a period of thirty days. The loss of such men for a month seriously affected the war effort on land, sea, and in the air. Most of the military personnel in Bari on the night of the German air strike were skilled men, needed for the openings in new and established units based in southern Italy; their loss was critical to the Allied war effort. Of course, some of the casualties were hospitalized much longer, some were so serious that they had to be evacuated eventually to better-equipped hospitals in North Africa or the United States. Many died.

Case 3

Clinical Sheet on Sub. Lieut. _____, R.N. Officer, 84 General Hospital.

2 Dec. 43 1930 hours. Was on deck of motor torpedo boat during air raid at Bari on 2 Dec. 43 when ammunition ship blew up. He was sprayed with water and oil but otherwise was not in the water. He was able to change clothes and have a bath at 0400 hours on 3 Dec. Noticed irritation of eyes and genitals an hour or so later.

3 Dec. 43 2300 hours. 1. Mild inflammation of mucous membrane that lines inner surface of eyelids. Atropine 1 percent. Saline washes. 2. Blistering of neck, lumbar region, elbows, scrotum, and penis. Blisters evacuated.

	Amyl salicylate to all except genitals. Calamine there.
5 Dec. 43	Complains of cough. Must stop smoking. Penis—vaseline gauze.
7 Dec. 43	Improving. Blister on back painful. Sulfonamide vaseline.
10 Dec. 43	Eyes normal. No further treatment. Penis and scrotum infected. Back very painful.
15 Dec. 43	Depressed. White cell count 11,400.
21 Dec. 43	Inflammation of penis. Dorsal slit performed.
22 Dec. 43	Saline dressings and flavine paraffin. Cod liver oil to back.
29 Dec. 43	Improving. Back still painful.
6 Jan. 44	Improving. Back painful. Two raw areas in lumbar region.
14 Jan. 44	Complains still of cough. No physical signs in lungs. X-ray lungs N.A.D. (No active disease).
15 Jan. 44	Fit to return to unit to continue treatment. Should receive one week convalescent and one week light duty.

Comment: This demonstrates the problem in the care of the genital lesions even though this was not a severe casualty.

If nothing else, the mustard disaster at Bari proved the fact that exposure to this toxic agent, especially when persons are immersed in a solution containing it, disables a man as far as performing his military duty is concerned for a considerable length of time. A minor wound received at the front lines could be healed and the victim back on full duty many days sooner than if the same man were exposed to mustard.

Of great interest to the doctors present at Bari during the tragedy was the cause of death among the mustard casualties. It was one of the few opportunities, tragic as it was, that the medical men had to study such a large number of victims, and much valuable information was gained that proved very useful in future years. Such a victim was hospitalized at the Ninety-eight General Hospital.

Case 4

Clinical Sheet on Seaman _____, age 18, 6 months
service, died 4 December 1943. 98 General Hospital.

2 Dec. 43   Brought in following air raid. Cold
              and shocked. No injuries requiring
              surgical attention. Received resusci-
              tation. Covered in oil. He was ra-
              tional.

3 Dec. 43   Oil has been removed. Marked uni-
              form erythema (excess of blood) with
              some blisters forming around neck.
              There was radial pulse. Able to sit
              up. Dangerously ill list.

4 Dec. 43   0915 hours. Patient unconscious.
              Gasping. No radial pulse and no
              cardiac sounds heard. Laid flat. Foot
              of bed raised and oxygen given. In-
              travenous plasma drip started and
              two pints run in under pressure in
              twenty minutes. Two capsules of
              anacardine given. Cardiac sounds
              gradually returned and the neck pulse
              was evident after about fifteen min-
              utes. Wrist pulse never returned.
              At 1150 hours two pints more plas-
              ma being run in at speed of 80
              drops per minute. Skin has bluish
              tinge.
              1530 hours. Patient died suddenly.
              A matter of seconds after asking
              nursing orderly for a drink. He was
              extremely congested in the skin of
              the face at the time.

Since this was one of the "mysterious" cases of death, a
post-mortem report of the autopsy was made.

General.

The body was that of a well-nourished man.
Externally the following features were observed: no
bruises on corpse noted though rigidity was marked;
there were dusky patches of skin seen over the
anterior chest, abdomen and thighs; the back also

displayed this phenomenon but to a lesser degree. The penis was much swollen. It was observed that the epidermis was easily dislodged on handling the body, the underlying cutis being of a livid pink. The lips were dull black in color.

The chest was opened.

There was no free fluid in the cavities and the lungs were shrunken in appearance. The tongue, oesophagus, trachea, and contents of the thorax were removed en masse. Tongue appeared normal, oesophagus displayed a curious black longitudinal streaking, most marked at its lower end. This did not wash off and was probably due to the presence of altered blood. There was excessive fluid in the tissue at the opening between the vocal folds at the base of the tongue with much enlargement of the windpipe throughout its length.

Lungs.

Both organs were light, airless, very congested and of a peculiar rubberlike consistency. Some sections were blackish red in color.

Heart.

No abnormality found.

Abdomen.

Stomach showed the same black areas as were observed in the oesophagus only they were more diffuse.

The remaining organs examined during the autopsy appeared fairly normal. This autopsy was conducted on December 5, 1943, only two days after the German air strike and before Alexander had uncovered the fact that the victims had been exposed to mustard. While there were some abnormal factors determined by the autopsy, there was not enough evidence at this time for the unsuspecting doctors to detect the toxic agent exposure symptoms. This death demonstrated the early type of death during the tragic episode at Bari and the total lack of response to the usual methods of resuscitation. Another victim admitted to the Ninety-eight General Hospital the same night reacted similarly. He was admitted smothered in oil, with a swelling of the upper lip, laceration of the right foot, and suffering from shock. Plasma drip was started immediately, but, by 6:00 P.M. on December 3, he was listed as critical. He had blisters of the neck, arms, chest, back and both legs which were opened and dusted with sulfanilamide and dressed with dry gauze. His pulse was very fast and at 4:30 A.M. on December 4 it stopped, then resumed. The patient was delirious and very restless. Oxygen was tried but he could not retain the mask. Toward the end his pain was relieved by morphia and at 2100 hours on the fourth of December he died.

The autopsy showed that this case was practically identical to that of the eighteen-year-old seaman who died earlier. There was the striking observation that the surface of the body failed to show the typical postmortem appearance of lividity, did not have the reddish or bluish discoloration usually associated with a corpse. The skin was pink and after removal of the outer layer looked like living tissue. Except for bleeding, the body was identical to those seen in an operating room. There was little wonder that the doctors were perplexed at this stage of the tragedy.

Another enigma was added to the medical mystery with the death of a twenty-two-year-old fireman at the Ninety-eight General Hospital.

Case 5

1. Clinical Sheet on Fireman ————, age 22 years, died 11 December 1943. 98 General Hospital.

2 Dec. 43 Involved in bombing of harbor. Ship sunk. Immersed oily water four (4) hours. Admitted in state of shock. Wrapped in blankets and given morphia.

3 Dec. 43 Appearance of erythema (excess of blood) in the skin of whole body with blistering developing all over neck, arms, trunk, back, and in area of scrotum.

5 Dec. 43 2300 hours. Collapsed—cold and clammy. Blood pressure not taken. Plasma started.

6 Dec. 43 1500 hours. Plasma changed to very slow. Still looks ill and constantly calling and complaining. Pulse full and strong. Dangerously ill list.

7 Dec. 43 Looking more exhausted. Copious spit.

8 Dec. 43 Pulse full and strong. Quieter and much less peevish. Cough less and looking generally fitter.

9 Dec. 43 Further improvement. Mentally normal and cooperative. Marked water-hammer pulse.

10 Dec. 43 Rise of temperature to 100.6. Pulse 140. Respiration 32. Represents a very sudden rise of all three. Can still speak but voice is hoarse and is quite rational but looks in dying condition (moribund).

11 Dec. 43 1330 hours, died.

Comment: This case demonstrates the blood pressure variation seen in the earlier stages. The patient recovered from the acute system upset only to die of pulmonary infection superimposed upon a blast injured lung.

This death occurred due to the action of the mustard on a lung that had been injured during the explosions in the harbor on the night of the German air raid. The lung injury itself would not have proven fatal, but the exposure to the toxic agent and the lack of treatment for this exposure due to the fact that the doctors were unaware of its existence led to the fireman's death and the death of many other victims. It became obvious, however, that the patients were dying due to the late results of some unknown factor and other autopsies were performed at British hospitals in an effort to uncover more clues.

Case 6

1. Clinical Sheet on 1st Seaman _____, age 24, died 12 December, 1943. 98 General Hospital.

2 Dec. 43 Admitted after raid. Was not entirely in the water. Was rowing in a boat, and put hands in water when helping survivors. When a bomb hit the ship, he was covered with oil and water. Was two hours in wet

clothes. Eyes commenced to burn almost immediately after the bomb explosion. Skin became irritable half an hour later, noticed that his arms and privates, and legs were especially bad when near the heat of the flames. Had sickness and vomiting on admission.

3 Dec. 43   Severe sore throat. Eyes very painful, and scrotum, arms and legs irritable. Body red, skin hot. Thickening of skin.

4 Dec. 43   Transferred to Ward 2. Throat worse, eyes improved, general condition improved slightly. Pulse rapid, volume good. Blisters large and tense both arms from above elbows to wrists, down both thighs to below knees. Skin hot, thickening.

6 Dec. 43   General condition unchanged. Throat still very painful. Thick yellow sputum, blood stained. Skin irritable. Generalized tiny white blisters on body and arms. Skin red and hot. Otherwise as before.

7 Dec. 43   Throat painful. Soreness center of chest. Cough with yellow pus tinged with blood. Pulse 120. Chest, windpipe, lungs are normal. Anterior surface of body, chest, abdomen still multiple tiny white blisters. Several new blisters on right arm and left thigh. Penis peeling, soggy.

10 Dec. 43   Condition poor. Throat still very sore. Cough and bronchitis. Pulse 120, soft, fair volume.

11 Dec. 43   General condition unchanged. Appeared to be taking slightly more notice of things and people around him. Skin peeling. Discoloration fading slightly. Throat still sore.

12 Dec. 43   Pulseless. General condition poor. Given oxygen but died at 1245 hours.

While these cases were being checked at Ninety-eight General Hospital, the medical staff at Three New Zealand General Hospital was also discovering that their patients were not responding to the normal treatment given to victims suffering from shock, exposure, and blast burns. Often, just when they thought the patient was on his way to recovery, he suddenly and inexplicably died. Such was the case of a fifty-two-year-old chief officer admitted shortly after the Luftwaffe attack.

Case 7

1. Clinical Sheet on Chief Officer _____, age 52 years, 27 years service. Died 14 December 1943. 3 New Zealand General Hospital.

2 Dec. 43 Injured during enemy air raid on 2 December 1943. Sustained burns of face, eyes, shoulders and arms. Was immersed in oily water. Very shocked when admitted. Burns were 2nd degree on shoulders, armpits and upper arms, 1st degree on chest and abdomen. Hoarse voice and cough. Put on intravenous plamsa drip.

4 Dec. 43 Blisters clipped and evacuated. Blood pressure 140/96.

5 Dec. 43 Slight improvement of eyes. Coughing a good deal. General condition improved on the whole.

(It was at this point in the patient's treatment at all the Bari hospitals that the doctors and nurses usually thought that he was on his way to recovery.)

6 Dec. 43 General condition fair. Coughing still, no blood. Burns redressed.

7 Dec. 43 Still coughing a good deal with a large amount of sputum. Fairly comfortable.

9 Dec. 43 Bronchitic still. Burns dry and fairly clean.

11 Dec. 43 Still coughing. Rather irrational.

13 Dec. 43 Voice—whisper only. Chest—bronchi both sides. Burns drying up

except on buttocks. 1800 hours—
condition somewhat worse.

14 Dec. 43 Died 1400 hours.

Comment: The severe increase in the concentration of blood cells resulting from the loss of plasma or water from the blood stream that initially threatened the life of this victim was resolved by the hospital staff only to have the patient succumb to an infection.

The infection was, of course, due to the late results of the mustard. As this fact became recognized after Alexander's investigation, there were still many deaths because the proper treatment for the mustard-oil-water exposure to part or all of the body for a considerable length of time was not known in 1943, but mention of the mustard began to appear in both the clinical sheets and postmortem autopsies.

Case 8

1. Clinical Sheet of 1st Seaman _____, age 21, 1 year service. Died January 1944. 98 General Hospital.

2 Dec. 43 Ship exploded. Jumped into water. Immersed for half-hour.

3 Dec. 43 Mild inflammation of the eyes. Legs, buttocks, wrists, arms discolored by excess of blood cells. Blistering of wrists, buttocks and legs extensive.

6 Dec. 43 Condition good. Blisters which increased considerably in extent were treated by puncture, sulfonamide powder and dry gauze.

10 Dec. 43 General condition poor. Querulous and irritable. Dangerously ill list. Temperature 99.2. Pulse 120. Blood pressure 110/30.

15 Dec. 43 General condition in status quo. Burns look very infected. Large patches of 3rd degree. Sputum blood stained.

16 Dec. 43 Half pint fresh blood.

19 Dec. 43 Burns dressed sterile Vaseline gauze.

Very weak and exhausted. Large amount of frothy sputum.

22 Dec. 43 Condition improving. Chest has numerous moist sounds all over.

26 Dec. 43 Condition much improved. Foul black-green sputum. Complains of pain in left chest.

(At this point it was considered that the patient was getting better, that it was merely a matter of time until he could be discharged.)

29 Dec. 43 Condition much worse. Breathing is labored. Color poor. Chest anterior NAD (no active disease) other than usual moist sounds. Impossible to examine back because patient is too weak. Very distressed.

30 Dec. 43 Drainage tube inserted between the ribs under local anesthesia. Patient more comfortable. Breathing less labored.

31 Dec. 43 Draining well. Drained 18 ounces.

1 Jan. 44 Worse. Trying to pull out tubes. Breathing very labored after coughing spells. Numerous moist sounds all over chest.

3 Jan. 44 Died, 0300 hours.

Comment: A late complication of the burns due to (enemy action) an unusual agent.

Since this death was one of the first that occurred after it was known that the victims had been exposed to the mustard, a part of the autopsy report is interesting.

Post Mortem Report on 1st Class Seaman _____, died 3 Jan. 1944.

General External Appearance.

The body was that of an adult blond male of average height and build. There was some loss of tissue beneath the skin but not to the state of emaciation. Post mortem rigidity was present and post mortem lividity was evident in the dependent parts. The whole body showed evidence of recent

peeling of the surface skin. Third degree burns were
present in the small of the back, the buttocks and
above the ankles. The skin over the right knee bone
was completely absent. A large dirty ulcer extended
into the knee sacs. The wrists and penis showed
destruction of the skin.

Neck and Thorax

On opening the chest the lungs were found to
be distended and failed to collapse. A thick pus was
found in the left lung. The right cavity contained
about three-quarters of a pint of fluid. The base of
the tongue and adjacent parts were not congested.
The oesophagus in its upper two-thirds appeared
normal; in the lower third the wall was thinner than
normal and presented the appearance of post mortem
auto-digestion [digestion of wall by gastric juice].
The windpipe was congested in lower extremity and
contained yellow pus.

Lungs

Both lungs were voluminous, pink, and somewhat firm to the touch. This was particularly obvious in the left lung and the right lower lobe. The
left lung was coated over almost its entire surface
with a layer of dense pus. The lobes themselves on
the left side were loosely gummed together. Numerous small abscesses were present in the lungs which
were mottled pink and mauve but showed little
evidence of blast.

There was little else in the autopsy that showed the
organs examined to be abnormal. The heart, except for that
fact that it was a little pale, showed nothing abnormal and no
valvular disease was found. The left side of the chest cavity
was covered with the same dense pus that had been found on
the lung surface. The liver was of normal size and did not
appear externally diseased as in the majority of cases. The
doctors initially thought that the mustard was affecting this
organ more violently than any other in the body and perhaps
causing death, but this theory was later abandoned. The
spleen, pancreas, bladder, prostate, and lymph glands, except for being pale, were all normal. It was discovered that
the kidneys were somewhat soft and, on section, the capsules

were found to strip very easily, leaving a pale, mauve surface. The stomach walls were so thin that they were transparent and certain areas ruptured on the slightest pressure. It was suggested that further tests of this organ, at a better-equipped laboratory, were required to obtain conclusive results.

It was decided by the medical staff at the Ninety-eight General Hospital that this case demonstrated very clearly the late effects of mustard vapor exposure. While the victim had been immersed in the oil-mustard mixture for approximately half an hour and had received severe external body burns, his death came because of the poison gas vapor he had inhaled. This vapor was present in the smoke which rolled over the harbor that night and also was emitted from the oil-mustard mixture on the surface of the water when the mixture caught fire. The hundreds of civilians, especially in the old section of Bari, who were subjected to the smoke-mustard vapor that night all inhaled the poison gas fumes. Without proper medical care a large percentage of these casualties died and their deaths were either not recorded or were listed as "due to enemy action." Military reports and memoirs written later mentioning this air raid indicated that "an offshore wind" carried the vapor out to sea. Those who were at Bari on the night of December 2, 1943, emphasize that the smoke covered the city, that in the part of the city bordering the Adriatic Sea it was so dense the citizens had trouble breathing or seeing because of its volumn, even before the mustard fumes affected their eyes and lungs.

The clinical sheet and post-mortem reports on a large number of the casualties who died in late December or early January clearly indicate the fatal "late results" of the mustard. The patient would have burns and blisters on his body and these would be treated and his condition would begin to improve. Suddenly he would have trouble breathing, he would lose his voice, he would expectorate large quantities of foul-smelling sputum that was often blood-stained and his pulse would weaken. Despite emergency measures, the patient would die. The true number of deaths, military or civilian, will never be known. Those who died in the Bari area hospitals were recorded and the cause of death accurately determined after it was known that the men had been exposed to the mustard. The patients who died from the toxic agent were known and their medical records were kept separate from those who died from blast burns or injuries, enemy fire, or drowning. But this was only a small number of the actual casualties. Many of the American patients were transferred to hospitals in other parts of Italy, to Sicily, North Africa, Great Britain, and the United States, and died before it was realized that they had been exposed to mustard. Thus, the records do not indicate the true reason for their deaths. Secrecy was another important factor in producing inaccurate records, since many U.S. and Allied military and political leaders agreed with Prime Minister Churchill that no mention of the poison gas should be made or the fact that there was mustard aboard an Allied ship in Bari harbor verified. They felt that the Axis would use the revelation as propaganda and possibly turn world opinion against the Allies.

Due to Churchill's decision that no mention of the mustard be made and that all deaths be attributed to "burns due to enemy action," British records were purged of any deaths caused by the mustard. This head-in-the-sand attitude of the British and especially Prime Minister Churchill, not only made an accurate count of the toxic agent casualties impossible, but his action in attempting to convince General Eisenhower at Allied Force Headquarters that no mention of the mustard should be made also resulted in additional civilian casualties. Even those Italians who returned from the countryside after abandoning the city the day after the German air strike and sought medical help for their mysterious ailments were not treated for mustard because of the delay in revealing the truth to the hospitals, because of Churchill's obstinate action. Italian doctors were not told the real reason for the deaths either, so patients they received were treated for the normal exposure, shock, and exhaustion besides the blast burns and injuries. Consequently, a much larger percentage of those who could possibly have been saved, since their exposure was minimal, died because of lack of proper treatment, even after Alexander had uncovered the mustard exposure.

Not all those exposed to the mustard died, of course. Some, such as Captain Heitmann, had a long, but successful, recovery never knowing what had actually happened to them at Bari that fateful night. Heitmann was considered well enough by December 29, 1943, that he was evacuated from the Seventy Station hospital in Naples to make room for seriously wounded frontline casualties and slept in a hospital tent near the airport that night awaiting transportation to

North Africa for further hospitalization. At 10:00 A.M. on December 30 he left Naples on a transport plane and, after a stop at Palermo, Sicily, arrived at the U.S. Army Twenty-four General Hospital at Bizerte. The hospital was cold, overcrowded, and understaffed and Heitmann decided he would be much better off if he could get back to the U.S. for further treatment. Despite the fact that he did not know the true cause of his symptoms, except for his injured back and shrapnel-lacerated hand, the captain sensed he needed expert medical aid and was determined to get it. His rank of sea captain helped him do just that.

On New Year's Day, 1944, Heitmann finally convinced the doctors at the Twenty-four General hospital at Bizerte that he was well enough to carry on if he could receive fast transportation to the U.S. He was evacuated from the hospital and stayed at the home of the war shipping representative that night while a priority letter for transportation was sought. The following day he flew to Algiers where he put up at the USS Club until January 3 when he received travel orders from Eisenhower's headquarters giving him a high priority for a flight home. Before he took off for the U.S. a doctor examined him once again.

"Avoid all unnecessary talking and get as much rest as you can," he advised the captain. "Your throat doesn't look good."

Heitmann nodded. He was well aware that after talking for an hour or so during the day he would lose his voice entirely. Something was radically wrong with his throat but he did not know what it was.

He finally arrived home, via airplane and ship, on January 18, 1944, where he insisted on reporting to the port director's office in New York to return the secret documents that he had saved from the *John Bascom*'s safe and carried with him during the ensuing weeks. He then, finally, submitted to further medical treatment.

Heitmann lived, and so did many of the other casualties who had been subjected to the mustard. Luck, prompt treatment at the hospital for symptoms not pertaining to the exposure to the toxic agent, a change of clothes, stronger personal resistance, and other factors often decided whether a patient lived or died after the Bari tragedy. It was nearly a flip-of-the-coin gamble among those exposed to the poison gas. Bari was a new experience for the Allies, one that was confusing and misunderstood, as a section of Alexander's "Final Report of Bari Mustard Casualties" indicates:

> While experimental studies will be necessary to answer the many questions raised by this group of casualties, it seems clearly established that the systemic effects of mustard, under certain circumstances, may be profound and the important factor in individual cases. This clinical picture is not that likely to be encountered in any tactical employment save in a chemical beach defense. If the opportunity for prolonged absorption is prevented, few serious casualties should result.
>
> The securing of complete and accurate data of a major accident or disaster is all too often not considered until the most profitable time for obtaining information has passed. All attention initially is directed to so-called life saving measures and alleviation of suffering. A disaster, such as this, or the initiation of a hostile chemical attack, presents an unusual and unique opportunity for the study of specialized type of trauma. At the same time it is imperative that guidance and assistance be immediately given the medical officers dealing with casualties, as the nature of the disaster must be known in order to proceed intelligently.
>
> To understand the type of trauma involved in each episode it is necessary to discern and delineate the pattern of the casualties as they are occurring. By appraising the nature and volume of the physical and chemical forces applied, the time intervals, and the clinical features and complications as they present themselves, it is possible to sketch the general pattern of disaster early in the chronology. When the pattern has been made clear, prompt and intelligent therapy procedures can be coordinated and standardized and in the long run better care rendered to all casualties more efficiently.
>
> This is best accomplished by having a skilled observer and technically trained professional man, promptly placed in charge to detail the medical aspects of the disaster and the casualty pattern. He should not be tied down by the immediate require-

ments of first aid and the care of patients or of hospital services. Ideally, he should be a specially qualified man, but the use of any competent clinical or laboratory investigator promptly is of more immediate value than a specialist several days removed.

These comments are not intended as a criticism of the handling of the situation by the authorities at Bari. It is felt that there was most exemplary devotion to duty upon the part of the medical personnel present; and that the professional care was splendid considering the difficulties and handicaps under which they were laboring. Rather, these comments are intended as a plea for more adequate planning for possible future episodes of disaster medicine.

19

"WE NEED SHIPS, MEN AND SUPPLIES!"

The German Air Force strike at Bari resulted in the second greatest shipping disaster for the Allies during World War II. The loss of seventeen merchant ships was a tragic blow since shipping was needed for several planned military operations decided upon at the Teheran Conference by Roosevelt, Churchill, and Stalin, in addition to the always-needed supplies for the forces already fighting in southern Italy. Then, too, the new Fifteenth Air Force at Foggia was depending upon its requirements coming through the port of Bari. When the Luftwaffe closed the port with its surprise raid on the night of December 2, 1943, the course of the war in Italy was changed drastically.

The one unalterable decision that had been made at Teheran by the "Big Three" and their respective staffs was that a cross-channel invasion of Europe would be made in May, 1944. Consequently, the bulk of the supplies and equipment coming from the United States after the Teheran Conference was sent to Great Britain to prepare for the greatest invasion in history. Other combat areas, especially the Mediterranean, suffered because of the plans for Operation Overlord. Churchill, who had always favored all-out effort in Italy, felt that the neglect of this theater of war was a serious mistake. A million or more British, British-controlled, and Allied armies were already engaged with the Germans in Italy and he wanted to wage a vigorous campaign regardless of the preparations for the cross-channel invasion. He had reason, some military, some personal.

Churchill believed that the Allied forces in Italy would not only take Rome early in 1944, but would also destroy or capture ten or eleven German divisions at the same time. This would weaken German resistance to Overlord and tie down replacement enemy divisions in Italy during the cross-channel invasion. Also, the Allied forces, once they had captured Rome, would then seize the airfields north of it which would enable the American heavy aircraft to bomb southern Germany. Prior to the Luftwaffe strike at Bari, the British prime minister was so confident of these objectives that he wondered what the Allied forces in Italy would do during the five or six months after the capture of Rome and the northern airfields and the scheduled cross-channel invasion in the spring of 1944.

Nor did the resourceful Churchill overlook the fact that the Italian battle area was mostly British controlled while the cross-channel invasion would primarily be an American operation. Great Britain had most of her troops in action in Italy and in the Pacific and had only a small number of divisions remaining to use in Overlord initially. He was determined that he would play his hand in Italy to the fullest extent—for the prestige of both Great Britain and Winston Churchill.

Unfortunately the conquering of Rome as predicted by Churchill was postponed indefinitely by the stubborn German defenses. With both the British Eighth Army and the Allied Fifth Army blocked by Kesselring's Gustav Line south of Rome, it appeared that any further advance up the Italian Peninsula during the winter months was definitely impossible. The "end run" amphibious landing aimed at putting an Allied force on the beaches at Anzio behind the Gustav Line also appeared doomed since its success depended upon the advance of the Eighth and Fifth armies up the spine of Italy to eventually link with the Anzio forces. During the long days immediately after the Bari raid, when the mustard victims were dying, Churchill's hopes for a successful Italian campaign were also dying. Ill with pneumonia in Carthage after leaving Teheran, the prime minister refused to recognize defeat, however, and, calling his senior Mediterranean commanders together, he tried to find a method of breaking the stalemate that had been imposed by the winter weather, the mountains, and the tenacity of the Germans. He ignored the fact that with the port of Bari closed, it would be many more times difficult to get supplies into Italy. Other ports, such as Naples, were available, but Bari was the best one available to the Allies prior to December 2. Now it was gone.

Shrewd enough to know that the Fifth Army could not possibly reach the Anzio area in time to prevent the amphibious landing force from being destroyed, Churchill looked for another solution to save the operation. He decided that he had found it when he gave orders to his commanders that the landing force should be strengthened so that it could stand by itself on the beach at Anzio against any German counterattacks until the Fifth Army did arrive. Unfortunately this change in plans required building up the assault force with more supplies than anticipated originally while still maintaining the normal flow of supplies to the land-bound troops. With seventeen ships destroyed at Bari, ships that regularly carried supplies to the land-bound troops, and the port itself closed to all shipping, Churchill's new plan for the landing at Anzio was in trouble before the men even boarded the assault boats.

The British commanders had no choice but to attempt the landing as outlined by the prime minister. British Field Marshal Harold Alexander, earl of Tunis, who supported Churchill's plan, prepared a one-page field order for the Fifth Army: "Fifth Army will prepare an amphibious operation of two divisions plus to carry out an assault landing on the beaches in the vicinity of Rome with object of cutting the enemy lines of communication and threatening the rear of the German XIV Corps. This operation will take place between 20 January and 31 January but the target dates should be as near 20 January as possible."

Alexander, more knowledgeable about the importance of the port of Bari, thought that the Italian harbor would be available for use within a few days after the German air strike. He realized that the enemy air raid had been very successful, that seventeen valuable ships and more than a thousand military casualties had been suffered, but he was certain that the "mess" in the harbor would be cleared by salvage crews within a short time and Bari would be back in operation. He was wrong.

Not that the Allied commanders did not make a heroic effort to get the port back into use. The U.S. Navy salvage ships arrived shortly after the disaster and started clearing the harbor under the direction of the Navy's number one salvage expert, Commodore William A. Sullivan. Sullivan, with the help of army engineers, sailors, soldiers, and civilians set about clearing up the "mess." He had experienced a similar situation when the Allied troops occupied Naples two months earlier. The departing Germans had left the harbor in a shambles, but Bari was worse in many respects. There had been no mustard contamination at Naples. However, in order to keep souvenir hunters and harbor thieves away from the sunken ships at Naples while waiting for the heavy-lift ships, Sullivan had posted warning signs, "Danger: Poison Gas!" At Bari there was no need for false warnings. The poison gas statement was true.

Working in complete harmony with the Royal Navy port command, Sullivan and his men cleared the piers of heaps of destroyed equipment, lifted the merchant ship wreckages from the bottom of the harbor where the Luftwaffe bombs had put them, prepared the docks for unloading, and access roads to the harbor were bulldozed through the ruins of buildings near the waterfront. They worked around the clock, but the German bombers had done an excellent job of blocking the port. All the while Sullivan and his men were laboring at the harbor area, bodies kept coming to the surface and were removed by the British. They used small boats to bring the bodies to the edge of the dock, then placed cargo nets under the bodies, and lifted them out of the water. Unloading the bodies into dump trucks, the British vehicles then left for parts unknown. The stench in the harbor area was terrible, nauseating.

Periodically during the salvage operations a ruptured bomb casing, or several such casings, would be brought to the surface with other material. Often these casings were the ones that had held the liquid mustard and, if the men working with Sullivan were careless—or unaware that mustard bombs had been aboard the destroyed *John Harvey*— they were burned by the chemical. The oil-mustard solution on the surface of the water was another hazard, since it dissipated slowly. While the salvage operations were in progress the Chemical Corps experts kept spraying the dock area and spreading lime in an effort to reduce the number of casualties. Three weeks passed before the harbor had any semblance of normal operation, twenty-one crucial days during which the British continued with their plans for the Anzio landing.

By this time even some of the top British military leaders were beginning to have their doubts about the possibility of supplying the troops that would make the amphibious landing on the beach at Anzio. General "Jumbo" Wilson, Eisenhower's successor as supreme allied commander, Mediterranean theater, stated, "Should maintenance not be possible, the force would have to be withdrawn with total loss of equipment, some loss of personnel, and serious risk to landing craft needed for later assault against France." During a meeting at the Villa Taylor in Marrakech, Morocco, where Churchill was still recovering from his pneumonia, it was suggested that the supplies needed for the landing forces be loaded on trucks at Naples with material brought to Italy by merchant ships docking at Bari and Naples, the trucks driven onto the LSTs, and, at the beachhead, the trucks driven off the landing craft directly to supply dumps. This procedure, however, was rejected by the prime minister and, while he gave no specific reason, it is thought that he finally realized that the closing of the port at Bari during December would not permit adequate supplies to reach Naples for the trucks and this obvious discrepancy in the plan for the landing at Anzio would become public knowledge.

Fortunately the Americans of the Fifth Army ignored the prime minister's rejection during the actual operation and loaded what supplies were available on trucks as they had previously suggested. There was a definite shortage since only a small percent of the expected supplies and equipment came across the peninsula to Naples from Bari because the German bombing had closed the port, but "a little was better than nothing."

The most adverse effect of the closing of the port at Bari was felt by the Eighth and Fifth armies, however, as they desperately tried to work their way north. The advance of the Fifth Army was particularly important since the troops scheduled to land at Anzio could only stand off the expected German counterattacks temporarily. They definitely would need the help of the Fifth Army as soon as possible. On January 12, short of men, supplies, and equipment, and with his personnel near exhaustion from continuous fighting over a long period, Clark reopened an offensive against the Germans. Initially it appeared that the Fifth Army was really on the move this time. The French Army Corps advanced ten miles the first day. Less than a week later the British Ten Corps of the Fifth Army moved across the Garigliano River despite heavy losses and, on January 20, only eight days after the offensive began, the U.S. Two Corps pushed across the

Rapido River and established a bridgehead with the idea of passing Monte Cassino and moving along Via Casilina.

It was a good plan, but the German Air Force, more than a month earlier and with no knowledge of the projected Rapido River crossing by the Fifth Army, had defeated the operation by bombing Bari harbor. Once the successful crossing of the river was made, Fifth Army commanders immediately suffered a shortage of supplies. Bad weather was one reason given for the shortage, but the real cause was the fact that the required amount of supplies was just not available. With the port of Naples being used to supply both the Fifth and Eighth armies, plus the Fifteenth Air Force and supporting units, shortages were unavoidable. This one port could not do the work of two. Bari harbor facilities and the ships that were sunk there on December 2 were the difference. Two days after the Rapido River bridgehead was established by the U.S. Two Corps, and on the very day of the Anzio landing, it had to be abandoned.

This defeat on the Rapido doomed the Anzio amphibious landing behind the Gustav Line to a long stalemate, if not actual failure. Kesselring, since he held the entire Italian Peninsula from Monte Cassino to Rome and north, was able to direct his attacks either against the Fifth Army or in the other direction against the troops that landed at Anzio. The German general took advantage of the situation and held both Allied forces at bay, containing the Anzio beachhead for a longer period than any other such amphibious landing force during World War II! Kesselring's surprise attack on Bari paid him handsome dividends during the long winter of 1943-44. The Gustav Line was not to be broken until May, four months after the Anzio landings.

The Bari disaster had a serious effect on the Fifteenth Air Force as well as the Allied ground troops fighting in Italy. Two days after the German air strike at Bari, the Combined Chiefs of Staff had designated the Combined Bomber Offensive, with the designated code name of "Point-blank," as the air operation of first priority for the Fifteenth Air Force stationed at Foggia. At that time little thought was given by the Combined Chiefs of Staff to the aviation fuel, bombs, and other equipment lost during the bombing of Bari nor the fact that the port would be closed to shipping for a considerable length of time. The overall planning for the cross-channel invasion the following spring or summer and the strategic bombing objectives that had to be accomplished prior to this invasion were uppermost in their thoughts. The bombing of Bari was only a single incident to them, one among many that they knew about, but often did not have the time to evaluate thoroughly. In the case of Bari, they glossed over the vital importance of the Adriatic seaport to the Foggia airfield complex.

Perhaps one of the reasons for overlooking the importance of the port at Bari to future plans for the Allied air forces in Italy was the reorganization that was taking place at this time. With Overlord planning taking top priority, many senior military leaders, such as Eisenhower, Doolittle, and others, were transferred to Great Britain for new duties. Lieutenant General Ira C. Eaker assumed command of the Mediterranean Allied Air Forces which was composed of three distinct air forces—strategic, tactical, and coastal. The Fifteenth Air Force was the strategic unit and was under the command of Major General Nathan F. Twining after Doolittle went to England to take over direction of the Eighth Air Force. Eaker was forced to divide his time between problems of organization and the pressing demands of combat and, at the moment, the bombing of Bari was an irritation, nothing more. The Tactical Air Force of the Mediterranean Allied Air Forces, under the command of Major General John K. Cannon, was given the prime task of providing air support for the landings at Anzio with the assurance that, if necessary, the Fifteenth Air Force would help. It was the Tactical Air Force's assignment to bomb enemy airfields to insure that the Luftwaffe would be unable to interfere with the landings, to bomb lines of communications between Rome and the north and between Anzio and the main battle area so that enemy reinforcements and supplies could not be brought in or shifted from one front to another, and to cut the supply line between Pisa-Florence and Rome. To insure the success of the Anzio landings, the accomplishment of these objectives was an absolute necessity. To accomplish the objectives, supplies such as aviation fuel, bombs, and ammunition were also an absolute necessity. Unfortunately, until December 2, 1943, most of these necessities arrived in Italy through the port of Bari, which was now closed.

B-25s of the Tactical Air Force began the pre-Anzio landing bombardments on January 2, 1944, by attacking the Terni railroad yards, while seventy-five B-26s bombed four

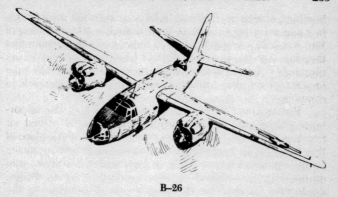

B–26

places on the railway east of Nice. For the following ten days the Tactical Air Force bombers of the Mediterranean Allied Air Force attacked the Italian railway system, concentrating on the western and central parts of the peninsula. Through the thirteenth of the month these air attacks on communications had been planned to slow down the building up of supplies by the Germans in the Anzio area. In the final week before the planned landings at Anzio by the Allies it was essential that the German supply lines, both above and below Rome, be completely blocked, since the battlefield had to be isolated if the Anzio landing was to have any hope of success. If the Germans were still able to rush down reinforcements to the Anzio area from Rome and the north or able to move large quantities of supplies to the same area, the beachhead forces would be in serious trouble.

On January 10, when it became evident to the officers of the Tactical Air Force that they needed help if these objectives were to be attained, the Strategic Air Force, namely the Fifteenth Air Force, was asked to help. The overall plan devised by Eaker at that time was for the Fifteenth Air Force to bomb the northern-most communications targets while the Tactical Air Force would take care of the railway lines nearer to Rome, notably those between that city and Arezzo, Viterbo, and Leghorn. What happened at this time has never been adequately explained, but, for some reason, several days elapsed before this joint operation actually started. In fact, the Fifteenth Air Force did not fly any of the Anzio missions until January 16, six days after the initial request. One explanation that was offered later was that the Tactical Air Force was waiting for a blanket order from the Mediterranean Allied Air Force Headquarters to detail to what extent the Strategic Air Force could be used while the Mediterranean Allied Air Force Headquarters was waiting for a bombing plan from the Tactical Air Force so it could issue a directive to the Strategic Air Force. Nearly one entire week of air attacks was lost at any rate, at a time when the bombing of the railway lines used by the Germans was critical.

Was this delay actually the result of the Fifteenth Air Force waiting for badly needed supplies to arrive? Supplies to replace those that were lost at Bari and those that were destined to be shipped to Bari for forwarding to Foggia during the period that the harbor was closed due to the German Air Force attack of December 2, 1943? Many military experts think this was the reason for the delay between the Tactical Air Force's request for help on the tenth of January and the Fifteenth Air Force's first mission in response to the request on the sixteenth. One fact is certain, however. The objective considered absolutely necessary by the planners of the Anzio beachhead landing—that of sealing off German reinforcements and supplies from the north—was not accomplished by the Fifteenth Air Force. The usual effectiveness of the heavy bombers was blunted during this period, resulting in the unfortunate situation that the Germans, instead of the Allies, sealed off the beachhead. Kesselring moved his divisions around the battle area and from other parts of Italy at will.

Initially, the Fifth Army forces that landed at Anzio on January 22 met little enemy resistance since Kesselring was caught off-balance. The German commander had his troops massed along the Gustav Line resisting the various attacks the Eighth and Fifth armies were making in their attempt to end the winter stalemate. If the Fifteenth and the Tactical air forces had blocked the highways and railways as expected, Kesselring would have found his position extremely serious and, in all probability, could not have rushed the necessary reinforcements to the Anzio beachhead to contain the Allied troops that had just landed. Unfortunately, he was able to move his divisions as he desired.

Kesselring immediately ordered elements of the Hermann Göring Division to the area. Alarm units from all over Italy and southern Europe were soon on their way to Anzio, over

He–111

the rails and roads that were supposedly impassable according to Fifteenth Air Force commanders. The Germans even sent three independent regiments, including the crack Infantry Lehr Regiment all the way from Germany, two heavy tank battalions from France, and a division, the 114 Jaeger, from Yugoslavia without trouble. In the first eight days after the Anzio landing, Kesselring brought the elements of eight divisions to surround the beachhead! Thus, by the first of February, the Allied force that was supposed to have opened the path to Rome was pinned down on a narrow beachhead under constant German artillery fire.

Unfortunately a lack of supplies and the loss of manpower caused by the Bari disaster, also prevented the Mediterranean Allied Air Forces from attacking German airfields prior to the amphibious landing at Anzio. The commanders had to choose between the roads and railways or the airfields, and they selected the former as the most important targets. It was estimated that the Luftwaffe had about 550 operational aircraft in Italy, the Balkans, southern France, and the Aegean. Most of the long-range bombers such as the ones that had attacked Bari the month before had been withdrawn from Italy, but there were fifty Ju-88s in Greece and Crete and sixty Ju-88s, He-111s, and Do-217s in southern France. If there had been sufficient aircraft, crews, and supplies, the

Allied planes would have bombed the German airfields in addition to the highways and railways, but there were not. Since it was considered unlikely that the Luftwaffe could do much damage during the Anzio operation, the fields were ignored until just a few days prior to the landing when several attacks were made. The only real achievement accomplished by these last-minute missions against the airfields was the bombing of the German reconnaissance base at Perugia. This raid was so successful that no reconnaissance plane could operate from it for four days, long enough for the Allied forces to land at Anzio without being spotted. Otherwise the Luftwaffe ground crewman filled up the bomb craters on the fields within hours, and their planes were taking off for missions against the trapped Allied troops on the beachhead. Once again the lack of supplies because of the closing of the port at Bari cost the Allied forces dearly.

On January 29 the Luftwaffe planes that were not expected to be a threat proved that once again Allied military leaders had misjudged the capability of the German Air Force, only this time, because of the lack of supplies, there was some excuse. On that night the Luftwaffe launched an attack on Anzio, using their radio-directed glide bombs, sinking the British cruiser H.M.S. *Spartan* and the Liberty ship *Samuel Huntington.* Even before that raid, German bombers had attacked shipping at Anzio on the twenty-third, twenty-fourth, and twenty-sixth and at Naples, the only large harbor the Allies had in full operation, on the twenty-third and twenty-fourth, usually bombing the ships at dusk when the Mediterranean Allied Air Force fighters had left for their home bases—reminiscent of the Bari raid timing. The mission on the twenty-ninth of January, however, was a much heavier raid. About 110 Do-217s, Ju-88s, and Me-210s delivered the blow. Kesselring had secretly strengthened his weak Italian-based bomber units by bringing in two Ju-88 groups from Greece and Crete and calling back a number of bombers that had left Italy the previous December to return to Germany and bomb London.

As February began and the port at Bari slowly resumed full operation, the required aviation fuel, bombs, ammunition, spare parts, and other material so desperately needed by the Fifteenth Air Force at Foggia began arriving and Twining's fighters and bombers attacked the German bases at Lavarino in Italy, Klagenfurt in western Austria, and at

Aviano and Udine, also in Italy. These missions reduced German long-range bomber operations to a very low level over the Anzio beachhead. Enemy fighter planes still plagued the beachhead, though. The U.S. Navy complained bitterly that it was losing four ships a day to German fighters, an exaggeration; but, because of its late start against the enemy airfields, the Mediterranean Allied Air Force never did completely stop the Luftwaffe attacks at Anzio. As late as February 6 and 7 the Germans flew 120 sorties each day over Anzio, causing considerable damage and many casualties. It was not until the following May, when supplies were once again flowing through the port of Bari on full schedule, that the Luftwaffe was actually contained.

The disaster at Bari on the night of December 2, 1943, and its serious consequences at Anzio were apparent within a short time, but the long-range effect on the cross-channel invasion plans was not so obvious, despite its importance. The Combined Bomber Offensive planners were depending upon the Fifteenth Air Force to help gain air superiority for the Allies over the Continent prior to the invasion of France early in 1944. On December 27, 1943, General H. H. Arnold, commanding general of the Army Air Forces, made the objectives very clear when he addressed the commanding generals of the Eighth and Fifteenth air forces:

a. Aircraft factories in this country are turning out large quantities of airplanes, engines, and accessories.

b. Our training establishments are operating twenty-four hours per day, seven days per week training crews.

c. We are now furnishing fully all the aircraft and crews to take care of your attrition.

d. It is a conceded fact that OVERLORD and ANVIL will not be possible unless the German Air Force is destroyed.

e. Therefore, my personal message to you—this is a MUST—is to "Destroy the Enemy Air Force wherever you find them, in the air, on the ground and in the factories."

Destroying the German Air Force, particularly its fighter strength, was designated as the objective that had to be accomplished before the Normandy D-Day. The Eighth Air Force, operating out of England, freed of its earlier assignment to bomb submarine facilities, began hitting such high priority targets inside Germany as the ball-bearing plants at Schweinfurt and aircraft factories at Regensburg, Bremen, and Marienburg, sometimes with extremely heavy losses. By late fall, however, it was obvious to the Allies that the German fighter strength was increasing, not decreasing and an all-out attack on the enemy aircraft industry by the Eighth and Fifteenth air forces was drawn up by Arnold and his staff and resulted in the speech to the commanders.

The powerful, better organized, and larger Eighth Air Force continued to bomb enemy targets during November, December, and January steadily despite the bad weather and lack of long-range fighter escort. Most of these radar bombing missions caused considerable damage to the German economy. During this same period, however, the Fifteenth Air Force had a great many more difficulties than the Eighth Air Force. The November 2, 1943, raid by the Fifteenth Air Force on the Messerchmitt airframe plant at Wiener Neustadt was very successful and cut production at this enemy plant by about 70 percent. Ironically, this air force that owed its formation to the fact that the weather for winter bombing of German targets was expected to be better in Italy than England was hampered during the remainder of the month of November by the horrendous Italian weather. Then came December 2, 1943, and the Luftwaffe raid on Bari harbor, the main supply port for the Fifteenth Air Force at Foggia. After this disaster, there was no hope of the Fifteenth Air Force accomplishing its share of the preinvasion bombing of German aircraft factories or flying missions into Germany to attract the Luftwaffe into the air to be destroyed by American fighters. Shortages of equipment, sunk with the merchant ships at Bari, plus the lack of trained personnel, many of whom were injured or killed during the Bari holocaust, kept the Fifteenth Air Force missions to a minimum. After the Wiener Neustadt raid of November 2, about all the new air force was able to do was support the ground troops fighting in Italy.

During the thirty-five days between January 17 and February 21, the Fifteenth Air Force bombed only four targets related to the strategic bombing program outlined by Arnold! It was not until the port of Bari was once again in full operation that the Fifteenth Air Force was able to contribute to the defeat of the Luftwaffe by flying missions into Germany, just as it had not been able to achieve its objectives at Anzio because of the lack of supplies and manpower due to the Bari harbor disaster.

Although the Bari tragedy was kept secret long after the end of World War II and is still little known even today, it had far-reaching consequences. One lesson that was obvious was the absolute necessity of knowing immediately that personnel have been subjected to a chemical agent. Very few of the known 617 military and merchant marine casualties need not have died if the knowledge of their exposure had been available to rescue parties, first-aid units, and the medical staffs of the Bari hospitals. Most of the deaths were due principally to the prolonged exposure, including inhalation of the vapor, to the diluted mustard. If the warning had been given at once, not only would the casualties have been treated differently, but many of the rescue personnel, crew members of ships not sunk, and hospital personnel would not have suffered burns, particularly of the eyes, as they did.

Secrecy, then and now, is the main cause of such tragedies. All matters pertaining to chemical warfare agents are cloaked in this "iron curtain" of secrecy, usually to the detriment of all concerned. Even Captain Knowles of the *John Harvey*, the ship carrying the mustard bombs, was not officially informed of his deadly cargo, nor was the crew. Most of them surmised what they were carrying in the hold because of the presence of Lieutenant Beckstrom and his six enlisted-man detachment of the 701st Chemical Maintenance Company on the Liberty ship. Once the *John Harvey* was sunk with all hands, only the British port authorities were aware of the mustard bombs that had been aboard her; but, once again, security restrictions kept them from spreading the alarm. For this action there was no excuse.

Nor can the action of Churchill be condoned when he insisted that the deaths at Bari which were caused by exposure to mustard be listed as due to "burns caused by enemy action." This action only added to the confusion at the scene, at the various outlying hospitals, and hindered the investigation into the tragedy. There was no need for secrecy concerning the incident, since Axis Sally was taunting the Allied personnel at Bari during her daily broadcasts about being casualties of their own "poison gas." Secrecy, when it causes death to innocent victims, is senseless.

Even when the mustard was not mentioned, the handling of the news of the Bari disaster by Washington and the Pentagon was a lesson in futility. In an apparent effort to cover up the lack of air defenses at Bari and the effectiveness of the Luftwaffe raid in an area where the Allies supposedly had overwhelming air superiority, Secretary of War Stimson kept the details to a bare minimum. The first release merely stated that "damage was done. There were a number of casualties." It was not until two weeks later, when the Washington *Post* learned how really devastating the enemy raid had been, that Washington admitted the news from Bari was bad. This lack of confidence in the American public to take bad news created a new suspicion of the government about the conduct of the war, a suspicion that lasted until the end of the conflict.

There can be no second guessing about whether the value of the Bari port was realized by the senior military commanders who planned the offensives attempted by the Fifth and Eighth armies up the spine of Italy during December and January of the winter of 1943-44 or the amphibious landing at Anzio. Facts indicate they underestimated the worth of the port, that those who should have known did not know that, with Bari harbor closed, it would be doubly difficult to get supplies into Italy for the ground or air forces. This error in judgment undoubtedly cost many lives during the Italian campaign and during the cross-channel invasion in June, 1944, since German resistance against the Normandy landings was much stronger than it would have been, on the ground and in the air, if the Fifth and Eighth armies and the Fifteenth Air Force had been able to meet their preinvasion objectives.

Bari was the only major poison gas incident of World War II, and it could have had severe repercussions in world propaganda and have led to all-out chemical warfare by both the Allies and Axis. This tragedy was a grim reminder that all nations have secret stores of chemical agents ready for use against each other if the need, in the minds of their leaders, arises. The victims of Bari, both those who died and those who survived, learned the horrors of chemical warfare. Even in an age when the nuclear bomb is the ultimate in weapons, poison gas is still feared just as much. It is hoped that never again will any man, woman, or child suffer the torments of another incident such as the Bari disaster.

On October 3, 1945, during a Service Salute to the New York National War Fund on the steps of the Subtreasury Building at Wall and Nassau streets in New York City, Captain Otto Heitmann was awarded the Distinguished Service Medal for the rescue of his crew at Bari on the night of December 2, 1943. This same slender, veteran captain of the S.S. *John Bascom*, who had so confidently walked to the War Shipping Administration office in Bari that December day after anchoring his ship at berth thirty-one on the East Jetty, was given the highest award in the Merchant Marine service by Captain Hewlett R. Bishop, Atlantic Coast director of the War Shipping Administration. It was a fitting tribute to a sea captain who not only personally survived America's secret poison gas tragedy at Bari, but also risked his own life to save the lives of his crew and the lives of many other seamen that night.

Saint Nicholas, the Santa Claus patron saint of mariners who is buried in the crypt at the Basilica of San Nicola, undoubtedly would have approved of the award.

20

THE AFTERMATH

The disaster at Bari certainly did not seem to have any bright side. All it brought was death and misery to thousands and, in the minds of many military experts, prolonged the war and increased the number of casualties during the Normandy Invasion. Yet, medical officers such as Stewart Alexander, the doctor who investigated the mystery deaths at Bari and discovered that they were caused by exposure to mustard, Colonel W. Bailey, RAMC, the British officer in command of Number Two District in Italy, and Colonel W. J. A. Laird, officer in command of the Ninety-eight British General Hospital, retained their interest in the catastrophe long after the bombing was forgotten by the majority of those who were aware of it. On December 27, 1943, less than a month after the Luftwaffe raid, Alexander wrote a preliminary report of the medical aspects of the mustard burns sustained in the harbor of Bari on the night of December 2, 1943. In the first paragraph of the introduction to the report, Alexander stated; "The facts [of this report] are related as of December 17, at which time many of the detailed data, and especially the histopathology, are not available. Many of the observations in this report are based upon statements made by casualties, or by medical officers and nurses who attended the cases, and only later study of the case records and data analysis will permit accurate appraisal and evaluation."

Copies of this preliminary report were distributed widely among military medical and research installations in the United States and Great Britain. One officer who was particularly interested in the report was Colonel Cornelius P. Rhoads, chief, Medical Division, Chemical Warfare Service. "Dusty"

Rhoads, as he was known throughout medical circles, civilian and military, was not only commander of the Medical Division of the Chemical Warfare Service, but at the same time was also head of New York's huge Memorial Hospital. This human dynamo, with enough energy for several normal men, had one smoldering obsession and that was to conquer cancer. Even a mention of the subject within earshot of "Dusty" Rhoads would make him twist his head toward the speaker and he would listen intently, his piercing blue eyes never still, hoping to find a clue to the problem that had the medical profession puzzled. When he heard about the Bari disaster and read Alexander's preliminary report, he immediately recognized an opportunity to prove or disprove, to some extent, certain theories he had concerning the use of chemicals in the battle against cancer. He immediately decided to investigate further. In April, 1944, he sent the following request to Alexander.

1. In connection with the slides of pathological specimens taken from casualties of the Bari incident, this office would appreciate being sent individual case reports so that the slides may be coordinated with individual cases.

2. Your cooperation in furnishing the previous report and the slides is greatly appreciated. It is felt that the report and slides make a distinct contribution to the medical aspects of the agent concerned.

By this time Alexander had nearly completed the "Final Report of the Bari Mustard Casualties" which was officially issued on June 20, 1944. He immediately sent the requested case histories to "Dusty" Rhoads with an accompanying letter that is interesting for several reasons. This letter not only points out several vital medical observations concerning the victims of the mustard, but also paragraph three gives an explanation of why the case histories compiled in the British hospitals did not mention the chemical agent, but used the term *NYD Dermatitis*. The command decision mentioned was the order given by Prime Minister Churchill.

HEADQUARTERS NATOUSA, OFFICE OF THE
SURGEON, APO 534, 29 May 1944

TO: Chief of the Chemical Warfare Service, War
Department, Washington, D.C.

THRU: Chief, Chemical Warfare Section, Allied
Force Headquarters, APO 512, U.S. Army

1. A copy of the medical case sheets and the
gross post mortem examinations of the 40 cases from
whom tissue blocks were dispatched are enclosed
herewith.

2. The two original sets of tissue blocks were
dispatched, one to Edgewood Arsenal and the other
to Porton. No tissue blocks were retained at this
headquarters for study as it was felt more important
to make this material available to the two large and
well-staffed research centers. It has not been possible to complete a final report of the episode because
of the absence of these histopathological data.

3. It is most necessary to point out that none of
the medical case sheets make any mention of a
vesicant agent because of the security regulations
that were immediately applied at the time. The use
of the term "N.Y.D. Dermatitis" was a command
decision. It is to be regretted that the tremendous
pressure under which the hospitals were working
prevented the accomplishment of many of the laboratory investigations that were desired and requested
at the time. By the same virtue, certain of the
recorded case sheets are scanty in relation to the
observations that were actually made.

4. Some of the impressions and opinions of the
preliminary report have been modified upon study
of the clinical material and of the various factors that
were involved. The effect of the subtotal body surface burns was probably a dominant factor in the
unusual hemodynamic changes noted. In the appraisal of the blood pressure changes observed, it is
probable that the extent of the skin burn per se was
of greater importance than that the causative agent
of the burn was a vesicant chemical. The part that
blast injury played in the clinical and pathological

picture can still not be clearly defined. It was hoped that the microscopic study of the lung sections would help properly to appraise this factor. There is no doubt that many if not most of the casualties sustained a certain degree of blast trauma. In some, this effect seems to be minimal while in others it was a major contributing insult. The systemic effects continue to be the most interesting aspect of the picture and the most provocative of thought.

5. It is planned to prepare a final report on this group of casualties when the microscopic study is completed and furnished by your office. Any advice, help, or suggestions would be most welcome so that the best possible use may be made of the information gained in this episode.

> Stewart F. Alexander
> Lieut. Colonel, M.C.
> Consultant, Chemical Warfare Medicine

High praise was given Alexander's final report on the disaster at Bari, a report that provided such complete information that it was considered a landmark in the history of mustard poisoning. It was not only used by military units but was also distributed as a model to the plants making mustard where there was a possibility that industrial accident might occur. But it was much more important than just this. After detailed study of the tissue blocks at the Edgewood Arsenal in Maryland, the reports were sent to scientists at Yale University, noting that there was no doubt that the mustard had damaged the lymphatic system and the bone marrow of the victims. These observations immediately suggested the significance of compounds of this type for the possible treatment of neoplastic disorders of the tissues that form white blood cells. At Yale University the mustard gases were tested as bone marrow depressants in the treatment of certain human tumors. Hodgkin's disease and leukemia appeared to be good possibilities for the application of this powerful agent.

The theory that the eventual cure for cancer would develop from the use of chemicals was not new in 1943. In the late 1930s Dr. Charles Huggins, a University of Chicago urologist, concluded that the growth of cancer of the prostate gland depended upon the male hormone. If this was correct, he decided that the cancer might be controlled by use of the female hormone. To test his theory, Huggins obtained permission to castrate a patient dying of prostatic cancer and then treated the man with the female hormone estrogen. The cancer was controlled and the patient lived comfortably and usefully for fifteen more years. This experiment by Huggins proved that some cancers could definitely be controlled by the use of chemicals. In 1966 Dr. Huggins shared the Nobel Prize for Medicine and Physiology in recognition of his initiation of the drug treatment of cancer.

The effectiveness of the drug estrogen in controlling cancer of the prostate gland naturally led to additional experiments and research into the use of chemicals for other cancers. In 1942, a year prior to the Bari disaster, Drs. A. Gilman, L. S. Goodman, and their colleagues prepared a report, under the mantle of military secrecy, on the effects of the intravenous administration of a nitrogen mustard known by the military code name of HN3 in seven patients with cancers that had been transferred from a primary area to a secondary area through the lymph channels or blood vessels. The idea for this test had come through the development work of the military during the early years of World War II with the family of compounds known as nitrogen mustards. Nitrogen mustards were related chemically to mustard gas; the basic molecule of the nitrogen mustards differing from that of mustard gas in that it contains an atom of nitrogen in place of sulfur. Extensive laboratory tests during the development period of the nitrogen mustards showed that both the mustard gas and the nitrogen mustards readily penetrated the skin to reach the circulatory system and destroy cells. This toxic agent was reflected first in the formed elements of the blood, particularly the white blood cells, and then in the lining of the gastrointestinal tract. Lymph tissue, bone marrow, and the intestinal tract were the sites that seemed the most susceptible to the effects of nitrogen mustards. During Gilman's and Goodman's experiment with the seven patients, they discovered that, although the nitrogen mustard caused considerable toxicity, there was a very definite regression of a solid tumor in the lymph gland of one patient.

Yet more proof was needed. Seven patients were not enough to prove the theory. During 1943 clinical trials were initiated with HN2, which became the most widely used of the nitrogen mustards, but these clinical experiences were inconclusive. Not until December of that year was there any real proof that the mustard would aid, and it came from Alexander after the Bari experience. This holocaust on the Adriatic Sea provided more patients—at least 617—than had been tested during all the years prior to this disaster and, after a study of the victims, Alexander recommended the use of mustard compounds in the treatments of certain cancers. His observations suggested at once the significance of compounds of this type for the possible treatment of neoplastic disorders of the tissues that form white blood cells.

Following up this clue, Drs. Thomas F. Dougherty and Abraham White, the former of the University of Utah, the latter of Albert Einstein Medical College in New York, injected a nitrogen mustard solution into a fat old mouse dying of leukemic blood corpuscles and the rodent became healthy and frisky within a short time. In November, 1947, using information gained from the Bari disaster, Dr. S. Farber and his associates at the Children's Cancer Research Foundation observed the first temporary remissions produced by any form of drug therapy in ten of a group of sixteen children seriously ill with acute leukemia! The remissions were characterized by shrinkage of enlarge lymph nodes, spleen, and liver, disappearance of all tumor masses, and return of the bone marrow to normal!

Rumors of a cancer cure spread rapidly around the research centers where chemotherapy experiments were taking place. Since security measures enforced by the military prevented the source of the vital information from becoming known, because U.S. authorities still did not want the public to learn that the nation had been prepared to wage gas warfare and actually had ships loaded with the mustard gas in the combat zone, nothing was said of the Bari disaster in this connection. Yet, the rumors continued. In New Haven the whispers of a cancer cure reached the ears of a man dying of a malignant tumor of the lymphatic tissue. The man was in such agony that when sitting or lying down he had to be supported from the ceiling by straps. Dr. Dougherty, who had experimented with nitrogen mustard injections on a mouse, was implored to test the rumored cure on the dying patient, and he finally agreed. The doctor injected the nitrogen mustard into the man's vein and for several weeks the victim enjoyed a pain-free, normal life. Then, as resistance to the drug developed, he died of the disease.

The remission had been brief, but was encouraging, and the experiments continued and broadened. The use of nitrogen mustard compounds led to the use of other drugs, especially compounds in the group known as alkylating agents. They are so called because they add an alkyl group (a type of alcohol radical) to compounds with which they react. By combining with protein and other essential molecules, they upset the metabolism of the cancer cell and block its growth and division. All as a result of the Bari disaster!

So far, no drug actually cures human cancer. The most the chemicals can do is restore a measure of health and prolong life, but the experimenting continues. "Dusty" Rhoads, the former chief of the Medical Division of the Chemical Warfare Service during World War II and the man who originally requested the case histories and tissue blocks from Alexander, launched an all-out war on cancer when he left the service. On his return to New York's Memorial Hospital he took many of his key army associates with him. He was convinced, after the Bari tragedy, that chemicals could be found that would kill cancer cells while leaving normal cells unharmed and he threw all his energies and knowledge into the search. His enthusiasm was contagious and he soon had the support of such men as Frank A. Howard, vice president of Standard Oil, and Alfred Sloan and Charles Kettering, two of the founders of General Motors. Sloan donated an initial four million dollars which started the construction of the Sloan-Kettering Institute, the first institute devoted entirely to cancer research. Naturally "Dusty" Rhoads directed the work of the new research center that has the motto, "Within these walls a few labor unceasingly that many may live." Though Dr. Rhoads died in 1959, his work at the Sloan-Kettering Institute continues, much of it a direct development from the information gathered by Alexander at Bari in 1943.

Others, too, keep experimenting, testing, developing the nitrogen mustard compounds. Surgeon Gordon D. Jack and his associates have worked many years with the highly poisonous family of nitrogen mustard, especially in the treatment of lung cancer. Jack put one or two large doses of tretamine, a nitrogen mustard drug, into the veins of forty-three lung cancer patients who, without treatment, were all within a few months of dying of their disease. In ten of the cases there was a very marked to complete regression of the tumor. However, three died within twelve days of the treatment, not of cancer, but of hemorrhaging from tumor masses which had been devastated by the drug. The other seven survived and, in four of them, the X-ray pictures of the cancerous lungs returned to normal or nearly normal. This was reported by Jack in 1966 and the experiments continue today.

His report emphasized the perils of putting a poison like tretamine into the veins, a verification of the dangers that the victims at Bari faced as they were exposed to the mustard for long periods. The nitrogen mustards kill cancer cells but, if not controlled properly, will also kill normal cells, particularly those that manufacture new blood cells. His patients, for instance, were nauseated within twenty-four hours, but within three days, because the drug was kept rigidly controlled, they were all feeling better.

Dr. Jack and his associates are members of the staff of a Manchester, England, hospital, an irony when it is remembered that the Bari victims were treated at British hospitals during the disaster and that England's Prime Minister Winston Churchill was the one individual who would not admit that mustard was present at Bari!

In 1961 the Follow-Up Agency of the Division of Medical Sciences, National Academy of Sciences, National Research Council, Washington, D.C., attempted to make a study of the physical condition of the survivors of the Bari disaster but obstacles were immediately encountered, even by this high-prestige organization. Edgewood Arsenal "couldn't find" the complete records of the incident; the British records "were not available"; few military officials knew or would admit that there had been any mustard at Bari, even at this late date. Once again, when dealing with poison gas, secrecy was the password. Even the director of the Follow-Up Agency was undecided how to approach the survivors about their health, even if he did locate them. "Should we frame our approach in terms of the Bari disaster or conceal our underlying interest in a general study of the subsequent health of men who served overseas in World War II?" he asked Alexander during the initial stages of the proposed study. What he really meant was, should he or should he not tell the survivors that they had been exposed to mustard at Bari that terrible night of December 2, 1943? Surprisingly, many of the survivors were completely unaware of the poison gas in the harbor that night!

How many eventually died or were disabled by their exposure to the mustard at Bari that night will never be known. How many eventually died of cancer because the mustard that entered their bodies was not controlled and killed normal cells or affected the bone marrow? No one knows. How many Italian civilians suffered the same fate in later years? No one knows.

It can only be hoped that the research drugs developed later, based on the information learned by Stewart Alexander at Bari that disastrous night, will eventually save more lives than were lost because of this secret World War II tragedy. Only time will tell.

APPENDIX

This preliminary report on the disaster at Bari was written by Stewart F. Alexander, the medical officer who discovered that the mysterious deaths were caused by mustard.

SECRET
(Equals British Most Secret)

HEADQUARTERS
NORTH AFRICAN THEATER OF OPERATIONS
Office of the Surgeon
APO 534

27 December 1943

SUBJECT: Toxic Gas Burns Sustained in the Bari Harbor Catastrophe

TO: Director, Medical Service, Allied Force Headquarters
Surgeon, NATOUSA

1. INTRODUCTION

This is intended as a preliminary report of the medical aspects of the mustard burns sustained in the harbor of Bari the night of December 2, 1943. The facts are related as of 17 December, at which time many of the detailed data, and especially the histopathology, are not available. Many of the observations in this report are based upon statements made by casualties, or by medical officers and nurses who attended the cases, and only later study of the case records and data analysis will permit accurate appraisal and evaluation.

2. THE AIR RAID

Enemy planes raided the harbor of Bari 2 December 1943. The raid began at 1930 hours and was over by 1950.

Hits were scored on several ships, probably only three or four. Only high explosive bombs were dropped.

The ship "John Harvey" loaded with 100 tons of mustard in 100-pound bombs, as well as a large quantity of munitions, was berthed stern on to berth #29 on the mole. Other ships were berthed side to side against the Harvey. Several ships away was another ship loaded with ammunition and explosives.

The John Harvey was not hit during the air raid. Shortly after the raid a petrol ship exploded and started to burn. There were apparently two big explosions the second of which blew up the Harvey and sank her at 2210. An order had been issued to scuttle the Harvey after the fires began but there is no information as to whether the message was received in time or at all. There were no survivors from the Harvey.

In the maelstrom of fire and explosion, sixteen ships were sunk and 4 others partially destroyed. Many survivors were blown into the water or forced to swim in the water at some time in the evening. The surface of the water was covered with oil to a very considerable degree in some locations in the harbor.

3. GAS THAT EVENING

It was fortunate that huge fires were raging as, undoubtedly, most of the mustard was burned. Empty bomb casings on the mole would account for the release of at least 2000-3000 pounds of mustard just above the mole.

It seems remarkable that no general alarm of gas was released that evening, but very few survivors identified any characteristic odor. In the fire and excitement any specific odor either was not detected or escaped recognition. On direct questioning, some of the survivors spoke of commenting earlier on a "garlicky odor", some even had joked about the odor during the evening, attributing it to the quantities of garlic consumed by the Italians.

At some time in the evening, someone aboard the ship Lyman Abbott called "Gas". The Lyman Abbott was lying in the harbor and later to be destroyed. Many of the crew put on their gas masks for about a half hour. None had recognized gas themselves. Masks were removed of their own volition.

No direct information concerning the possibilities of mustard exposure was communicated to the hospitals that evening. A rumor had been heard at one hospital of this possibility, but it was authoritatively (?) denied by an unknown naval officer.

Such mustard as was not burned, either sank to the bottom of the harbor or was mixed and dissolved in the oil. It was the mixture or solution of mustard in oil that produced most of the severe casualties and deaths. The amounts of mustard in the oil must have varied considerably from one part of the harbor to another. Some casualties were due to vapor alone, but the great majority, and the important ones, were those who had become covered with oil. Some became so contaminated while swimming, some by the oil being thrown up against them or on to their clothes, and a few by sitting or standing in the oil in life boats, or hanging from life rafts.

4. THE CASUALTIES

More than 1000 men were killed or missing following the disaster.

More than 800 casualties were hospitalized following the raid. Of these casualties, 628 were suffering from mustard exposure. Sixty-nine deaths, wholly or partly caused by mustard, had occurred as of 17 December.

5. FIRST AID TREATMENT

It must be repeated that rescue squads at the port and hospital personnel at the hospital had no idea or information that the casualties were, or had been, exposed to mustard.

The casualties were covered with crude oil and, under the supposition that they were suffering from immersion and exposure, the casualties were wrapped in blankets and given warm tea. Surgical cases were given priority care and those just covered with oil were left wrapped up in blankets for as long as 12 or even 24 hours. No attempt was made to decontaminate or wash this mustard-in-oil solution from them. Oil contaminated clothing was not removed.

A few individuals, on their own initiative, cleaned all the oil from themselves promptly that night. These individuals sustained only minor burns.

No anti-gas treatment was employed.

Many of the cases, after several hours, appeared in good condition and were permitted to be sent to an Auxiliary Seaman's Home (still clothed in their oil contaminated clothing). All cases showing shock or other injuries were given concentrated care and resuscitation.

In the hustle and rush of work no odors were detected,

and many cases covered with oil remained wrapped in their wool blankets for many hours awaiting their turn for special care.

Very few of the medical attendants sustained burns, although several had irritation of the eyes, which would tend to indicate that, for the most part, the solution of mustard-in-oil was quite dilute. Cases were hospitalized in the 98th General Hospital (British), 14th Combined General Hospital (Indian), 3rd New Zealand Hospital, 70th General Hospital (British), and the 84th General Hospital (British).

6. GENERAL OBSERVATIONS

The main explosion in the harbor that evening was of tremendous violence. Window glass seven miles away was shattered, and considerable other damage done in Bari. With this in mind, it was expected by the hospitals that many blast injuries would be admitted, and cases, initially, were considered either as such or as immersion and exposure.

The first indication of unusual proceedings that evening was noted in the resuscitation wards. Men were brought in supposedly suffering from shock, immersion and exposure. Pulse would be imperceptible or just barely palpable, blood pressure would be down in the realm of 40-60 mm Hg, and yet the cases did not appear to be in clinical shock. There was no worried or anxious expression or restlessness, no shallow rapid respirations, and the heart action was only moderately rapid, 110-120, considering the condition of pulse and blood pressure. These cases did not complain of chest pain, have altered respiration, injured ear drums, or blood tinged sputum as in typical blast injuries. They were rather apathetic. Upon being spoken to they could sit up in bed and would state that they felt rather well at a time when their pulse was barely perceptible and their systolic blood pressure perhaps 50.

A striking feature was the lack of response of the hypotension to the usual resuscitation measures. Plasma infusions, at best, gave only a small and transient rise of blood pressure, and most cases showed no response to plasma, warmth, stimulants, and morphia. Adrenalin gave no rise in tension, even when given as intravenous infusion. Coramine gave a transient, but not significant, effect.

About six hours after the disaster, cases began to have eye symptoms. Patients in the hospital and cases not yet admitted noted burning of the eyes and lachrymation.

Lachrymation became very marked and was associated with severe blepharospasm and photophobia. Within 24 hours, the eyes were swollen and the individuals complained that they were blind. There was no actual loss of vision but the blepharospasm was so severe that they would not open their eyes.

Erythema of the skin was noted early the next morning as it became light. Blisters were noted also about this time some 12-14 hours after initial exposure. It was at this time that the hospitals first were notified of the possibility of "blister gas" exposure among their casualties.

Nausea and vomiting were present in nearly all cases upon admission. Little information was gathered as to the character of the vomitus.

The first death occurred 18 hours after exposure. Several other deaths occurred at 24 hours. There were 14 deaths within the first 48 hours. The type of early death deserves special mention as it was as dramatic as it was unpredictable. Individuals that appeared in rather good condition, save for hypotoia, conjunctivitis, and skin erythema, within a matter of minutes would become moribund and die. There was no respiratory distress, marked cyanosis, or restlessness associated with their deaths. Cases that were able to talk and say they felt well, would be dead within a few minutes after speaking, and there were no prognostic signs of this possibility noted. Some cases just rapidly went down hill, as for example: one case was pulseless but warm, and able to talk; though still with a clear sensorium—he next was pulseless but cold; and soon his heart stopped beating. Their hearts, lungs, abdomens, and C N S showed no or only very minimal findings at these times. They did not complain of chest pain or have any blood tinged sputum.

The plotting of deaths of 54 studied cases (not selected) showed this distribution of the time of death:

1st day — 5 deaths		8th day — 8 deaths
2nd day — 8 deaths		9th day — 6 deaths
3rd day — 6 deaths		10th day — 3 deaths
4th day — 4 deaths		11th day — 3 deaths
5th day — 4 deaths		12th day — 0 deaths
6th day — 3 deaths		13th day — 1 death
7th day — 2 deaths		14th day — 1 death

This demonstrated two peaks in the death curve, the first peak on the second to third day, and a second on the eighth to ninth day. Upper respiratory tract symptomatology began to appear by the second or third day and was characterized by hoarseness and soreness of the throat, especially marked on swallowing. Cough, at first, was brassy and, only later, productive of purulent sputum. However, lower respiratory tract involvement was not prominent until well towards the end of the first week. Physical findings in the lungs in the patients who were to die early were not striking save for tracheal rhonchi.

The general apathy of the patients was quite consistent and impressive. They could be roused, but, when the external stimulus was removed, they returned to their apathetic state. The casualties included men of at least twelve nationalities or races and the apathy was as striking in one as in the other.

7. CLINICAL OBSERVATIONS

Eyes. The eyes were involved to some degree in almost every case that sustained any other mustard lesion. In this group of cases the *initial* eye symptomatology was severe and distressing, but it is believed that practically none of the eye lesions will produce permanent damage. The lesions were due either to vapor or to the mustard-in-oil solution.

Burning and soreness first was noted by casualties four to six hours after exposure but was not of appreciable significance until several hours later. The eyes, at first, felt gritty, "as though sand particles had gotten in the eyes". This soon became associated with marked lachrymation, actual pain and burning, photophobia, and intense blepharospasm. Many cases believed they had been blinded and it was necessary to force them to open their eyes to prove that vision was still possible. By 24-30 hours, symptomatology was maximal and many men were casualties only because of their eye lesions.

The eyes showed marked oedema of the lids and conjuctival surfaces and profuse lachrymation. Some congestion was noted but the oedema and lachrymation completely overshadowed the picture. There were very few corneal lesions, only one showing diffuse, though not marked, corneal clouding. There was no frank denuding of the corneal epithelium or development of corneal ulcers.

Symptoms remained especially severe for three to four days and then the acute features rapidly subsided. By the end of the first week, most of the eyes were not causing further difficulties.

Secondary infections were not severe and did not play a large part in the acute picture. In the small, somewhat more severe group, infection was not a tremendous problem, though it must be remembered that the eye lesions, on the whole, could not be classed as severe, or comparable to liquid mustard splash lesions, or saturated vapor lesions. On the other hand, the significance of the acute eye lesions cannot be overemphasized. For example; the destroyer, Bistera, was in the harbor of Bari that night, and, after picking up about thirty casualties from the water, put to sea for Taranto. Six hours out of port, eye symptoms appeared in the ship's officers and most of the crew. This became so severe that it was only with great difficulty that the ship was brought into Taranto harbor eighteen hours later, as the staff was practically blinded by their eye lesions.

After the acute phase had passed, the problem of exposure ulcers of the lower portion of the cornea, in the severely ill patients, required special attention.

The more severe eye lesions were associated with the more severe face lesions, and, after the first week, the burns of the skin surface of the eye lids accounted for much of the remaining eye trouble.

Eye Treatment. No first aid was given to any of the cases. The two cases that wore gas masks that evening did not suffer from eye lesions or respiratory tract lesions.

All eyes were irrigated gently one to three times a day to remove the matter and for cleaning. Atropine solution drops were used in almost all cases (three times daily in most instances).

Albucid solution was used only on a portion of the cases, 2.5% solution was used initially as drops after irrigation. The strength was raised as lacrymation was intense and most of the solution rapidly was washed out. Albucid solution had no effect upon the initial acute phase, and the albucid cases did no better nor worse than the others.

In the more severe cases, and in those that did develop secondary infections, 10% albucid solution was used in one group and penicillin solution used in another comparable group.

A detailed ophthalmological report will be made by an attending ophthalmologist.

The use of "Eye teams" was initiated in one hospital, placing the responsibility for the care of all the eye lesions on the ophthalmological service. After the ophthalmologist saw the cases, all treatment of the eyes was done by the eye service. The eye team might be one or more nurses with one or more corps men and they would travel from one ward to the next, taking care of the eyes only. The ward nurses and corps men were not permitted to deal with the eyes at all in this situation. By this method, the treatment was standardized and regular, and the eyes were not overlooked, as they often are in a busy ward.

Skin. No skin lesions were noted the night of the accident, and first evidences of erythema became apparent the morning of December third. There was no pain associated with the skin changes. Erythema and vesicle formation became more marked in the 18-36 hour period. In many instances, the vesicles, initially, did not seem to be surrounded by erythema and, as the blistering was extensive, it was difficult to delineate the outlines of the vesicles. The vesicles, for the most part, were quite superficial. The extent of the skin lesions showed to be more and more extensive over the course of the first three or four days, as wider areas of erythema and blistering became apparent. In a few, there was marked erythema and little vesicle formation, while in others there was general vesicle formation over the skin surface.

Almost from the first observations, oedema of the skin was noted. This was of a strikingly brawny character. The skin was thickened and not of normal texture. It did not pit and was tender on pressure. Later, a subcutaneous oedema developed. This did pit, but should not be confused with the oedema into the substance of the skin. These whole areas of skin later were to strip off their superficial layers, covering, in some cases, up to 80-90% of the body surface.

The coloration that developed was most striking, bronze, reddish brown or tan in some, and very red in others. Many resembled sun burn and sun tan. Part of the coloration was erythema and could be faded out with pressure, and part was due to changes in the skin and disappeared when the skin later was desquamated.

The distribution of the burns was quite varied but certain patterns were present, depending upon how the individual had been exposed. Burns were found where mustard-in-oil had been in contact with the skin. Some that were immersed were burned in all areas. Those individuals that had only their feet or arms in the water (and oil) were burned only in those areas. Individuals in P.T. boats that were showered by oil and water from the harbor were burned where the mustard-in-oil landed. Vapor burns were more marked on the exposed areas and in the axillae and groin. Mustard-oil mixture burns were not more marked in exposed areas. Several who had sat in the mixture had burns only of the buttocks. The soles of the feet and the palms of the hands were remarkably free from burns.

The subcutaneous oedema was most severe and distressing in the genital region. The penis in some cases was swollen to three to four times its normal size and the scrotum was greatly enlarged. The skin here, and in the fold of the groin, sloughed and local sepsis rapidly began in the region, as well as within the prepuce of the penis. Paraphimosis was common. These local lesions were quite painful and, in addition, caused much mental anguish.

Treatment of Skin. The simplest treatments were the most satisfactory.

Keeping the lesions clean, in itself, presented a prodigious nursing problem. Vaseline-gauze dressings or bland ointment dressings were very satisfactory, but, if Vaseline gauze is to be used, adequate amounts of Vaseline must be in the gauze or it will stick.

About 10 cases were treated with Amyl Salicylate. These cases did not seem to dry up any faster than those with no treatment. Most cases were cleaned and then simply dusted with sulfanilamide powder or a bland powder. Many of the cases were just cleaned and no local therapy used. Some were treated with 1-10000 acriflavin solution. As this particular group of lesions was, for the most part, superficial, it did not seem to make much difference what local therapy was used.

In one of the hospitals, tannic acid tanning was performed. Several were tanned with triple dye. These cases did a bit more poorly, if anything. They were not benefited.

The blisters and skin loss were quite superficial and many of the minor ones were well healed by 14 days. Loss of full thickness of the skin was minimal and present only in a few of the buttock and neck lesions. It was interesting to note that some of the very mild burns did not make their appearance until a very late date, and some small patches of erythema or coloration appeared as late as the eighth day.

A few of the burns were due to vapor only, as the individual had not been in the water. However, the great majority was burned with the mustard-oil preparation. Mustard can form a true solution in crude oil up to 20%, but the strength of mustard in the oil must have been far less than this. The concentrations in different areas must have varied considerably but, on the whole, were very dilute. The burns sustained depended upon the amount of mustard in the oil that contaminated the man *and* the length of time this oil remained in contact with the skin. As there was no thought of toxic agent in the oil, no attempt was made to wash or decontaminate the men. Many men in wet, oil-contaminated clothes were wrapped in blankets, given warm tea and allowed to lie with the oil on their skin all night. The opportunity for burn and absorption must have been tremendous. A few cases were cleaned with liquid paraffin and then with warm water and soap. They showed only a diffuse and mild erythema and no toxic effects, and it is certain that early cleansing saved their lives.

Only a few of the doctors, nurses, and attendants sustained injuries to their hands, and/or mild eye lesions. All of these did well. This also points to the solution of mustard-in-oil being rather dilute. A longer period of exposure would have been necessary to sustain significant lesion.

A rather interesting oedema developed in several cases. This was a straightforward, pitting oedema of the ankles and feet or wrists and hands, with *no* lesion of the hands or feet. In these cases, there was always a lesion of the upper arm or thigh, extending completely about the limb and there would be oedema of the skin *itself*, and just under it, in the local area of the burn. This probably interfered with the lymphatic drainage of the limb, and was aided by gravity distribution. There was not a venous obstruction.

Systemic Effects. It always has been assumed that the systemic effects of mustard were insignificant in its usual employment, and this probably is true of simple exposure to liquid splash or to vapor. In this group of cases, however, the individuals, to all intent purposes, were dipped into a solution of mustard-in-oil, and then wrapped in blankets, given warm tea, and allowed a prolonged period for absorption.

Blood Pressure. Men were admitted and considered in shock. Their blood pressure would be down to 40-60 mm Hg, and their pulse often would be imperceptible. They were treated as shock and wrapped in blankets, given hot tea, morphia, and plasma infusions. Their blood pressure did not rise and they did not respond to resuscitation as ordinary shock cases. This was observed and commented on repeatedly before any information was had as to the possibilities of mustard being present. These cases did not complain of chest pain. They were not anxious and restless, but, rather, were very apathetic. Another feature was that patients with imperceptible pulses and systolic blood pressures of over 40 mm Hg could be roused easily and would say that they felt rather well. As soon as the stimulus was removed they lapsed back into their apathetic state. With the failure of response to adequate plasma and other resuscitation measures, several cases were tried on adrenalin, even to the point of adrenalin infusion. There were several observations of absence of response of the blood pressure to adrenalin. The response to Coramine was observed, in several cases, to be transient.

By the second or third day, if the patient still lived, the hypotension had resolved and normal tension reestablished, but, in many cases, the systolic tension more than compensated and rose to as high as 180-190 mm Hg. The diastolic pressure did not rise comparably. By the fifth to sixth days most of the systolic tensions had settled to normal levels but the pulse pressures remained abnormally large, and pulse pressures of 90-100 were observed. In certain cases, the diastolic readings continued as variable for some time. Most cases that showed severe changes in the blood tension did not survive.

Blood. There was a marked hemo concentration when the individuals were admitted. This extended to as high as 135%-140%, hemoglobin and 6,000,000 R.B.C. During this time, the white blood cell count tended to be in the range of 9,000-11,000. The hemo concentration in those who survived was corrected by the second or third day. Beginning on the third or fourth day, W.B.C. counts began to drop and rapidly fell, in some cases, to as low as 50 or 100 per cu mm. At first, the relative number of granulocytes was raised, although the total number was diminished. The lymphocytes were most severely affected first but the granulocytes also were affected and just as severely. Not every case demonstrated this fall in

W.B.C. Those with the extremely low counts recorded all died.

Urine. No significant or consistent urinary tract findings were present.

Respiratory Tract. There were no respiratory complaints the first 36 hours. After that, hoarseness began to develop, accompanied by roughness and soreness of the throat. This was followed by cough. By the fifth and sixth days, these had progressed to severe degrees. There was voluntary aphonia in several cases and marked pain on swallowing. At this time, they started raising sputum, progressively purulent. There was some blood showing at this period, but *none* before. A few of the cases had certain respiratory distress throughout the course of their illness, but respiratory distress and cyanosis were not features of most of the early deaths.

Physical findings were not marked in the chests. The most striking feature, in some of the cases, was the diminution of breath sounds. Burns of the chest made examination difficult, but, from accounts, parenchymal sounds were not prominent. In the cases with hoarseness, painful throats, and cough, there were large rhonchi originating from the trachea and large bronchi. Towards the end of the first week, certain of these cases developed more typical findings of pneumonitis and died shortly thereafter. Throughout, the scarcity of physical findings in the lung except for rhonchi was impressive.

In the second week, the milder cases showed some improvement of the hoarseness and cough. Painful swallowing was very marked in six or seven cases. Secondary pulmonary involvement appeared in almost all of the cases that died in this period.

Prophylactic sulphonamide therapy was instituted for all patients who had any involvement of the respiratory tract. At the first evidence of upper respiratory symptoms, prophylactic dosages were started in the attempt to reduce lower respiratory tract infection. Sulfadiazine was used in most instances.

Pathological Findings. The following pathological observations are based only on gross examination as no histopathological study has been possible as yet. All statements should be regarded as tentative, pending confirmation:

There was a marked absence of post mortem lividity in the early deaths. There were varying extents of first and second degree burns covering, in some cases, up to 90% of the body surface. The surface layers of the epithelium came loose in large strips, leaving a normal pinkish skin underneath, but the skin strips often took the hair with them. Third degree burns were quite uncommon and were confined, for the most part, to the buttocks or neck regions. In the early deaths, the skin appeared somewhat thickened, as though odeamatous, and there was subcutaneous oedema. Towards the end of the week the skin oedema no longer was evident but the subcutaneous oedema was present in many burned areas.

Most of the autopsies showed at least some evidence of trauma to the lung, compatible with blast injury. Some of the dead showed no manifestations of blast injury at all. In the deaths at 48-72 hours many of the autopsies showed nothing, while others of the early deaths showed only evidence of blast injury. In a few of these there was extensive blast injury, but not in most. In many there were sub-pleural hemorrhages, some of which would extend down into the lung substance. Later deaths showed a similar distribution of this type of lesion. There was some oedema in cases that had been given large plasma transfusions.

Tracheal and bronchial lesions were present, in some degree, in almost every case. In some cases, where vapor exposure had been more severe, there was oedema, congestion, ulceration, and denuding of the whole laryngeal organ, trachea and bronchii. Several areas showed a complete stripping of the lining of the trachea and bronchi in one piece, as a large cast.

Broncho pneumonia, or descending suppuration of the lung, first was noted significantly in gross pathology after the first week. Secondary lung infections were of much less extent than might have been expected. However, toward the end of the second week, they had become much more nearly constant.

There were no mouth lesions but there was congestion, inflammation and local irritation in the oro pharynx and, especially, in the pyriform sinuses.

The liver showed changes which were very apparent, grossly. The normal liver markings were distinguished with difficulty and, in some cases, were not discernible. There was a yellowish coloration of the whole liver background, and multiple irregular patches of a more intense and more homogenous yellow color. The liver was quite full in size and its texture more friable than usual.

The stomach, in many cases, showed areas of irritation and inflammation of the fundus and near the cardiac orifice. The intestines showed no significant gross lesions.

The spleen was of firm texture, its cut surface sank below the capsule edge, and stroma markings were quite evident. Lymph nodes appeared generally small and pale, save for the carbon pigmented nodes in the broncho-pulmonary area.

8. DISCUSSION

Many of these patients were exposed to blast injuries and many of the cases demonstrated some pathological evidence of blast trauma, but, save in a few of the early deaths, blast cannot be considered as a prime factor in the cause of death.

The striking features of this group of patients were the severity of the systemic effects and the physiological changes leading to death.

The initial changes in the blood pressure and pulse might be explained on the basis of sub-total body surface burns with fluid loss into the skin and subcutaneous tissue, hemo concentration, and fall in blood pressure. However, if the above were true, the clinical picture should have been that of shock and such shock should have responded, to some degree, to resuscitation measures. The point is to be raised as to whether or not there was a direct toxic action on the peripheral blood vascular bed. The temporary rise in systolic tension above normal levels after the third day, and its later recession, but still with a large pulse pressure, also would indicate some grave derangement of peripheral blood pressure control.

The profound changes of the blood leucocyte levels can be explained only by systemic toxic effects, and the liver changes, whatever they prove to be histologically, point also to a profound systemic insult. The mental apathy was quite consistent and difficult to explain save as a central depression.

The respiratory tract infections were, on the whole, much less than would have been expected from a parallel of last war cases. In this respect, the following points are to be considered; (1) that the vapor exposure was a relatively small part of the total exposure, (2) all of the cases were on prophylactic dosage of sulfadiazine.

The point should be clearly made that these exposures were to mustard and not to other agents. It was not a new agent, but a new, and rather unique, method of applying an old agent. The major portion of the body surface in some patients was covered with a dilute solution of mustard-in-oil; this was allowed to remain on the skin for 12 to 24 hours; the individual was wrapped in blankets, kept warm, and given hot tea—all of which factors were optimal for absorption of the mustard. The fact that those few patients who were washed (decontaminated) sustained only mild diffuse burns, but no significant systemic effects, would indicate that the absorption took place over a protracted period of time.

In addition, considerable quantities of the mixture may have been swallowed by some of the men. Stomach lesions indicated that some, undoubtedly, had been swallowed, but the absence of mouth burns indicated that the amounts of the agent in any given portion of oil probably were quite small.

It seems clearly established that the systemic effects of mustard, under certain circumstances, may be profound and the important factor in individual cases. In other cases, it must have been a highly important auxiliary factor, if still not a prime lethal effect.

The severe systemic effects induced in this episode are not likely to be reproduced to this degree in any tactical employment of mustard, since such an opportunity for prolonged absorption will not be the common situation.

Warning must be given that it still is too early to evaluate properly all factors in this group of cases, and that study of the collected data and pathological material will permit a more nearly complete and factual presentation. This preliminary report is believed warranted in the effort to have such information as is now available dispatched to the centers in Porton and Edgewood for early consideration. Pathological specimens of forty representative cases, dying within the first twelve days, also will be dispatched to these centers for microscopic examination and study.

9. SUMMARY

1. A preliminary report of the mustard casualties which occurred in the Bari Harbor is submitted.

2. Of 628 mustard casualties, 69 died within the first two weeks. Some of these casualties had associated injuries, primarily blast effects.

3. Casualties were due to mustard vapor and to a

mustard-in-oil solution's being in contact with the skin for prolonged periods of time.

4. The systemic effects were very severe and of far greater significance than has been associated with mustard burns in the past. This is attributed to prolonged absorption over an enormous body surface exposure.

STEWART F. ALEXANDER
Lt. Colonel, Med. Corps
Consultant, Chemical Warfare Medicine

This is the official Navy Department report on the sinking of the S.S. *John Bascom* at Bari, Italy, on the night of December 2, 1943. Captain Otto Heitmann was master of the *John Bascom*.

NAVY DEPARTMENT
Office of the Chief of Naval Operations
WASHINGTON

28 February 1944.

MEMORANDUM FOR FILE
ALL TIMES GCT

SUBJECT: Summary of Statements by Survivors of the SS JOHN BASCOM, 7176 G.T., U. S. Liberty Ship, owned by War Shipping Administration operated by Moore-McCormick Lines, Inc.

1. The JOHN BASCOM was bombed without warning at 1845 2 Dec. 1943 while moored to the seawall at Bari, Italy. Ship sailed from Augusta 25 Nov. and arrived at Bari 1 Dec. carrying 8300 tons of general Army cargo, high test gasoline in 50 gallon drums, and acid. Ship sank on an even keel at 1910 in 40' of water.

2. Ship was moored to seawall stern to, blacked out, although port was lit up and ships at dock were working cargo, radio silent, 4 Armed Guard lookouts, 2 on bow and 2 on stern guns, one merchant crew on gangway watch. The weather was clear, wind SW force 2, visibility good, other ships tied up along seawall to starboard.

3. At approximately 1830 enemy planes flew over harbor

and attacked shipping at anchor. First planes just dropped bright flares which seemed to hang in mid-air and could not be shot out by gun fire. At 1845, 3 bombs struck ship at Nos. 1, 3, and 5 holds. Damage caused by bombs unknown but fire broke out immediately. No distress signal sent. Counter offensive offered by 3″ and 20 mm. guns with unknown results. After ship was abandoned, lines were parted by the flames and ship drifted down toward the ammunition ship JOHN L. MOTLEY which was adjacent to port. When ship was 50′ away from the MOTLEY that ship blew up and caved in whole port side of BASCOM causing her to sink almost immediately. All coincidental papers were burned in master's cabin except for 2 U. S. codes retained in Master's possession.

4. Ship was abandoned at 1900 on orders of the Master when advice was received that fires on the JOHN L. MOTLEY, loaded with ammunition, were out of control. Only 1 lifeboat could be launched. The wounded were placed in this and other survivors clung to the sides of the boat. Total ship's complement was 72 consisting of 43 merchant crew, 28 Armed Guard and 1 Army Security Officer. There are 40 merchant crew survivors and 3 known dead. Of the Armed Guard there are 19 survivors and 9 known dead.

5. Attacking planes were not seen by survivors due to bright flares dropped and, owing to violent barrage from ships and shore batteries, could not be heard.

6. The following information has been obtained from the interviews of survivors and personnel aboard other merchant ships which were in Bari, 2 Dec. Survivors stated there was no advance warning of the attack. There was no AA fire until after the first bombs had been dropped and the barrage even then was described as weak. It was reported that enemy planes, believed to be ME-210, were over the harbor nearly every day from 26 November to 2 December, apparently engaged in scout observations and taking of photographs. When plane appeared during the afternoon of 2 December a convoy had just arrived, filling the harbor. Ships had received instructions concerning coordination of anti-aircraft fire. They were not to open fire until attacked and were to coordinate their fire with a radar controlled gun ashore firing white tracers. It was reported that this gun was knocked out of action early in the attack.

Survivors commented that those ships which were not

illuminated by the flares were outlined by the fire from their own guns and thus made better targets for the planes. It was reported that the town of Bari was not blacked out.

As the attack began, the bright lights illuminating the piers and harbor were promptly extinguished, except for a spotlight (or searchlight) situated on a shore crane. This crane was abandoned by panicky Italian personnel and the light remained on for about 9 minutes until shot out by British Military Police. (This is probably the light that illuminated the SS SAMUEL J. TILDEN). The Captain of the SS LOUIS HENNEPIN, stated that scarcely a bomb was wasted and attributed the success to the combined factors of the crowded condition of the harbor, the careful scouting and observation prior to the attack, and the extreme accuracy of the bombers, plus the failure to receive any advance warning of the approach of bombers and the confusion in defense measures.

For several weeks before the attack it had been the practice of all ships when they had finished discharging, to throw all their dunnage into the harbor; other ships had discharged a lot of fuel oil. This oil saturated wood was driven by a Southwesterly wind between the ships and the Mole and consequently caught fire. Upon abandoning ship, survivors were met by this wall of fire, causing the death of many seamen and hampering the rescue of men in the water.

Survivors of the MV DEVON COAST stated that after the explosion everything was blurred. It was learned that one of the damaged ships had mustard gas on board and that sooner or later everybody was temporarily blinded by this gas. Most of the men's burns were caused not by fires but by coming into contact with this mustard gas in the water.

Another source stated that the British authorities were alert and trying to do their best with what facilities they had. The British officers who gave instructions for coordination of anti-aircraft fire stated that the harbor was a "bomber's paradise" and that defense against air attack was largely up to the ships. He said at that time that no fighter planes for harbor protection could be expected despite the proximity of the Foggia airbase, as all planes were being used on offensive missions.

Note: The following merchant ships were also sunk as a result of the attack at Bari:

U. S.	— JOHN BASCOM, JOHN L. MOTLEY, JOSEPH WHEELER, JOHN HARVEY, SAMUEL J. TILDEN.
BRITISH	— TESTBANK, LARS KRUSE, FORT ATHABASKA, DEVON COAST.
NORWEGIAN	— LOM, BOLLSTA, NORLOM.
ITALIAN	— BARLETTA, FROSINONE, CASSALA.
POLISH	— PUCK, LWOW.

The following ships were damaged during the same attack but were not sunk:

U. S.	— LYMAN ABBOTT.
BRITISH	— CRISTA, FORT LAJOIE, BRITTANY COAST.
DUTCH	— ODYSSEUS.
NORWEGIAN	— VEST.

Robert G. Fulton,
Lieutenant, U.S.N.R.

CC: 16-E-2, 16-P-1(Lt.(jg) Judd), 16-P-1, 16-Z(5 copies), Cominch, Cominch 41 and 42, F-48, FX-45, (ASWORG-Dr. Olshen, Rm. 4311), FX-37 (C&H), FX-43, F-21, Op-20G-M, Op-23-L, Op-30, Op-39 (2 copies), BuShips, BuOrd (Re-6-a), BuOrd, Atlantic Fleet Anti-Sub Unit, BuPers-222,222-23, CG(2 copies), DIO 1, 3, 4, 5, 6, 7(3 copies), 8(2 copies), 10(4 copies), 11(3 copies), 12, 13, 14(4 copies) 15 ND's, JAG (Comdr. M. H. Avery, Rm. 2327), Coord. Res. & Dev. (Lt. Parker, Rm. 0142, 2 copies), Op-16-FN, Op-31, Op-35, Op-16-1-V, Op-28.

It is not considered that any of the deaths in this series can be primarily attributed to blast injury; or expressed another way, it is not considered that any of the deaths reported in this series would have occurred if no other factor than blast had been present.

Sketch #1 indicated the location of various ships in a portion of the Bari Harbor on the evening of the raid. It is interesting to correlate the deaths in hospitals *primarily attributable to mustard* with the ship positions. It must be kept in mind that these are only the casualties that actually

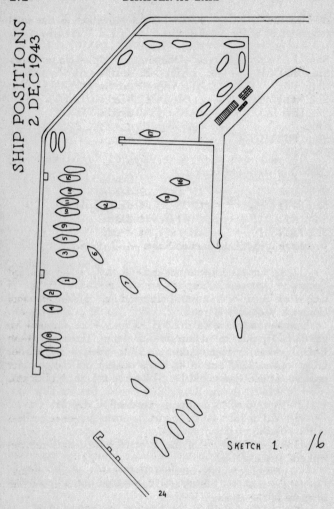

SHIP POSITIONS
2 DEC 1943

SKETCH 1.   16

24

This sketch helped pinpoint the S.S. *John Harvey* as the ship causing the trouble and later led to the discovery that the *John Harvey* was carrying mustard gas bombs.

died in the hospitals and are not a reflection of the total casualties or of the total deaths.

Ship #1 — John Harvey — the mustard ship — No survivors
Ship #2   18 deaths
Ship #3   9 deaths
Ship #4   11 deaths
Ship #5   3 deaths
Ship #6   10 deaths
Ship #7   2 deaths
Ship #8   0 deaths
Ship #9   0 deaths
Ship #10   11 deaths
Ship #11   2 deaths
Ship #12   4 deaths
Ship #13   1 death
Ship #14   1 death
Unknown and Miscellaneous Ships — 11 deaths

These figures indicate in general that of the mustard casualties that were hospitalized the greatest number of deaths attributable to mustard occurred among the personnel closest to the John Harvey.

Among the mustard deaths, pneumonia or suppurative pneumonitis was the dominant feature in 35 cases. These were the later group of deaths, in contrast to the earlier group of deaths. Thus in 48 cases neither blast injury nor pulmonary infection could be allowed as *the* cause of death.

This group of 48 deaths is explained as due to

(1) total or subtotal body surface burns per se regardless of the specific etiology, mustard.

(2) systemic effects of the mustard burns upon the peripheral vascular bed.

(3) toxic effects of the mustard upon remote organ systems.

(4) the sublethal effects of a blast injury added to any one or more of the above.

(5) undetected bacterial infection in a body severely weakened by 3 and 4 above.

BIBLIOGRAPHY

Alexander, S. F. "Toxic Gas Burns Sustained in the Bari Harbor Catastrophe." Allied Force Headquarters, Office of the Surgeon, APO 512, 1943.

————. "Final Report of Bari Mustard Casualties." Allied Force Headquarters, Office of the Surgeon, APO 512, 1944.

Baumbach, Werner. *The Life and Death of the Luftwaffe.* New York: Coward-McCann, Inc., 1949.

Beigh, George S. and Erickson, Reuben F., eds. "History of the Twenty-Sixth General Hospital." Minneapolis: Bureau of Engraving, Inc., 1954.

Bekker, Cajus. *The Luftwaffe Diaries.* New York: Doubleday & Company, Inc., 1968.

Brophy, Leo P., and Fisher, George J. B. *The Chemical Warfare Service: Organizing for War.* Washington, D.C.: Office of the Chief of Military History, Department of the U.S. Army, 1959.

Brophy, Leo P., Miles, Wyndham D., and Cochrane, Rexmond C. *The Chemical Warfare Service: From Laboratory to Field.* Washington, D. C.: Office of the Chief of Military History, Department of the Army, 1959.

Cahill, James L. "Official Statement, S.S. *John Harvey.*" Washington, D.C.: War Shipping Administration, 10 January 1944.

Churchill, Winston S. *Closing the Ring.* Boston: Houghton Mifflin Co., 1951.

Cocks, E. M. Somers. *Kia-Kaha: Life at 3 NZGH 1940–1946.* Christchurch: Caxton Press, 1958.

Conard, B. A. "Summary of Statements by Survivors S.S. *Samuel J. Tilden.*" Washington, D.C.: Office of the Chief of Naval Operations, 18 January 1944.

————. "Summary of Statements by Survivors S.S. *Fort Lajoie*." Washington, D.C.: Office of the Chief of Naval Operations, 26 April 1944.

Cope, Zachary, ed. *Medical History of the Second World War: Surgery*. Her Majesty's Stationery Office, 1953.

Craven, Wesley F., and Cate, James L. *The Army Air Forces in World War II*. Vol. 2. Chicago: University of Chicago Press, 1949.

————. *The Army Air Forces in World War II*. Vol. 3. Chicago: University of Chicago Press, 1951.

Douglas, Lord, with Wright, Robert. *Combat and Command*. New York: Simon and Schuster, 1963.

Eisenhower, Dwight D. *Crusade in Europe*. New York: Doubleday & Company, Inc., 1948.

Filewicz, Chester B. "U.S. Coast Guard Report on S.S. *John L. Motley*." Washington, D.C.: Office of Merchant Marine Safety, 18 January 1944.

Fulton, Robert G. "Summaries of Statements by Survivors M.V. *Devon Coast*, S.S. *Testbank*, S.S. *Fort Athabaska*, S.S. *John Bascom*." Washington, D.C.: Office of the Chief of Naval Operations, 28 February 1944.

Hays, Captain W. R. "Report of Anti-Aircraft Action Against the Enemy." U.S. Fleet Mediterranean (Bari), 5 December 1943.

Heitmann, Captain Otto. "Report of Captain Otto Heitmann." War Shipping Administration, 24 January 1944.

Hersh, Seymour M. *Chemical and Biological Warfare*. New York: The Bobbs-Merrill Company, 1968.

Hurth, John J. "Status of Persons MIA from S.S. *John Harvey*." Washington, D.C.: Adjutant General's Office, 29 April 1944.

Jackson, W. G. F. *The Battle for Italy*. New York: Harper & Row, 1967.

Johnson, Bruce. *The Man with Two Hats*. New York: Carlton Press, Inc., 1968.

Karig, Walter, Burton, Earl, and Freeland, Stephen. *Battle Report: The Atlantic War*. New York: Farrar & Rinehart, Inc., 1946.

Kleber, Brooks E., and Birdsell, Dale. *The Chemical Warfare Service: Chemicals in Combat*. Washington, D.C.: Office of the Chief of Military History, Department of the Army, 1966.

McKinney, J. B. *Medical Units of 2 NZEF in Middle East and Italy*. Wellington: New Zealand Department of Internal Affairs War History, 1950.

Morison, Samuel Eliot. *Sicily-Salerno-Anzio*. Boston: Little, Brown & Company, 1962.

Newkirk, Roy J. "U.S. Coast Guard Report of Investigation, S.S. *Joseph Wheeler*." Washington, D.C.: Office of Merchant Marine Safety, 5 January 1944.

Price, Alfred. *Pictorial History of the Luftwaffe*. London: Ian Allan Ltd., 1969.

"War Diary of 3 New Zealand General Hospital."

"War Diary of the German Naval Staff." December 1943.

INDEX

Join the Allies on the Road to Victory
BANTAM WAR BOOKS

William L. Shirer

A Memoir of a Life and the Times Vol. 1 & 2

☐ 34204 TWENTIETH CENTURY $12.95
         JOURNEY, The Start 1904-1930
☐ 34179 THE NIGHTMARE YEARS, $12.95
         1930-1940
☐ 32335 WM. SHIRER BOXED SET $25.90

In Volume 1, Shirer recounts American/European history as seen through his eyes. In Volume 2, he provides an intensely personal vision of the crucible out of which the Nazi monster appeared.

Anthony Cave Brown

☐ 34016 BODYGUARD OF LIES $12.95

The extraordinary, true story of the clandestine war of deception that hid the secrets of D-Day from Hitler and sealed the Allied victory.

Charles B. MacDonald

☐ 34226 A TIME FOR TRUMPETS $11.95

The untold story of the Battle of the Bulge.

John Toland

☐ 34518 THE LAST 100 DAYS $12.95

The searing true drama of men and women caught in the final struggles of the epic conflict, World War II.

Prices and availability subject to change without notice.

Special Offer
Buy a Bantam Book
for only 50¢.

Now you can have Bantam's catalog filled with hundreds of titles plus take advantage of our unique and exciting bonus book offer. A special offer which gives you the opportunity to purchase a Bantam book for only 50¢. Here's how!

By ordering any five books at the regular price per order, you can also choose any other single book listed (up to a $5.95 value) for just 50¢. Some restrictions do apply, but for further details why not send for Bantam's catalog of titles today!

Just send us your name and address and we will send you a catalog!
